PRINCIPLES
OF
PROGRAM DESIGN

A.P.I.C. Studies in Data Processing
General Editor: C. A. R. Hoare

A.P.I.C. Studies in Data Processing
No. 12

PRINCIPLES
OF
PROGRAM DESIGN

M. A. JACKSON

1975

ACADEMIC PRESS
LONDON   NEW YORK   SAN FRANCISCO

A Subsidiary of Harcourt Brace Jovanovich, Publishers

ACADEMIC PRESS INC. (LONDON) LTD.
24/28 Oval Road
London NW1

United States Edition published by
ACADEMIC PRESS INC.
111 Fifth Avenue
New York, New York 10003

Library of Congress Catalog Card Number: 75 15033
ISBN: 0 12 379050 6

Printed in Great Britain by Page Bros (Norwich) Ltd, Norwich

PREFACE

1.

This book is about programming. In particular, it is about programming for data processing applications. The main theme of the book is that programs can, and should, always be simple, even if the tasks they perform are complex. The main subject matter is a design technique which allows this simplicity to be achieved.

Traditionally, programming is distinct from system design. The system designer, usually called "systems analyst", decides what files and programs are needed in the system, and specifies these for the programmer; the programmer then writes his programs according to the designer's specifications. This traditional division of labour is absurd: it has had several damaging effects on our understanding of computer systems and on the way we build them.

First, it has helped to perpetuate the primitive idea, derived from the earliest batch-processing systems, that there is a hard boundary between the tasks of system design and program design. We expect to apply different techniques and different design criteria, and to use different tools, when the elements of our design are programs and files from those we apply and use when the elements are subroutines, machine instructions and core storage. The distinction is beginning to break down now; we recognize that JCL is a programming language (of a bizarre and unsatisfactory kind), and that the word "program" loses much of its meaning in the context of an on-line transaction processing system. The design technique discussed in this book, especially the aspects considered in Chapters 7 to 11, undermines the distinction between programs and systems in the context of batch processing also.

Second, it has obscured the nature of the systems analyst's task. He is expected to do two very different jobs: he must analyse the application needs to determine what the system ought to do if it is to serve the user well; at the same time he must design the higher levels of that system, configuring programs and files so that the work can be carried out efficiently on the computer. The first job is concerned with the techniques of inventory control, sales forecasting, production planning—whatever the particular application may be—and demands knowledge of the relevant parts of business management. The second job is concerned with computer system design, and demands knowledge of computer science. An unusually versatile person is needed to do both of these jobs successfully. What tends to happen in practice is that the analyst concentrates on the job he likes better. Too often the needs of the user are inadequately considered; the tedious business of understanding the application and planning an ergonomically sound system is hurried through so that the pleasures of flowcharting and of laying out file and record formats can begin. Too often the resulting system specification consists of a perfunctory description of what the system will do, with a a detailed and loving account of how it will do it.

The third effect, the effect on the programmers, concerns us most directly. In many installations there is no career path in applications programming; the job is bounded above by the design work already done by the analyst, while the lower bound is being continually pushed upwards by the introduction of high-level languages, report generators and data-base software. Programmers who are technically ambitious escape into systems programming, where they can become learned in the intricacies of the manufacturer's software; programmers who are ambitious for money or position become systems analysts. Those who remain in applications programming often take refuge in an understandable, but disastrous, inclination towards complexity and ingenuity in their work. Forbidden to design anything larger than a program, they respond by making that program intricate enough to challenge their professional skill.

2.

It is already widely recognized that intricacy and complexity are programming vices; the virtues are clarity and simplicity. As we build ever larger and more powerful systems it becomes ever more important that those systems, and the components of which they are made, should be transparently simple and self-evidently correct. As Professor Dijkstra points out (Structured Programming, Academic Press, 1972):

"If the chance of correctness of an individual component equals p, the chance of correctness of a whole program, composed of N such components, is something like

$$P = p^N.$$

As N will be very large, p should be very, very close to 1 if we desire P to differ significantly from zero!"

The purpose of this book is to present a coherent method and procedure for designing systems, programs and components which are transparently simple and self-evidently correct. The main emphasis is on structure—on the dissection of a problem into parts and the arrangement of those parts to form a solution.

The examples used throughout the book are necessarily small and simple;

a large and complex problem would demand too much of the available space merely to define the problem and to show the program text of the solution. The examples are therefore used to illustrate the principles of design, and the solutions given are intended to be generally valid. Little or no attention is paid to finding solutions which make best use of special facilities of a particular operating system or programming language. Above all, optimization is avoided. We follow two rules in the matter of optimization:

Rule 1. Don't do it.

Rule 2 (for experts only). Don't do it yet—that is, not until you have a perfectly clear and unoptimized solution.

Most programmers do too much optimization, and virtually all do it too early. This book tries to act as an antidote. Of course, there are systems which must be highly optimized if they are to be economically useful, and Chapter 12 discusses some relevant techniques. But two points should always be remembered: first, optimization makes a system less reliable and harder to maintain, and therefore more expensive to build and operate; second, because optimization obscures structure it is difficult to improve the efficiency of a system which is already partly optimized.

3.

Although most of the example problems are drawn from a batch data processing environment, the design principles are applicable also to on-line systems and to scientific programming. Solutions to the problems are given mainly in schematic logic, a kind of abstract programming language which can be readily translated into any of the procedural languages in common use.

Where coding is shown, it is mostly COBOL. COBOL is still the most widely used language for data processing, and it is relatively easy for non-users to read and understand. Further, it is a very simple language, and we have restricted ourselves to an even simpler subset which is described in the appendix. So the coded solutions do not depend at all on the power of COBOL: they can be easily transcribed into ALGOL, FORTRAN, PL/I or any assembler language. They are not intended to show COBOL at its best, still less to exemplify a recommended usage; they merely show that the designs resulting from the technique can be coded without difficulty.

4.

When you read this book, you should try hard to solve each problem for yourself before reading the solution given. Most of the problems, especially in the earlier parts, can be solved in an hour or two, and sometimes in a few minutes; some of the later problems will take longer. If you have your own solution to compare with the solution given in the book you will get more value and pleasure from what you read. Where the solutions agree, you can proceed in a warm glow of mutual approbation between writer and reader; where they disagree, you can read on in a more alert and critical frame of mind.

Exercises and questions for discussion are given at the end of almost every chapter. Each exercise is graded (a), (b), or (c). The exercises graded (a) are easy, and usually call for minor modification to a program already discussed or for practice in the use of a notation. Those graded (b) are harder, and present a non-trivial design task. Those graded (c) are harder still, and usually call for the design of a difficult program.

The questions for discussion may be of value to teachers who care to use this book, and may also give food for thought to the individual reader. Some of the questions raise topics and difficulties which are discussed later in the book.

ACKNOWLEDGEMENTS

Many of the sources of ideas for this book are already in the public domain: informed readers will recognize these, perhaps better than I can recognize them myself. I would like here to mention two sources which might otherwise go unacknowledged. First is Barry Dwyer, a colleague with whom I worked closely for several years. He provided many insights and many imaginative solutions to difficult problems, and he gave me, constantly, the benefit of his strong intellectual conscience. Second are all the people who have come to my program design courses. Their questions, criticisms and ideas have been a stimulus and an aid to refining and developing the design technique presented in this book. I never cease to be amazed that there is always something new to say about even the simplest programming problem.

CONTENTS

1. INTRODUCTION

1.1

The beginning of wisdom for a programmer is to recognize the difference between getting his program to work and getting it right. A program which does not work is undoubtedly wrong; but a program which does work is not necessarily right. It may still be wrong because it is hard to understand; or because it is hard to maintain as the problem requirements change; or because its structure is different from the structure of the problem; or because we cannot be sure that it does indeed work.

This book is about how to design structured programs so that they will be free from these faults. The basic ideas of structured programming have become widely accepted. We may summarize them briefly as follows:

Problems should be decomposed into hierarchical structures of parts, with an accompanying dissection of the programs into corresponding structures and parts.

At each level of decomposition we should limit ourselves to the use of three structural forms: concatenation (sequential flow), repetition (DO WHILE or REPEAT UNTIL) and selection (IF THEN ELSE or CASE).

The GO TO statement should be avoided completely or so far as possible.

There is a brilliant description of these basic ideas, and of much more, in Professor E. W. Dijkstra's Notes on Structured Programming.

An uncomfortable analogy can be drawn between today's wide acceptance of these ideas and the acceptance by an earlier generation of programmers of the ideas of Modular Programming. The basic ideas of Modular Programming were these:

Each program should be dissected into modules which can be separately compiled.

1

Modules should be as small and simple as possible within the limits dictated by the efficient use of the programming and operating systems.

Modules should be separately tested before integration into the programs which use them.

Modular Programming was not always successful in practice, for various reasons. Some compilers imposed very large overhead costs in space and time on separately compiled modules; the smallest practicable size for a module was therefore very large, and the technique useless for any but the largest problems. Some users found great difficulty in integrating modules into workable programs; during "integration testing" many interfaces between modules had to be respecified and many modules rewritten, at a cost greater than the savings achieved in originally constructing the modules. Certain promised benefits were obtained only rarely: few users managed to create a library of general-purpose modules and so reduce the amount of new code to be written for each successive project; many users found that program maintenance became harder, not easier, because many modules had to be amended and recompiled where previously only one monolithic program was affected. Almost all users became conscious that they had a major new problem in program design: what was the best way to dissect a program into modules? —or, more succinctly, what is a module?

This last problem was crucial. But there were no good answers to the questions. Some answers were useful for a limited range of simple problems: "the program should have a main-line control module with subordinate modules to process transactions". But for the most part the answers permuted a standard range of buzz-words—"logical entity", "functional integrity", "generalized logical function" and many others—and no-one was any wiser for them. Programmers who had previously written good monolithic programs now wrote good modular programs; programmers who had previously written bad monolithic programs now wrote bad modular programs.

1.2

We face a similar difficulty in Structured Programming. It is not enough to decide that a program should be built of DO WHILE and IF THEN ELSE constructs: the crucial problem is to decide what particular DO WHILE and IF THEN ELSE constructs are needed for this particular program, and how they should be fitted together. If the structure is wrongly designed we will not be saved by the fact that each individual part is well formed.

As an illustration, consider the following trivial problem.

PROBLEM 1—MULTIPLICATION TABLE

A multiplication table is to be generated and printed. The required output is:

1									
2	4								
3	6	9							
4	8	12	16						
5	10	15	20	25					
...	...	...	...						
10	20	30	40	50	60	70	80	90	100

The table is to be printed on a line printer, using the statement DISPLAY PRINT-LINE to print each line as it is generated.

Here is a very badly designed program to solve this problem.

```
...
DATA DIVISION
WORKING-STORAGE SECTION
77   LINE-NO PIC 99.
77   COL-NO PIC 99.
01   PRINT-LINE.
   02   NUM OCCURS 10 PIC ZZZ9.
PROCEDURE DIVISION.
PSTART.
        MOVE SPACES TO PRINT-LINE.
        MOVE 1 TO LINE-NO.
        MOVE 1 TO NUM (1).
        PERFORM PLINE UNTIL LINE-NO = 10.
        DISPLAY PRINT-LINE.
        STOP RUN
PLINE.
        ADD 1 TO LINE-NO.
        MOVE 0 TO COL-NO.
        DISPLAY PRINT-LINE.
        PERFORM PNUM UNTIL LINE-NO = COL-NO.
PNUM.
        ADD 1 TO COL-NO.
        MULTIPLY LINE-NO BY COL-NO GIVING NUM (COL-NO).
```

The program was designed by drawing a flowchart, and coded from the flowchart. It works correctly, producing the required output. The coding itself is well-formed: the PERFORM statements are correctly coded repetitions and the rest of the logic is sequential flow with no GO TO statements. And yet the structure is hideously wrong.

Consider what changes we would need to make to the program if the problem were changed in any of the following ways:

print the upper-right triangular half of the table instead of the lower-left triangular half; that is, print:

1	2	3	4	5	6	7	8	9	10
	4	6	8	10	12	14	16	18	20
		9	12	15	18	21	24	27	30
						...	...	...	...
								81	90
									100

print the lower-left triangular half of the table, but upside down; that is, with the multiples of 10 on the first line and 1 on the last line.

print the right-hand continuation of the complete table; that is, print

11	12	13	14	15	17	18	19	20
22	24	26	...	...	...	...	...	...	40
...	...	...	...	...	...	...	...	...	...
110	120	130	140	150		...	...	190	200

All of these changes are awkward—or as awkward as changes can be when the problem is so trivial and the program so small. The first change affects only the choice within each line of which numbers are to be printed and which omitted; instead of beginning at NUM (1) and continuing to print up to and including NUM (LINE-NO), we want to begin with NUM (LINE-NO) and continue up to an including NUM (10). We ought to be able to make a localized change to the program—perhaps to the second and fourth statements of PLINE—but we cannot. The changes needed in the program amount almost to a complete rewriting. We are defeated similarly by the second and third changes.

The essence of the difficulty is this. We wanted to make simple and localized changes to the specification: to alter the choice of numbers to be printed within each line; to alter the order of printing the lines; to alter the choice and values of numbers to be printed in each line. We therefore looked to make similarly localized changes to the program: where is the component which determines the choice of numbers to be printed? where is the component which determines the order of the lines? where is the component which determines the values of the numbers? And the answers were not so simple as we hoped. PLINE appears superficially to be the component which processes each line. In fact, however, PLINE prints line N and generates line N+1 when it is executed for the Nth time. So PLINE is executed only 9 times, and the first line is generated by PSTART and the 10th line is printed by PSTART. Furthermore, the printable values in each line persist in the next line, unless they are overwritten; PRINT-LINE is cleared only once, at the beginning of PSTART. So in considering what is to be printed in each line we have to bear in mind what was in the previous line.

In short, the program structure does not match the problem structure. The program should instead have been as follows:

```
...
DATA DIVISION.
WORKING-STORAGE SECTION.
77   LINE-NO PIC 99.
77   COL-NO PIC 99.
01   PRINT-LINE.
   02   NUM OCCURS 10 PIC ZZZ9.
PROCEDURE DIVISION.
PTABLE.
      PERFORM PLINE VARYING LINE-NO
            FROM 1 BY 1 UNTIL LINE-NO > 10.
      STOP RUN.
PLINE.
      MOVE SPACES TO PRINT-LINE.
      PERFORM PNUM VARYING COL-NO
            FROM 1 BY 1 UNTIL COL-NO > LINE-NO.
      DISPLAY  PRINT-LINE.
PNUM.
      MULTIPLY LINE-NO BY COL-NO GIVING NUM (COL-NO).
```

The paragraph PTABLE processes the whole table. The paragraph PLINE processes each line. The paragraph PNUM processes each number. The table

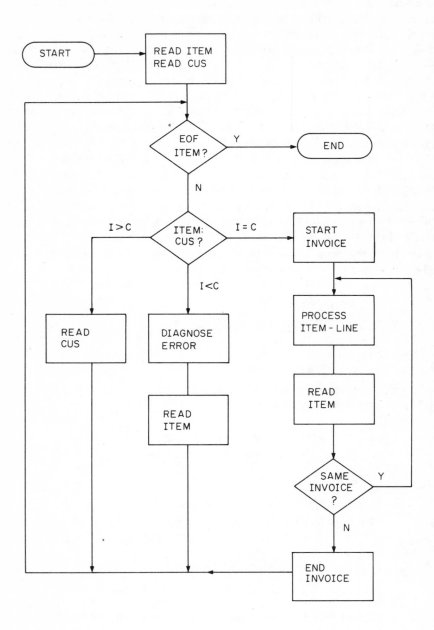

consists of 10 lines, and **PTABLE** executes **PLINE** 10 times. Each line consists of LINE-NO numbers, and **PLINE** executes **PNUM** LINE-NO times. There is a perfect correspondence between the program structure and the structure of the problem.

1.3

Here is another illustration of the difference between right and wrong in program structures.

PROBLEM 2—PRINTING INVOICES

A serial master file contains customer name and address records, arranged in ascending sequence by customer number. Another serial file contains billable item records, arranged in ascending sequence by date within invoice number within customer number.

These two files are to be used to print invoices. There may be more than one invoice for a customer, but some customers will have no invoices. Due to punching errors, there may be billable item records for which no customer record exists; these are to be listed on a diagnostic file of messages.

Shown opposite is a flowchart of a solution. We assume that at the end of each file the associated record area is filled with artificially high values.

Here, in abbreviated and informal style, is skeleton coding for a COBOL program corresponding to the flowchart. . . .

```
    ...
PROCEDURE DIVISION.
PSTART.
        Read item file.
        Read customer file.
        PERFORM PROCESS-ITEM UNTIL end of item file.
        STOP.
PROCESS-ITEM.
        IF CUSNO IN ITEM-RECORD > CUSNO IN CUS-
                                            RECORD
        Read customer file
        ELSE IF CUSNO IN ITEM-RECORD < CUSNO IN CUS-
                                            RECORD
```

> Diagnose error
> Read item file
> ELSE PERFORM PROCESS-MATCH.

PROCESS-MATCH.
> PERFORM START-INVOICE.
> PERFORM PROCESS-ITEM-LINE-AND-REC
>   UNTIL end of item file or new invoice.
> PERFORM END-INVOICE.

PROCESS-ITEM-LINE-AND-REC.
> Process item record, producing invoice line.
> Read item file.

Once again, the program works, and the coding is impeccable. But the structure is utterly wrong.

Again, we can see how wrong it is by considering some likely changes to the problem specification. This time, the changes are to be applied cumulatively:

> Print on the diagnostic listing the customer numbers of those customers for whom at least one invoice has been produced

> Print on the diagnostic listing, and mark with an asterisk, the customer numbers of those customers for whom no invoice has been produced

> To each customer number printed by the first change append the total amount invoiced for that customer

> Instead of diagnosing each item record in error, print only the customer number, marked with an "E", for each number for which at least one error item exists.

None of these changes is impossibly difficult. Anyone who has worked in data processing has seen programs changed in this kind of way, and probably successfully changed. But the changes are much more difficult than they ought to be, and as we make each successive change the conviction grows that we are storing up further difficulties for ourselves. Sometimes, after many changes, the program becomes so hard to understand that any further change is dangerous, and a complete redesign is then necessary.

What makes the changes so difficult? They all call for the insertion of coding into the program to process one customer. For the first change we need to insert a statement "print customer number" at a place in the program where it will be executed once for each customer who has at least one invoice. For the second change we need to insert a similar statement at a place where it will be executed once for each customer who has no invoice. The fourth change presents a similar problem again. The third change is related to the first; at the start of processing each customer who has at least one invoice, we want to zero the total amount; when we process each invoice we want to add the invoice total to this total amount; at the end of processing the customer we want to print the total amount.

To make the changes, we look for the appropriate places in the program to insert the required statements. We easily find where each invoice is processed: the paragraph PROCESS-MATCH processes one invoice each time it is executed; the invoice total is available after all the items of the invoice have been processed. This accounts for a part of the third change, but the rest is much harder. There is no program component which processes each customer with invoices, or each customer without invoices, or each customer with error items. So there is nowhere appropriate to put the statements needed for the changes.

Of the components which do exist in the program structure, PROCESS-MATCH, although misnamed, is intelligible: it processes each invoice; and PROCESS-ITEM-LINE-AND-REC processes each item within an invoice. But what does PROCESS-ITEM do? The flowchart seems plausible: we have a customer record and an item record, and PROCESS-ITEM compares their keys and takes the appropriate action according to the result of the comparison. This seems natural on the flowchart, but less natural if we ask what data is processed by each execution of PROCESS-ITEM. The answer, after we have examined the program carefully, turns out to be:

either one billable item record for which no customer record exists,

or one complete invoice,

or one customer record for which there may or may not have been invoices.

It is not surprising that we found difficulty with the changes. The program structure was always absurd, although it may have seemed reasonable on the flowchart: the changes only forced us to recognize what we should always have known.

1.4

One lesson to be learnt from these examples is that we should avoid flow-charts.

For many people it has long been an article of faith that flowcharting should precede coding. There is a kernel of important truth here: coding cannot be the first stage in building a program; it must be preceded by design. But flowcharting is not designing. Design is about structure, and flowcharts, as their name suggests, are about the flow of control. At the time when the designer should be thinking about the shape of his problem, the flowchart encourages him to think about execution of the program inside the computer. Of course, some programmers who draw flowcharts do produce well structured programs; but their success is in spite of the technique, not because of it. Flowcharts tend to conceal structure. For a given flowchart, there are many ways of arranging the symbols on the page, and the programmer must exercise superhuman foresight if he is to achieve the arrangement which exhibits the structure he has in mind. So we will draw no more flowcharts.

Another, more positive, lesson is that program structures should be based on data structures. There are deeply underlying reasons why this is so, and we depict them in the following diagram.

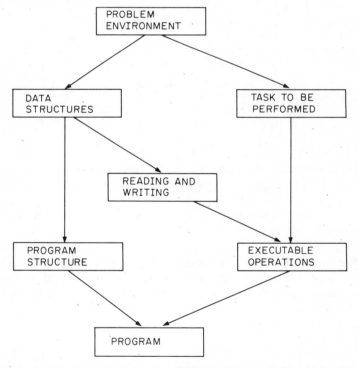

The problem environment is the real world, or that part of it which affects and is affected by the computer system. In Problem 2 this world contains a number of customers, individually identifiable; these customers have purchased items from the organization served by the computer system; they now owe money in payment for those items, and that money is to be collected by sending out invoices; there may be more than one invoice per customer, perhaps because he has purchased items from more than one part of the organization.

The computer system sees the world through the medium of its data structures. The customer file is a model, intelligible to the computer, of the set of customers; each customer is represented by a record and is individually identifiable by the customer number, the key of the record. The item file is a model of the set of items purchased by the customers. The invoice file is a model of the customers' debts, and at the same time plays a direct part in the real world.

The task to be performed must make sense in the real world; a customer owes money because he has purchased some items, and the total of his debt is the total price of those items. So we collect together all of the item records and write out the required number of invoices. The total line on the invoice is formed by adding up the item prices, and the invoice is mailed to the customer's address.

The program we are trying to build consists essentially of operations to be executed by the computer. Some of these operations are concerned with finding our way around the data structures: when we are ready to pass on to the next item we must execute the operation "read item file"; when we are ready to start a new invoice we must skip to the top of a page. Other operations are more directly concerned with the task to be performed: for each item in an invoice we must execute the operation "add price to invoice total". Each operation must appear somewhere in the program text, in some program component. To make an intelligible and correct program we must ensure that for each operation there is an appropriate component in which it may appear; "add price to invoice total" must appear in a component which processes each item in an invoice; "skip to top of page" must appear in a component which processes the start of each invoice.

In general, both types of operation, those concerned with finding our way around the data structures and those more directly concerned with the task to be performed, can be associated with components of the data structures. If, therefore, we give our program the same structure as the data it processes we can expect that we will have no difficulty.

These ideas are the basis of the design techniques discussed in this book. We start by considering the data structures, which we then use to form a program structure. We list the executable operations needed to carry out the task, and allocate each operation to a component of the program structure. There are, of course, further steps in the design process, but these three are the first and the most important: the quality of the work we do as we take these steps will determine the quality of the programs we write.

EXERCISE 1.1 (a)

Make the three suggested changes to the second (good) program for Problem 1.

EXERCISE 1.2 (b)

Make the three suggested changes to the first (bad) program for Problem 1.

EXERCISE 1.3 (b)

Design a program to solve Problem 2, and make the suggested changes to it.

QUESTION 1.1

How would you test a solution to Problem 1? Is testing often as easy as this?

QUESTION 1.2

Why do you suppose the designer of the first (bad) program for Problem 1 placed the statement MOVE SPACES TO PRINT-LINE where he did? What did he gain? What did he risk losing?

QUESTION 1.3

Can the structure of a file be determined objectively? If so, how? If not, what are the constraints on the structures we may choose? Why did we choose to regard the multiplication table as a structure of lines instead of a structure of coloumns?

2. STRUCTURES AND COMPONENTS

2.1

We may usefully think of programming in the following way. We are given a problem and a machine; the problem is the task to be performed by the program; the machine is a hardware and software system which is capable of executing a certain set of primitive operations—the executable instructions of our programming language. The programmer's job is to express the task in terms of these primitive operations.

If the task is entirely trivial, we may be able to express it directly in primitive operations. For example, a program to exchange the values of two variables can be written down immediately as

    MOVE A TO TEMP.
    MOVE B TO A.
    MOVE TEMP TO B.

But not many programs are as trivial as this. A realistic program may contain hundreds or thousands of instructions, and cannot be written down directly: the task is too large and complex to be held, all at one time, in a human mind. We need some way of tackling the work which allows us to devote our attention to only a small part of it at any one time.

Hierarchical structuring is such a way. We wish to create a program P which, when executed, performs the desired task T. We decompose T into a number of subtasks—say, T1, T2 and T3—and we make a corresponding decomposition of P into program components P1, P2 and P3; when P1 is executed it performs T1, and so on. We now have four components to create: P1, P2, P3 and P itself. P is needed to bring P1, P2 and P3 into the correct relationships with each other. Having decided what those relationships are, we have effectively completed our consideration of P: all that remains is to settle some details of coding. But P1, P2 and P3 are probably too complex to be written down directly in the programming language, and we apply the same technique of decomposition to them in turn. We decompose T1 into subtasks —say, T11, T12, T13 and T14—and we decompose P1 correspondingly.

15

The process continues, level by level, until no component remains which is too complex to be coded directly in the programming language as a single executable instruction.

Hierarchical structuring is powerful because it allows us to create large and and complex programs without using large and complex components: the complexity and size of the program is reflected only in the number of components and in the number of levels in the hierarchy. The components are of two kinds: elementary and composite. The elementary components are single instructions in the programming language; the composite components consist only of the coding needed to bring together, in correct relationships, the parts of which they are directly composed.

The subject of this book is program design: how to make the right dissection of the problem. The subject of this chapter is the nature of the components we shall use and the notations by which we shall describe them.

2.2

We will restrict ourselves to four component types. They are:

elementary components, which are not further dissected and have no parts

three composite types:

(i)   sequence, which has two or more parts occurring once each, in order

(ii) iteration, which has one part, occurring zero or more times

(iii) selection, which has two or more parts of which one, and only one, occurs once.

The parts of the composite types may themselves be composite or elementary, without restriction. There is therefore no limit to the size of structure which can be created or to the number of components.

The three composite types form an effective structuring system. Each is easy to understand, in the sense that the relationship between its parts corresponds to an intuitively acceptable idea which is simple and easy to remember. Also, it has been shown that any program which can be expressed in a flowchart can be expressed as a structure of sequences, iterations and selections, so there is no restriction on the programs we may write. More precisely, there is no restriction on the programs we may write for a serial machine: certain kinds of parallel processes cannot be expressed by flow-charts, and cannot be directly executed in a serial, deterministic, machine; however, they can be simulated, so the restriction is not important,

All four types of component are manifested in data structures no less than in program structures. This is especially significant because, as explained earlier, we intend to base our program structures on the structures of the data processed. In the discussion which follows, examples are given of each of the four types both in data and in program form.

2.3 Sequences

A sequence has two or more parts, occurring once each, in order. Here are some examples of sequences in COBOL and PL/I data and procedure coding.

```
PA.   ADD X TO Y.
      CALL "Q" USING Y, W, Z.
      PERFORM PB.
```

The paragraph PA is a sequence of three parts: the ADD operation, sub-program Q and paragraph (or section) PB. Each time PA is executed, each of these is executed once, in the order given.

```
01   RECORD-A.
  02   FA1 PIC 99.
  02   FA2.
    03   FA2-1 PIC X(24).
    03   FA2-2 PIC S9(4) COMP.
  02   FA3 PIC X(36).
  02   FA4 PIC S9(8) COMP.
```

The group item RECORD-A is a sequence of four parts: the elementary item FA1, the group item FA2, the elementary item FA3 and the elementary item FA4. Each instance of RECORD-A consists of one instance of each of these parts, in the order given.

```
DO;
    A=1;
    B=C;
    CALL X (C);
END;
```

The DO-group is a sequence of three parts: the assignment to A, the assignment to B and the call of X.

```
DO;
    A=1;
    B=C;
    DO;
        D=E;
        CALL Y (F);
    END;
END;
```

The outer DO-group is a sequence of three parts: the assignment to A, the assignment to B and the inner DO-group.

```
DCL 1 YYMMDD, 2 (YY PIC "99", MMDD),
                    3 (MM, DD) PIC "99";
```

YYMMDD is a sequence of two items: the field YY and the structure MMDD.

```
XYZ:  PROC;
        PUT SKIP LIST ("PROC XYZ CALLED");
        PUT SKIP DATA (I, J, K);
        END XYZ;
```

The procedure XYZ is a sequence of two parts: the PUT LIST operation and the PUT DATA operation.

Evidently there are many different ways in which sequences may be written in a programming language. Each of these ways is highly specific, incorporating choices among different forms of the sequence itself and of its parts. This variety is useful and necessary in a programming language, to allow us to choose the most appropriate and efficient form of each particular sequence; but it is very inconvenient at the early stages of design, because it forces us to make our choice prematurely. We therefore need notations of a more general nature. We want to be able to describe structures without specifying how they will be eventually written in the finished program.

We will use both a diagrammatic and a verbal notation. The diagrammatic notation for a sequence A, with parts B, C and D, is:

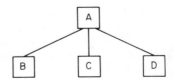

Note that the diagram is not a flowchart. Each line in the diagram, connecting two components, means that the component at the lower end of the line is a part of the component at the upper end. B is a part of A, and so too are C and D.

The diagram may be extended to as many levels as required. For example, we may represent the COBOL item RECORD-A, shown above, as

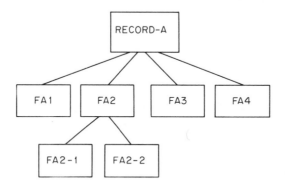

We will use structure diagrams for both program and data structures. The verbal notation, called schematic logic, will be used chiefly for program structures. Schematic logic for the COBOL paragraph PA, shown above, is:

```
PA   seq
     Y:=Y+X;
     do Q;
     do PB;
PA   end
```

There are three forms in which we may write the parts of a component in schematic logic; two of them are shown in this example. First, we may write an elementary operation directly into the schematic logic text: the operation may be written in the programming language ("ADD X TO Y"), or in any conveniently brief notation ("Y:=Y+X"). Second, we may denote the presence of a non-elementary component by writing the word "do" followed by the component name, as in "do Q" and "do PB". The non-elementary component is expanded elsewhere into schematic logic; we choose to write it in the form "do Q" merely for visual convenience, and there is absolutely no implication that Q will be written as a sub-program or a section or, indeed, in any particular manner in the programming language. Third, we may write the schematic logic for a non-elementary part directly into the schematic logic of the containing component. Thus, if PB is itself a sequence of PC followed by PD, we could write PA as:

```
PA  seq
     Y:=Y+X;
     do Q;
     PB      seq
             do PC;
             do PD;
     PB      end
PA    end
```

2.4 Iterations

An iteration has one part, which occurs zero or more times for each occurrence of the iteration component itself. Here are some examples of iterations in COBOL and PL/I data and procedure coding.

PERFORM PB 5 TIMES.

This statement is itself an iteration: the iterated part is PB, which occurs 5 times for each occurrence of the statement.

```
01   TABLE.
  02   ENTRY OCCURS 100.
     03   ENTRY-KEY PIC X(8).
     03   ENTRY-VALUE PIC X(4).
```

The group item TABLE is an iteration: the iterated part is ENTRY, which occurs 100 times for each occurrence of TABLE.

```
PRINT-REST-OF-TABLE SECTION.
PRT1.
     IF ENTRY-KEY (S) = HIGH-VALUES
         GO TO PRTX.
PRT2.
     DISPLAY "ENTRY", S, "=", ENTRY-VALUE (S).
     ADD 1 TO S.
PRT3.
     GO TO PRT1.
PRTX.
     EXIT.
```

The section PRINT-REST-OF-TABLE is an iteration: the iterated part is the paragraph PRT2, which is executed zero or more times each time that PRINT-REST-OF-TABLE is executed. The coding other than PRT2 is logically equivalent to the statement

PERFORM PRT2 UNTIL ENTRY-KEY (S) == HIGH-VALUES.

Note that PRT2 will be executed zero times if ENTRY-KEY (S) = HIGH-VALUES for the initial value of S.

```
A:   DO     I = 0 TO 9;
            X(I) = X(I)+I;
            Y(I) = Y(I)*I;
     END    A;
```

The DO-group A is an iteration. Its iterated part is not named, and is itself a sequence of two parts—the assignment to X(I) and the assignment to Y(I); the iterated part is executed 10 times for each time that A is executed.

DCL 1 D, 2 C(N), 3 B FIXED, 3 A FLOAT;

The structure D is an iteration: the iterated part is C, which occurs N times for each occurrence of D.

The diagrammatic representation of a structure A whose iterated part is B is:

The asterisk in the box for B indicates multiple occurrences of B within A. Note that A is the iteration, and that the multiplicity of B's occurrences is an attribute of A, not of B. The PL/I structure D, shown above, may be represented diagrammatically as

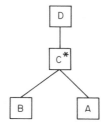

Schematic logic for an iteration A whose iterated part is B is:

A   **iter**
   do B;
A   **end**

The iterated part may, of course, be written in any of the three forms described above for sequences. We may add to the schematic logic a specification of the number of occurrences of the iterated part. For example, the iteration PRINT-REST-OF-TABLE shown above may be written as

PRINT-REST   **iter until** key (S) = high-values
    PRT2   **seq**
        print entry number and value;
        S:=S+1;
    PRT2   **end**
PRINT-REST   **end**

in which the condition written specifies the condition under which the iteration terminates. We may instead specify the condition for a further occurrence of the iterated part, in the form

PRINT-REST   **iter while** key (S) ≠ high-values
    PRT2   **seq**
        print entry number and value;
        S:=S+1;
    PRT2   **end**
PRINT-REST   **end**

All of the iterations described above have the same logic flow: the condition is tested before every potential execution of the iterated part, including the first. This logic flow is shown explicitly in the COBOL section PRINT-REST-OF-THE-TABLE, where the test "IF ENTRY-KEY (S) = HIGH-VALUES" is made before every potential execution of PRT2.

This logic flow has three important implications, which are fundamental to the use we shall make of iteration throughout this book:

the condition test asks whether there is another occurrence of the iterated part yet to come; it must therefore always be a test which can be made before processing each occurrence of the part and in particular before processing the first occurrence;

zero occurrences of the iterated part is a legitimate instance of the iteration; if, therefore, a particular instance of A consists of zero occurrences of B, it would be wrong to say "A is not executed" or "the data component A is not present";

the iteration always consists of the maximum possible number of occurrences of the iterated part; truth of an "until" condition is a necessary as well as a sufficient condition for termination; truth of a "while" condition is a sufficient as well as a necessary condition for a further occurrence.

There is another possible form of iteration, in which the condition test is at the tail of the iteration, following each occurrence of the iterated part. This form of iteration is used in FORTRAN, and is sometimes referred to as "REPEAT UNTIL", contrasted with "DO WHILE" which is the form we will use. There are some situations in which the "REPEAT UNTIL" form is more convenient, but we will avoid it altogether. The additional complexity in design which would be created by having alternative forms of iteration is too high a price to pay for the small improvement in convenience. More importantly, the "REPEAT UNTIL" is significantly harder to use correctly: because the first occurrence of the iterated part is not preceded, in this form, by execution of the condition test, we are obliged to consider two distinct contexts for the iterated part; the context for the first occurrence is the context on entry to the iteration component, while the context for each subsequent occurrence is determined by the condition test. This difficulty is not trivial; it can be a source of gratuitous error.

Sometimes, where it is particularly important to emphasize that an iteration must contain at least one occurrence of the iterated part, we will be forced to show the first occurrence separately. For example, if A consists of one or more B's, we may be forced to represent A in the form:

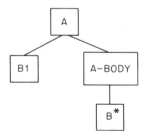

We will usually find in such cases that there is some special characteristic of the first occurrence which makes it proper to depict it separately in this way.

We may think of iteration as a development of sequence. As a trivial example, consider the following component TABLE:

```
01  TABLE.
    02  ENTRY-1 PIC 99.
    02  ENTRY-2 PIC 99.
    02  ENTRY-3 PIC 99.
```

TABLE is a sequence of three parts, and we may appropriately process it by a program component of the same structure:

```
PTABLE.
        ADD 1 TO ENTRY-1.
        ADD 1 TO ENTRY-2.
        ADD 1 TO ENTRY-3.
```

Now if we observe that each part of the sequence is like each other part, we may rewrite TABLE as an iteration:

```
01  TABLE.
    02  ENTRY OCCURS 3 PIC 99.
```

and we may rewrite the program component similarly:

```
PTABLE.
        PERFORM PENTRY VARYING S FROM 1 BY 1
                UNTIL S > 3.

PENTRY.
        ADD 1 TO ENTRY (S).
```

What we have done is to generalize the concepts ENTRY-1, ENTRY-2 and ENTRY-3 into the more general ENTRY. This provided us with some economy in our description of the data and in the program procedure text, the economy being proportional, roughly, to N-1, where N is the number of occurrences of ENTRY.

The next step in development of the iteration from the sequence is more powerful. The number of parts in a sequence must be known when the program is designed and written: for the sequence version of TABLE we must know in advance that there are three parts. In an iteration, by contrast, the number of occurrences of the iterated part may be determined at program execution time. We may write TABLE in some form such as

```
01   TABLE.
  02   NUM-E PIC 999.
  02   TABLE-BODY.
    03   ENTRY OCCURS 500 DEPENDING ON NUM-E
         PIC 99.
```

and we may then write PTABLE as

```
PTABLE.
    PERFORM PENTRY VARYING S FROM 1 BY 1
        UNTIL  S > SNUM-E.
    . . .
PENTRY.
    ADD 1 TO ENTRY (S).
```

in which the number of entries is determined when the program is executed.

This idea of the development of iteration from sequence is important because it focuses our attention on the generalization of the parts of the sequence. We must answer the question "what characterizes each iterated part and how do we recognize an interated part"? In this case we may recognize an iterated part ENTRY (S) by the constraint on S

$$0 < S \leqslant NUM\text{-}E$$

and we know therefore that the iteration has the form

```
P-TABLE-BODY   iter while  0 < S ⩽ NUM-E
                   process one entry;
P-TABLE-BODY   end
```

Adding the necessary operations to find our way through the table—they are $S:=1$ (point to first possible entry) and $S:=S+1$ (point to next possible entry)—we arrive at the form

```
P-TABLE   seq
              S:=1;
          P-TABLE-BODY   iter while  0 < S ⩽ NUM-E
                             process one entry;
                             S:=S+1;
          P-TABLE-BODY   end
P-TABLE   end
```

It is now apparent that the condition $0 < S$ is otiose: it will always be satisfied because S is initialized to the value 1 and is never subsequently decremented. So we eventually arrive at the final form in which the iteration continues so long as $S \leqslant$ NUM-E and terminates when $S >$ NUM-E.

Of course it is not suggested that every programmer must go through all these stages in designing a simple iteration: it will usually be possible to formulate the iteration correctly by drawing on accumulated experience. But the principles should always be in our minds, as the following small example will show.

A file contains three types of record: T1, T2 and T3, containing the values 1, 2 and 3 respectively in the first position of the record. The first record is always a T1, and the last is always a T3, while those in between are all T2's. Evidently the structure of the file is:

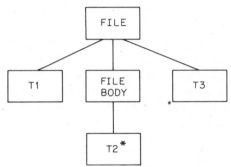

and the gross structure of the program to process it is:

```
PFILE    seq
            process T1;
     PBODY    iter
                process T2;
     PBODY    end
            process T3;
PFILE    end
```

The question now arises: what is the correct condition to write for the iteration PBODY? It seems simple enough to write "until T3", but this would definitely be a mistake. The component "process T2" cannot validly be performed unless there is a T2 record which is its object; the presence of a T2 record can be properly assured only by the condition "until not T2" or, equivalently, "while T2".

The point is simple, but must not be ignored. The iteration FILEBODY consists of some number of occurrences of T2; each occurrence is recognizable by the condition T2, that is, by the value 2 in the first position of the record. If we use the condition "until T3", we are relying on a property of the sequence FILE, which we ought not to do. We would be punished for our error if the specification of FILE were changed so that a T4 record is interposed between FILEBODY and the final T3 record: we would then have to change FILEBODY although the specification of FILEBODY itself has not been changed. An accumulation of small difficulties of this kind can have a large effect on the cost of program maintenance.

2.5 Selections

A selection has two or more parts, of which one, and only one, occurs once for each occurrence of the selection component. Here are some examples of selections in COBOL and PL/I data and procedure coding.

```
IF X =  0
    MOVE A TO B
ELSE MOVE C TO D.
```

The IF statement is a selection; its parts are the two MOVE statements. Each time the IF statement is executed, one, and only one, of the MOVE statements is executed.

```
01   TRANSACTION.
   02   TRANS-CODE PIC X.
   02   CREDIT.
      03   CREDIT-NOTE-NO PIC X(5).
      03   CREDIT-AMOUNT PIC 9(8).
      03   CREDIT-TYPE PIC X.
   02   DEBIT REDEFINES CREDIT.
      03   CUSTOMER-REF PIC X(8).
      03   DEBIT-AMOUNT PIC 9(8).
      03   ITEM-CODE PIC X(6).
   02   TRANSFER REDEFINES CREDIT.
      03   FROM-LEDGER PIC X(4).
      03   TO-LEDGER PIC X(4).
      03   TFR-AMOUNT PIC 9(8).
      03   TFR-NOTE PIC X(30).
```

The three group items CREDIT, DEBIT and TRANSFER are the parts of an unnamed selection component. The group item TRANSACTION is a sequence of TRANS-CODE and the unnamed selection component. For each occurrence of the unnamed selection (that is, once in each TRANS-ACTION) there is one, and only one, occurrence of either CREDIT or DEBIT or TRANSFER.

```
A:  DO;
          IF CODE = 5 THEN CALL P (INREC);
          ELSE DO;
                    I=1;
                    J=M;
          END;
    END A;
```

The DO-group A is a selection: its parts are P and the inner DO-group consisting of the two assignment statements.

```
IF CODE = 5 THEN;
ELSE CALL X;
```

The IF statement is a selection: its two parts are null and the procedure X.

As in the case of an iteration with zero occurrences of the iterated part, a selection is considered to have been executed in the program, or present in the data, even when the selected part is null for the particular instance considered. If CODE = 5, the above IF statement may be legitimately executed and its execution will consist of doing nothing. It would be quite wrong to say that when CODE = 5 the IF statement is not executed.

The diagrammatic representation of a selection A whose parts are B, C and D is:

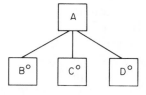

The circles in the boxes for B, C and D indicate that A is a selection.

The diagram for the structure TRANSACTION above is shown on p. 29. Note that we are forced to create a name for the selection which was unnamed in the COBOL description.

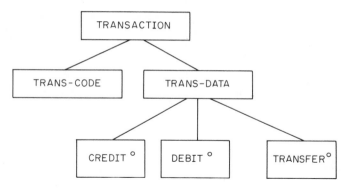

Schematic logic for a selection A whose parts are B, C and D is:

A   **select**
    do B;
A   **or**
    do C;
A   **or**
    do D;
A   **end**

We may, and will almost always wish to, write conditions in the schematic logic for a selection, indicating how the choice among the parts is made. Suppose, for example, that we wish to process the structure TRANSACTION, and that TRANS-CODE has the values "C", "D" and "T" for CREDIT, DEBIT and TRANSFER respectively. Then we may write the schematic logic for an appropriate component as follows:

PTRANSDATA   **select** trans-code = "C"
                do process-credit;
PTRANSDATA   **or** trans-code = "D"
                do process-debit;
PTRANSDATA   **or** trans-code = "T"
                do process-transfer;
PTRANSDATA   **end**

The logic flow for a selection is shown by the following COBOL coding for PTRANSDATA:

```
PTRANSDATA SECTION.
PTDSLCT.
    IF TRANS-CODE NOT = "C" GO TO PTDOR1.
```

```
    . . .
  process credit transaction

    . . .
  GO TO PTDEND.
PTDOR1.
      IF TRANS-CODE NOT = "D" GO TO PTDOR2.

        . . .
      process debit transaction

        . . .
      GO TO PTDEND.
  PTDOR2.

        . . .
      process transfer transaction

        . . .
  PTDEND.
  EXIT.
```

There is an obvious discrepancy between the COBOL coding and the schematic logic. In the schematic logic we write a condition for each part of the selection, while in the COBOL coding we omit the condition for the last part. The reason is instructive. Schematic logic is a design language, and should be fully explicit in those matters which pertain to design and structure; if our design assumes that each instance of TRANS-DATA is either a CREDIT or a DEBIT or a TRANSFER, and that the value of TRANS-CODE is accordingly either "C" or "D" or "T", then we should say so in the schematic logic. We are recording the fact that our design is based on this assumption, and that the resulting program can not reasonably be expected to work when the assumption is false. In the coding, for the very same reasons, it is nonsensical to test the value of TRANS-CODE once we have determined that it is neither "C" nor "D": the design is explicitly based on the assumption that the value must then be "T".

At first sight, these ideas seem to contradict established good practice. Surely we should check, as conscientious programmers, that the data is valid? The point is taken up briefly later in this chapter, and is discussed at

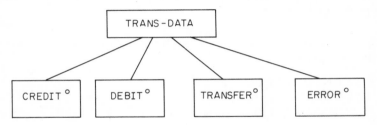

length in Chapter 5. For the moment, we may observe that nothing prevents us from respecifying TRANS-DATA in the form shown on p. 30 and rewriting PTRANSDATA as

PTRANSDATA	**select** trans-code = "C"
	do process-credit;
PTRANSDATA	**or** trans-code = "D"
	do process-debit;
PTRANSDATA	**or** trans-code = "T"
	do process-transfer;
PTRANSDATA	**or** trans-code ≠ "C", ≠ "D", ≠ "T"
	do process-error;
PTRANSDATA	**end**

taking explicit account in the design of the possibility of an erroneous transaction.

Observe that the logic flow of a selection is like that of an iteration: the condition test for each part precedes processing of that part. The condition must therefore be such that the test can be made before the part is processed. This point may seem too obvious to be worth mention; but we will discover, later on, that there are certain problems where the logic flow of a selection is inadquate precisely because the condition test must precede processing of the selected part.

We will allow ourselves one minor abbreviation in respresenting selections of a special type. If a selection has two parts exactly, and one of them is null, then according to our notation we should represent it as

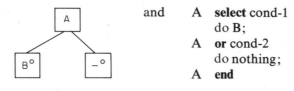

	and	A	**select** cond-1
			do B;
		A	**or** cond-2
			do nothing;
		A	**end**

for brevity we will sometimes use the representations

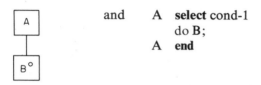

	and	A	**select** cond-1
			do B;
		A	**end**

This abbreviation should not be used for selections of more than two parts; nor should it be used when cond-2 is anything other than the complement of cond-1 (that is, cond-2 = NOT cond-1): if we adhere to these rules we can avoid ambiguity.

2.6   Elementary Components

The programming language we use provides us with a set of elementary components. More precisely, with two sets: one for data and one for programs. To design a system we must dissect the problem data into a structure of which the lowest level components are the elementary data types of the programming language; similarly we must dissect the program into a structure of which the lowest level components are the elementary executable operations of the language.

By definition, an elementary component has no parts, and can not be dissected into a structure of smaller components. For example, if we declare an elementary COBOL data item

```
03   FLDA PIC S9(4) COMP.
```

we can execute certain operations on the item taken as a whole, but we cannot legitimately execute any operation on an individual digit. It is sometimes possible to devise ingenious coding which will operate on something less than the whole of an elementary item; such coding always relies on knowledge of how the item is represented by a particular compiler in a particular machine, and is not a proper use of the programming language.

Of course, we know very well that components which are elementary in the programming language are composite from the point of view of the generated machine instructions and the internal workings of the machine. For example, we may declare an item

```
02   FLDB PIC X(20).
```

and use the elementary operation

```
MOVE SPACES TO FLDB.
```

Inspection of the generated code shows that it consists of two instructions

```
MVI    FLDB, C' '
MVC    FLDB+1(19), FLDB
```

whose action is to move a space into the first position of FLDB and then propagate that space through the remaining positions. Further, inspection of the internal workings of the machine shows that the MVC instruction is implemented by an iteration. So the structure of the operation MOVE SPACES TO FLDB is

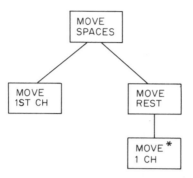

And there are further levels to be discovered by delving deeper into the machine. But these levels do not concern us as COBOL users. The MOVE statement is elementary in COBOL; its effect is well defined in the language specification; we need not, and should not, look further than that.

The usefulness of the elementary operations depends heavily on the fact that we can use them in many different programs, and in many different places in each program. This is not in general true of components created during the process of top-down design. In top-down design we are concerned to limit our span of attention. We start with the idea of a program P, and dissect it into, say, P1, P2 and P3, giving the structure:

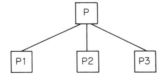

The effect of the dissection, if we do it properly, is that we can now consider each of P1, P2 and P3 in isolation: this was our original purpose, since P is too complex to be considered as a whole. The dissection of P1 is carried out without paying attention to P2 or P3, and so on until we arrive at the final structure. This final structure is, perhaps, as shown at the top of p. 34.

This structure is an example of what is called a tree. (To see why, you have

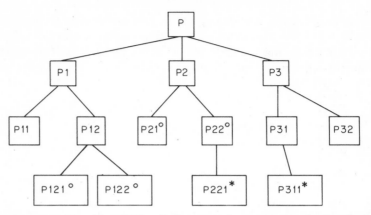

to stand on your head or, if that is inconvenient, to turn the book upside down.) The essential property of a tree is that there is only one path from the root (P) to any node; P122, for example, can be reached from P only by passing through P1 and P12. The effect, for the resulting program, is that we have only one context for each component. The context of P122 is set by P12; the context of P12 by P1; the context of P1 by P. We never have to ask "how did we get here?", because the answer is always the same for a particular component and is immediately visible from the program structure diagram.

If, by contrast, we allow ourselves during top-down design to treat a component as a part of two or more higher level components, we create a structure such as this:

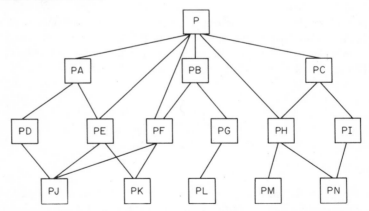

This is not a tree. PJ can be reached from PD, PE or PF; PE can be reached from PA or from P; PF can be reached from PB or from P. So the context of PJ, for a particular execution, depends on the path taken by the program before PJ is entered. This uncertainty will cause difficulties and errors. If the program fails during execution, we will need some kind of trace facility to help us to determine why it has failed, to determine the history of execution before the failure. We may also wonder about the design process: was PE designed originally as a part of PA or as a part of P? Or did the designer have both PA and P in mind when he designed PE? In designing PJ, did he then have in mind PD, PE as a part of PA, PE as a part of P, PF as a part of PB and PF as a part of P, all at the same time? If so, his span of attention must have been uncomfortably wide.

All this discussion has been based on the assumption that we are practising top-down design; it leads to the conclusion that the result of top-down design should be a tree structure. But top-down is not the only possible technique. There is also bottom-up. In top-down design we say, in effect, "this problem is too complex for me; I shall dissect it into a number of smaller problems, and those into smaller problems still, until I have a set of problems simple enough to solve". In bottom-up design we say instead "this machine is not well suited to my problem, because the elementary operations are too elementary; I shall therefore use the elementary operations to create a more powerful machine, and the operations of that machine to create one still more powerful, until I have a machine on which my problem can be easily solved".

In bottom-up design we are paying only the most general attention to the original problem: the main impetus of the work is to create a new machine which will be more suitable than the old one. For example, if we were forced to write a set of mathematical programs in COBOL, involving manipulation of matrices, we might reasonably begin by designing a new machine COBOL-M which was capable of arithmetic operations on matrices. We might specify a new COBOL-M data type, the matrix, and a set of operations MATRADD, MATRSUB, MATRMUL and MATRDIV; we would find it convenient to introduce new figurative constants MZERO and M1, to represent the zero and unit matrices. To implement our new machine we might decide that the new data components should be defined as members of the source-statement library and that the operations should be written as sub-programs. Just as in COBOL we can multiply two numbers, A and B, assigning the result to another number C, by the statement

MULTIPLY A BY B GIVING C

so in our new machine we could multiply two matrices by the statement

CALL "MATRMUL" USING A, B, C.

Effectively, the matrix operations are elementary operations in the COBOL-M machine. They should be so well designed and so carefully specified that we need never ask how they work or how they were built: it should be enough to ask what they do, and the answer should be clear from the specifications. The COBOL-M programmer can use them as elementary operations, writing the statements CALL MATRMUL, CALL MATRADD and the others with the same freedom as the COBOL programmer writes MULTIPLY, ADD and the other COBOL arithmetic verbs.

Our conclusions, then, are these. First, that components of general utility do not (and should not) emerge from top-down design; second, the converse of the first, that such components can and should be created by the processes of bottom-up design; third, that such components must be thought of by their user, the top-down designer, as elementary components of the machine he is using and therefore not susceptible to internal examination; fourth, that the top-down designer must create tree structures, working at a level at which there can be no shared components.

Once again we seem to be flying in the face of established good practice. Surely it is every programmer's ambition and duty to design so that a high proportion of his code can be used for more than one purpose, thus economizing on valuable storage space? The objection contains its own answer. Shared components, other than elementary components, are an optimization device; they are discussed in Chapter 12.

2.7

A program structure, and the coded program written from it, is a general pattern defining a set of possible computation processes. Each time the program is run one particular member of that set of processes is executed:

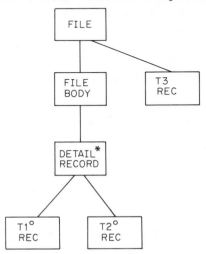

it is unlikely, for most realistic programs, that exactly the same process would be executed on two different occasions; if we were to keep an exact trace, statement by statement, of each execution of the program, we would be very surprised to find two identical traces. The set of possible complete processes is very large, but at the same time it is tightly constrained by the program structure.

The same is true of the data structures on which we base our program structures. A data structure for a file is a general pattern defining the set of all possible instances of that file: the set of all possible instances is large, but at the same time it is tightly constrained by the structure. Consider, for example, the file structure shown opposite.

A T1 record has the value 1 in position 1, a T2 record has the value 2, and so on. The following instances of files are all properly described by this structure:

    T1, T1, T3;
    T2, T1, T1, T1, T3;
    T3;
    T2, T2, T2, T2, T2, T3;

but the following are not:

    T1, T2;
    T4, T3;
    T3, T1, T1, T2, T3;

Now, if we base our program structure on the file structure given, because that is the structure of the input file which the program is required to process, we cannot usefully predict the operation of the program on those files which are not properly described by the structure. We will say that those files are not valid input to the program, and that its operation on those files is unspecified.

Sometimes it is right to draw an exceedingly general data structure. If a program processes a punched card file, it would be very inconvenient if the behaviour of the program were unspecified merely because of a keypunching error or because a card had been dropped from the deck. So in such a case we would devise a structure which could accommodate all possible card files, and the resulting program would operate in a specified manner on any deck of cards we cared to present.

But this is not the usual case. More often we will want to define data structures which are quite tightly constrained. We must then ensure, at a higher level of design, that invalid data cannot reach the program.

C

2.8

Our programs are designed for essentially sequential machines, and are written accordingly in a sequential language. Some machines are not purely sequential, but can carry out more than one operation at a time; for example, in a machine with two arithmetic processors the following two operations can be performed in parallel:

> ADD A, B GIVING X.
> MULTIPLY C BY D GIVING Y.

one processor calculates X while the other simultaneously calculates Y.

In the present state of computing technology we are almost always quite happy to leave it to the compiler and the hardware between them to recognize the possibility of such parallel computation. We are not disturbed by the necessity of writing a program which is, in an important sense, overspecific: we have chosen to write the MULTIPLY second and the ADD first, while we could equally well have made the opposite choice; ideally, perhaps, we would have written the program in a form which left the order unspecified.

To write such programs we would need a different set of structuring rules from those described in this chapter. We would need to be able to write components which were like sequences except that their parts were unordered; like selections except that the conditions were tested in any order, or in none; like iterations except that the occurrences of the iterated part were taken in any order, or in none.

While we are designing sequential structures for sequential machines we will occasionally feel the need for an unordered component; this need arises in one of the exercises at the end of this chapter. But the discomfort is small. Where the discomfort is large, as when we are dealing with a multi-threading problem, we need to find some way of simulating parallel operation of several processes: the topic is discussed in Chapters 10 and 11.

EXERCISE 2.1(a)

Transcribe the following structure diagram into schematic logic without using the "do" notation except for I, J, F, K and H.

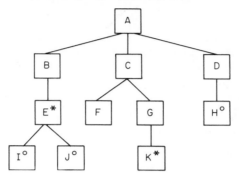

EXERCISE 2.2(a)

Draw a structure diagram from the following schematic logic.

```
A     seq
      B       seq
              do C;
              do D;
              E       iter
                          do F;
              E       end
      B       end
      G       select
              do H;
      G       or
              I       select
                      J       select
                                  do K;
                      J       or
                                  do L;
                      J       end
              I       or
                      do M;
              I       end
      G       end
A     end
```

EXERCISE 2.3 (a)

Draw a structure diagram of the following COBOL paragraph.

```
    A.
        IF X = 0
            MOVE Y TO Z
        ELSE PERFORM B UNTIL W =  0
            IF V = 0
                MOVE T TO U
            ELSE ADD R TO S.
        IF Q =  0
            PERFORM C
            PERFORM D
            PERFORM E.
```

EXERCISE 2.4 (a)

Draw a data structure diagram of a conversation: a conversation consists of messages, alternately from the user (a "user-message") and from the system (a "system-message"). The conversation always begins with a user-message and always ends with a system-message.

EXERCISE 2.5 (a)

Draw a data structure diagram of Utopia: Utopia is divided into two parts, Western Utopia and Eastern Utopia; all of the people who live in Western Utopia have green eyes, but in the Eastern part people have either blue or brown eyes.

EXERCISE 2.6 (b)

Draw a data structure of a meal: a meal is defined by the following invitation:

"We hope you will enjoy your meal. Please help yourself to any of the starters; then choose from three delicious soups, with roll and butter, and follow with any number of helpings from our cold buffet. There is tea or coffee to finish off your meal. We regret that the high price of caviar forces us to ask you not to have soup if you have chosen caviar as your starter."

EXERCISE 2.7 (c)

Design a COBOL matrix manipulation facility along the lines suggested in Section 2.6.

EXERCISE 2.8 (c)

Examine the two following flowcharts, and say precisely why they cannot be coded directly into schematic logic. Redraw them, without changing their effective operation, so that they consist only of proper sequences, iterations and selections, and code them into schematic logic.

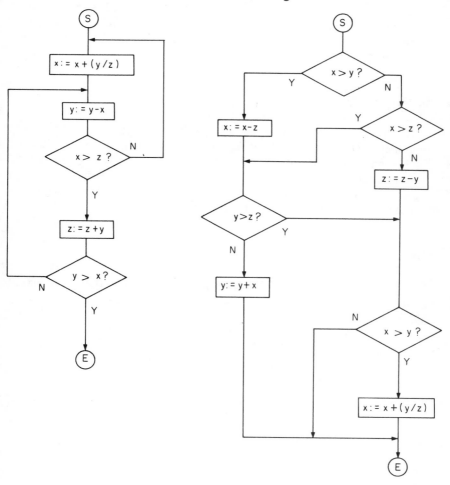

QUESTION 2.1

Most programming languages embody a degree of bottom-up design: some operations and some data types are, by design, composite structures of more elementary parts of the language; some languages provide facilities to allow you to carry the bottom-up design to a further stage. Examine the facilities of COBOL or PL/I or FORTRAN or ALGOL in this light.

QUESTION 2.2

Look at the problem specifications for Exercises 2.1 and 2.2. The component names have been allocated in an obvious manner. Now look at your solutions to those exercises. What has happened to the ordering of the component names? Why?

QUESTION 2.3

In Section 2.6 two structures are shown for program P; the first, with components P1, P11 etc, is a tree; the second, with components PA, PB, etc., is not. You may have noticed that no iteration or selection symbols ("*" or "o") were written on the second structure. Why not? How would we have to change our notation to allow the second diagram to show sequence, iteration and selection without ambiguity?

QUESTION 2.4

Elaborate the data structure FILE shown in Section 2.7 so that it can accept as valid any file whatsoever. How many different ways are there of doing this? How does your choice of elaboration affect the treatment of those records which would have fitted validly into the original structure?

3. BASIC DESIGN TECHNIQUES

3.1

The foundation of the design technique is the following three-step procedure:

(i) consider the problem environment and record our understanding of it by defining structures for the data to be processed;

(ii) form a program structure based on the data structures;

(iii) define the task to be performed in terms of the elementary operations available, and allocate each of those operations to suitable components of the program structure.

When the program structure is formed from the data structures it is only a skeleton: we will usually need to add some components when we come to allocate the executable operations.

We begin by illustrating the technique in its application to the following simple problem.

PROBLEM 3—CANTOR'S ENUMERATION OF RATIONALS

A rational number is a number which can be expressed with perfect accuracy as the ratio of two integers: thus 3/5 is a rational number, but the square root of 2 is not. The question arises: how many rational numbers are there? Clearly, there is an infinity of rational numbers, but there are different sizes of infinity: for example, it can be shown that there are more non-terminating decimal fractions than there are integers, although there is an infinity of each.

Cantor showed that the number of rationals is the same as the number of integers. He did this by arranging the rationals in a 1–1 correspondence with the integers, from which it follows that there must be the same number of each. If we write the rationals in an array:

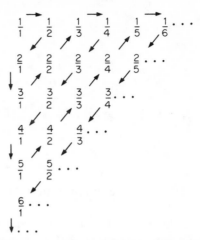

then by following the arrows we can read off the rationals in a pre-specified order and be sure that each one occurs once and once only.

The problem is to design a program which will print out the rationals in the order shown, stopping as soon as the number 100/1 has been printed. Print one number on each line.

We begin, as we always will, by considering the data structure. The set of rationals forms a zigzag pattern as shown by the arrows in the array. In fact, it is an iteration of zigzags, where each zigzag consists of a diagonal ("zig") pointing upwards and to the right followed by a diagonal ("zag") pointing downwards and to the left. Each diagonal is an iteration of rationals; the first diagonal of all consists of one rational only, the number 1/1. Conveniently, we wish to stop when the hundredth diagonal is complete, that is, at the end of the fiftieth zigzag.

The data structure is therefore:

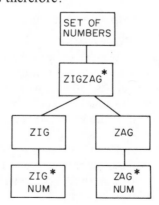

We may ignore the structure of the output; it will be enough to DISPLAY each rational as we encounter it. The program structure may be formed directly from the structure of the set of numbers by trivially changing the names of the components:

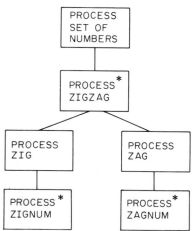

We have now completed the first two steps in the design process. Life will not often be so easy! We now turn our attention to the third stage.

Because we have structured our solution as an iteration of zigzags, we will need a variable to identify each zigzag: let us call it Z. We will also need two variables, S and T, for the numerator and denominator respectively of the rationals. We must initialize Z to the value 1, and we must increment it by 1; we must initialize S and T to 1, and both increment and decrement them by 1; we must intialize S and T from Z; and we must display each generated rational and stop when we have finished. So the list of operations is this:

  1. $S: = 1$
  2. $S: = S+1$
  3. $S: = S-1$
  4. $S: =$ some function of Z
  5. $T: = 1$
  6. $T: = T+1$
  7. $T: = T-1$
  8. $T: =$ some function of Z
  9. $Z: = 1$
  10. $Z: = Z+1$
  11. DISPLAY S/T
  12. STOP

D

Before embarking on the allocation of these operations to the program structure, the reader should remind himself of the form of iteration we use. If A is an iteration of B, then full schematic logic for A is:

> . . .
> get 1st potential B;
> A **iter until** no more B's
> process B;
> get next potential B;
> A **end**
> . . .

It is always necessary to get the 1st potential occurrence of the iterated part in this way, before entering the iteration proper: otherwise the test at the entry to the iteration could not be made.

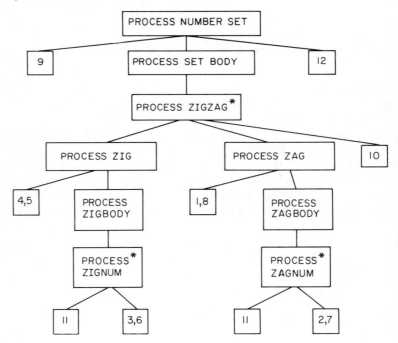

We now set about allocating the operations to the program structure.

1. $S := 1$ must be executed once at the beginning of each zag.
2. $S := S + 1$ must be executed once at the end of each zagnum, as part of getting the next potential zagnum.

3. S: =S−1 must be executed once at the end of each zignum, as part of getting the next potential zignum.

4. S must be initialized from Z once at the beginning of each zig; we can now see that the required operation is S: =2*Z−1.

5. T: =1 must be executed once at the beginning of each zig.

6. T: =T+1 must be executed once at the end of each zignum, as part of getting the next potential zignum.

7. T: =T−1 must be executed once at the end of each zagnum, as part of getting the next potential zagnum.

8. T must be initialized from Z once at the beginning of each zag; we can now see that the required operation is T: =2*Z.

9. Z: =1 must be executed once at the beginning of the program.

10. Z: =Z+1 must be executed once at the end of each zigzag, to get the next potential zigzag.

11. DISPLAY S/T must be executed once for each zignum and once for each zagnum.

12. STOP must be executed once at the end of the program.

Adding the necessary components to the program structure, and representing the operations by their serial numbers, we arrive at the structure shown opposite. Transcribing the structure diagram into schematic logic, we have:

```
PNSET   seq
        Z: =1;
    PSBODY   iter until Z > 50
        PZIGZAG   seq
            PROCZIG   seq
                      S: =2*Z−1;
                      T: =1;
                PZIGBODY   iter until S < 1
                    PZIGNUM   seq
                              display S/T
                              S: =S−1;
                              T: =T+1;
                    PZIGNUM   end
                PZIGBODY   end
            PROCZIG   end
            PROCZAG   seq
                      S: =1;
                      T: =2*Z;
```

```
                    PZAGBODY   iter until T < 1
                      PZAGNUM   seq
                                display S/T;
                                S: =S+1;
                                T: =T−1;
                      PZAGNUM   end
                    PZAGBODY   end
                  PROCZAG   end
                        Z: =Z+1;
              PZIGZAG   end
        PSBODY   end
            stop
  PNSET   end
```

The conditions on the iterations are derived from the definitions of the iterated parts. For a zigzag we must have $0 < Z \leqslant 50$; for a zignum we must have $1 \leqslant S \leqslant 2*Z-1$; for a zagnum we must have $2Z \geqslant T \geqslant 1$.

Evidently, the program is less efficient than it could be. For the moment, we will ignore the obvious possibilities of optimization, leaving them as an exercise for the reader at the end of this chapter, and hurry on to the coding. Here is one of many possible ways of coding the program in COBOL·

```
    . . .
    77   Z PIC 99.
    77   S PIC 999.
    77   T PIC 999.
    . . .
    PROCEDURE DIVISION.
    PNSET.
        PERFORM PZIGZAG VARYING Z FROM 1 BY 1
                UNTIL Z > 50.
        STOP RUN.
    PZIGZAG.
        ADD Z, Z, −1, GIVING S.
        MOVE 1 TO T.
        PERFORM PZIGNUM UNTIL S < 1.
        MOVE 1 TO S.
        ADD Z, Z, GIVING T.
        PERFORM PZAGNUM UNTIL T < 1.
    PZIGNUM.
```

```
        DISPLAY S, "/", T.
        SUBTRACT 1 FROM S.
        ADD 1 TO T.
    PZAGNUM.
        DISPLAY S, "/", T.
        ADD 1 TO S.
        SUBTRACT 1 FROM T.
```

We have not attempted to print S/T in an edited form—the task is purely one of COBOL manipulation. Nor have we made any effort to choose the most efficient data types for Z, S and T: the choice depends largely on the way in which the various data types are represented by the particular compiler we are using, so throughout this book we will choose merely the most obvious types for our data. A practising COBOL programmer must, of course, make choices appropriate to his compiler and machine.

3.2　Reading Serial Input

Problems 1 and 3—the Multiplication Table and Cantor's Enumeration of Rationals—have an artificial air: it is hard to imagine a real need for such programs; certainly, since they produce the same output each time they are run, it is hard to imagine that anyone would want to run them more than once.

The reason is essentially that they have no serial input; reading and processing serial input forms a vital part of almost any useful program. Furthermore, as we shall discover later in this book, there are many awkward problems which yield quickly to treatment as problems in serial file processing although at first sight they appear to be nothing of the kind.

Here is a problem with a serial input file.

PROBLEM 4—COUNTING BATCHES

An input file of card images is to be analysed. There are three card types, T1, T2 and T3, with the values 1, 2 and 3 respectively in position 1 of the card. The required analysis is as follows:

Count the cards preceding the first T1 (count A);

Display the first T1;

Display the last card, which is always the first T2 following the first T1;

Count the batches following the first T1, where a batch is either an uninterrupted succession of one or more T1 cards or an uninterrupted succession of one or more T3 cards (count B);

Count the T1 cards after the first T1 card (count C);

Count the batches following the first T1 card which consist of T3 cards (count D).

All counts are to be displayed following the display of the last card. The file is known to be in correct format; that is, there is at least one T1 card, the last card is a T2, and no T2 intervenes between the first T1 and the last card.

Here is a data structure diagram for the input file.

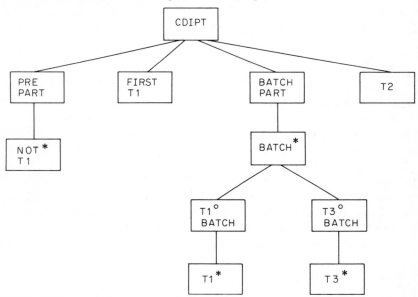

This diagram reflects our understanding of the problem as seen in the input file structure. The PREPART is the set of cards preceding the first T1; between the first T1 and the last card is a set of batches (BATCHPART), and each batch may be either a succession of T1 cards or a succession of T3 cards. Note that we have shown both types of batch as simple iterations: to be completely explicit we should have shown each type as consisting of a first card followed by a set of further cards, as shown opposite.

The program structure can be based directly on the CDIPT structure: once again we will print our output by DISPLAY statements, and pay no

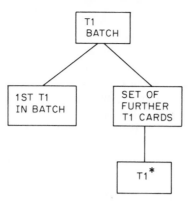

particular attention to the output structure. The program structure is therefore obtained by redrawing the CDIPT structure with the word "process" added to the name in each box.

The list of executable operations is obvious. It is:

1.   CA: =0
2.   CB: =0
3.   CC: =0
4.   CD: =0
5.   CA: =CA+1
6.   CB: =CB+1
7.   CC: =CC+1
8.   CD: =CD+1
9.   display first T1
10. display last card
11. display counts
12. open CDIPT
13. close CDIPT
14. stop
15. read CDIPT

Allocation of these operations to the program structure is also obvious: for example, we wish to increment count A once for each card preceding the first T1, so operation 5 is allocated to the program component PROCESS NOT T1. The last operation, however, read CDIPT, may cause us some difficulty. Our initial inclination may be to allocate the operation simply to each program component which processes a card: the component then reads the card and processes it. But remembering that iterations and selections have their condition tests at their points of entry we can see that something a little more sophisticated is needed.

3.3   Reading Ahead

What is needed is that we should always keep one record ahead of the processing. We read the first record at the time we open the file, and subsequently we read whenever the processing of a record is complete. Each program component which processes a record therefore takes the form "process this record and then read another".

Leaving Problem 4 aside for the moment, we can see how the need for the technique arises from a trivial illustration. If we have a file which is a sequence of just two cards, say a T1 followed by a T2, we can process the file by the program:

```
P   seq
      open file;
      P1   seq
             read;
             process T1;
      P1   end
      P2   seq
             read;
             process T2;
      P2   end
      close file;
P   end
```

There is no difficulty in placing the read operations; the T1 record is always present, and P1 merely reads it and processes it; similarly P2 reads and then processes the T2 record. There are no decisions to be made. Now we introduce a minor complication: we allow the T1 record to be omitted; the file now consists of

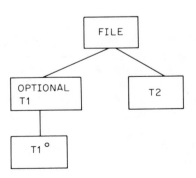

and we wish to modify our program accordingly. We ought to be able to modify it by changing only P1—after all, it is only the first part of the sequence that is affected—but this proves surprisingly hard. For example, the program

```
P    seq
     open file;
     POP1    seq
                 read;
             POPTL1    select T1 present
                       process T1;
             POPTL1    or T1 absent
                       do nothing;
             POPTL1    end
     POP1    end
     P2    seq
           read;
           process T2;
     P2    end
     close file;
P    end
```

will not work. When the optional T1 record is absent, the T2 record has already been read (in POP1) when we arrive at P2; the read statement in P2 then obliterates the T2 record by reading the end-of-file marker. Nor can the problem be solved by writing POP1 in the form

```
POP1    select T1 present
        read;
        process T1;
POP1    or T1 absent
        do nothing;
POP1    end
```

because the condition on the selection cannot be evaluated: we must read the first record, whatever it may be, before we can decide whether the T1 record is present.

We may attempt an *ad hoc* solution by writing

```
P    seq
     open file;
     POP1    seq
                 read;
```

```
        POPTL1    select T1 present
                  process T1;
                  switch: =1;
        POPTL1    or T1 absent
                  switch: =0;
        POPTL1    end
    POP1   end
    P2    seq
        P2X    select switch=1
               read;
        P2X    end
               process T2;
    P2         end
        close file;
  P    end
```

When switch=0, the T2 record has already been read by POP1 and no read operation is required in P2; when switch=1, POP1 has read the T1 record, and the T2 record is still to be read by P2. It should be clear that this is a very bad solution: with more complex file structures it will lead to a mass of confusing and error-prone statements for setting and testing the necessary switches.

The technique of reading ahead solves the problem perfectly. As soon as we open the file we read the first record. This is then available for examination, as often as we wish, by the condition tests in iterations and selections: it is the next record to be processed. Examination of the record does not, of itself, affect it; if we decide that it is not what we are looking for, we simply leave it alone and it is available for further examination elsewhere in the program. When the record is finally processed by some program component, the sequence of events is:

stop thinking of the record as the next record to be processed, and think of it instead as the current record;

process the current record completely;

read another record so that a new next record will be available for examination.

This arrangement, reading one record ahead, allows the program to explore the input file structure by examination of the next record to be processed. Some input file structures will be such that we cannot explore them effectively without reading two or more records ahead· the questions we need to ask cannot be answered by looking only at the single next record. File structures of this kind, and the technique of multiple reading ahead, are discussed later in the book.

The single read ahead technique may be summarized by these two rules for allocating the read operation:

read the first record immediately following the open;

read again at the end of each program component which processes an input record.

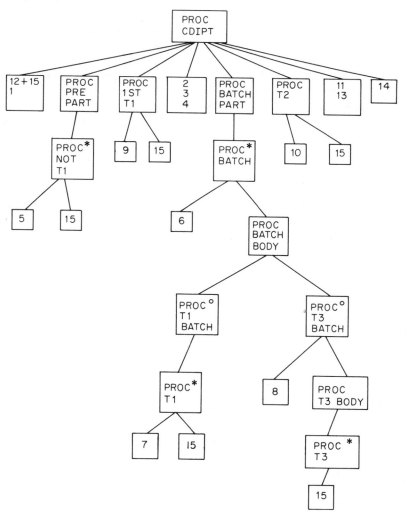

3.4

Returning to our consideration of Problem 4, we may now complete the allocation of operations, giving the program structure shown on p. 55.

It is essential to recognize that the third step, allocating the executable operations, provides the criterion of correctness for the work done in the first two. For example, operation 6, incrementing the count of batches, must be allocated to a program component which is executed once per batch: if we were unable to find such a component in our program structure, or to add one by a trivial extension, we would know that the structure was incorrect. The third step in design must therefore be taken with great care and with a scrupulous consideration for the placing of each operation: if there is the slightest difficulty we must re-examine the program structure to find the source of the difficulty. The program structure diagram represents our model of the problem: if one of the operations cannot easily be be fitted into that stucture, there is something wrong with our model.

Writing schematic logic is left as an exercise for the reader. Here is a possible form of COBOL coding:

```
      ...
77    CDEOF PIC X VALUE SPACE.
      ...
PROCEDURE DIVISION.
PROCCDIPTSEQ.
      OPEN INPUT CDIPT.
      READ CDIPT AT END  MOVE "E" TO CDEOF
      MOVE 0 TO CA.
PPREPARTITER.
      IF T1 GO TO PPREPARTEND.
      ADD 1 TO CA.
      READ CDIPT AT END MOVE "E" TO CDEOF.
      GO TO PPREPARTITER.
PPREPARTEND.
      DISPLAY INCARD.
      READ CDIPT AT END MOVE "E" TO CDEOF.
      MOVE 0 TO CB, CC, CD.
PBATCHPARTITER.
      IF (NOT T1) AND (NOT T3) GO TO PBATCHPARTEND.
      ADD 1 TO CB.
```

```
PBATCHBODYSLCT.
    IF NOT T1 GO TO PBATCHBODYOR.
PT1BATCHITER.
    IF NOT T1 GO TO PT1BATCHEND.
    ADD 1 TO CC.
    READ CDIPT AT END MOVE "E" TO CDEOF.
    GO TO PT1BATCHITER.
PT1BATCHEND.
    GO TO PBATCHBODYEND.
PBATCHBODYOR.
    ADD 1 TO CD.
PT3BATCHITER.
    IF NOT T3 GO TO PT3BATCHEND.
    READ CDIPT AT END MOVE "E" TO CDEOF.
    GO TO PT3BATCHITER.
PT3BATCHEND.
PBATCHBODYEND.
    GO TO PBATCHPARTITER.
PBATCHPARTEND.
    DISPLAY INCARD.
    READ CDIPT AT END MOVE "E" TO CDEOF.
    DISPLAY CA, CB, CC, CD.
    CLOSE CDIPT.
    STOP RUN.
PROCCDIPTEND.
```

3.5   End of File

The physical representation of a serial file must include a special end-of-file record of some kind; in general, we can recognize that the file has been completely processed only by encountering this special record.

In Problem 4, however, we were able to recognize the end of the input file by the terminal T2 record. The T2 record acts as a trailer or sentinel, but in addition it plays the role of an ordinary record of the file and may be processed in whatever way we wish. This is not true of the special end-of-file record, which is directly recognized only by the input–output software and is inaccessible to the programmer. Conventionally, in COBOL, PL/I, FORTRAN and other commonly used languages, recognition of the end-of-file record is fugitive: it raises a condition which can be evaluated only as part of the read operation itself, and the programmer must ensure that the condition is recorded in a form capable of subsequent evaluation.

For example, in COBOL he must write

READ INFILE AT END imperative-statement

where imperative-statement is an assignment statement, a GO TO, a PER-FORM or some other unconditional statement. In FORTRAN he may write

READ (3,100,END=99) A, B, C

specifying that control is to be transferred to statement 99 when the special end-of-file record is read. In PL/I the end of file is handled by an on-unit:

ON ENDFILE (INFILE)
    EOF_FLAG="E";

when a read statement is executed which causes the end-of-file record to be read, the assignment to EOF_FLAG is executed and control returns to the point following the read statement.

Whatever the facilities, or obstacles, provided by the input–output software, we must adopt a technique which satisfies these requirements:

the read operation must remain closed with respect to the flow of control; that is, processing must continue at the point in the text following the read statement, whether or not the end-of-file has been reached;

the end-of-file record must be effectively recognizable as a possible value of "next record", and the test for the value must be capable of being made anywhere in the program and not only during or immediately after the read operation.

One obvious technique is to place some unique value in the record area:

READ INFILE AT END MOVE HIGH-VALUES TO KEY-FIELD.

However, this technique is not sufficiently general. First, there is no reason why the records of a serial file should not be bit-strings, able to take all possible values; there is then no unique value available to designate the end of file. Second, some software has been designed (wrongly) in such a way that main storage for the record area is released when the end of file is encountered; the area then becomes unaddressable, and any attempt to assign a value to it or to test its value will cause an illegal program-check.

The only sufficiently general solution is to provide an additional data item which is conceptually, but not physically, part of the record area, and to set the unique value in that item. CDEOF, in the COBOL coding for Problem 4, is such an item; if we have a need to test for the end of file we may write

```
   ...
77   CDEOF PIC X VALUE SPACE.
   88   EOF-CDIPT VALUE "E".
   ...
     READ CDIPT AT END MOVE "E" TO CDEOF.
     ...
     IF EOF-CDIPT...
     ...
     ...
     IF EOF-CDIPT...
     ...
```

3.6

Here is another simple problem concerned with processing an input file.

PROBLEM 5—STORES MOVEMENTS SUMMARY

The stores section in a factory issues and receives parts. Each issue and each receipt is recorded on a punched card: the card contains the part-number, the movement type (I for issue, R for receipt) and the quantity. The cards are copied to magnetic tape and sorted into part-number order. The program to be written will produce a simple summary of the net movement for each part. The format of the summary is:

```
A5/13672   NET MOVEMENT     −490
A5/17924   NET MOVEMENT   175000
B31/82     NET MOVEMENT      127
   ...
```

The lines of the summary are to be printed by DISPLAY statements; no attention should be paid to such refinements as skipping over the perforations at the end of each sheet of paper. Note that the part-number is not numeric or strictly alphanumeric: any encodable character can appear in any position.

Clearly the data structure of the sorted movements file is:

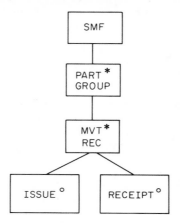

We may take the program structure directly from the data structure. The list of executable operations is:

1. open SMF
2. close SMF
3. read SMF
4. display summary line
5. PARTNO: =part-number of next input record
6. NETMVT: =0
7. NETMVT: =NETMVT+quantity
8. NETMVT: =NETMVT−quantity
9. stop

Allocation of the operations, and the attendant elaboration of the program structure, is left as an exercise for the reader. The resulting schematic logic is.

```
PROCSMF   seq
              open SMF; read SMF;
        PSMFBODY   iter until eof-SMF
            PPARTGROUP   seq
                    PARTNO: =part-number;
```

$$\text{NETMVT:} = 0;$$

PPARTGPBODY   **iter until** eof-SMF or
$$\text{PARTNO} \neq \text{part-number}$$

    PMVTREC **seq**

      PMVTRECDATA   **select** code $= I$
$$\text{NETMVT:} = \text{NETMVT}$$
$$-\text{quantity}$$

      PMVTRECDATA   or code $= R$
$$\text{NETMVT:} = \text{NETMVT}$$
$$+\text{quantity};$$

      PMVTRECDATA **end**

      read SMF;

    PMVTREC **end**

PPARTGPBODY **end**

      display summary line;

  PPARTGROUP **end**

PSMFBODY **end**

    close SMF;

    stop;

PROCSMF **end**

A possible COBOL program is ·
  ...

```
PROCSMF.
    OPEN INPUT SMF.
    READ SMF AT END MOVE "E" TO SMF-EOF.
    PERFORM PPARTGROUP UNTIL EOF-SMF.
    CLOSE SMF.
    STOP RUN.
PPARTGROUP.
    MOVE PART-NUMBER TO PARTNO.
    MOVE 0 TO NETMVT.
    PERFORM PMVTREC UNTIL EOF-SMF OR
            (PART NUMBER NOT=PARTNO).
    DISPLAY PARTNO, "NET MOVEMENT" NETMVT.
PMVTREC.
    IF CODE = "I"
        SUBTRACT QUANTITY FROM NETMVT
    ELSE ADD QUANTITY TO NETMVT.
    READ SMF AT END MOVE "E" TO SMF-EOF.
```

Even a simple problem such as this can be badly mangled. Here is a traditional, and very bad, solution:

```
...
77   FIRST-TIME-SWITCH PIC X VALUE "Y".
...
PROCEDURE DIVISION.
START-PROGRAM.
    OPEN INPUT SMF.
READ-LOOP.
    READ SMF AT END GO TO END-PROGRAM.
    IF FIRST-TIME-SWITCH = "Y"
       OR PARTNO NOT = PART-NUMBER
       PERFORM CONTROL-BREAK-PROCESS.
    IF CODE = "I"
       SUBTRACT QUANTITY FROM NETMVT
    ELSE ADD QUANTITY TO NETMVT.
    GO TO READ-LOOP.
CONTROL-BREAK-PROCESS.
    IF FIRST-TIME-SWITCH = "Y"
       MOVE "N" TO FIRST-TIME-SWITCH
    ELSE DISPLAY PARTNO, "NET MOVEMENT", NETMVT.
    MOVE 0 TO NETMVT.
    MOVE PART-NUMBER TO PARTNO.
END-PROGRAM.
    IF FIRST-TIME-SWITCH = "N"
       DISPLAY PARTNO, "NET MOVEMENT", NETMVT.
    CLOSE SMF.
    STOP RUN.
```

The fundamental error in this solution is that it is based on an implicit data structure:

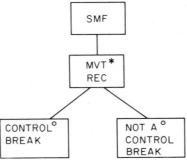

The file is regarded as an iteration of records, and the program, accordingly, consists of a main loop which processes one record on each iteration. A record may be either a control-break record or an ordinary record; a control-break record is one whose part-number is different from the part-number of the immediately preceding record. From this wrong structure many difficulties arise. The processing of a control-break record must include both the ending of the preceding part group and the initialization of the new part group. We must arrange that the first record of all is treated as a control-break record, and that the end-of-file record is also treated as a control-break record. But for the first record there is no preceding part group to be ended, and for the end of file there is no new group to be initialized. We need the first-time-switch to ensure that the first record is treated as a control-break, because there is no value we could set initially in PARTNO which would certainly differ from the part-number in the first record. We must also test the switch at the end of the program to cater for the possibility that the file contains no records: there would be no last part group to be ended at the end of the program.

The resulting program is more complex than it need be; it is harder to understand, and will certainly be harder to maintain. And yet this style of programming is traditional in some places. We may attribute this strange tradition, at least in part, to the treatment of end of file by statements of the form:

READ SMF AT END GO TO END-PROGRAM.

This treatment is unnecessary in COBOL, as we have seen, but is forced upon us in FORTRAN and in some low-level languages, where end of file must always cause an unconditional GO TO statement to be executed. This GO TO statement gives rise to serious difficulties in any program containing more than one READ statement: how can we know which READ was last executed? A spurious piece of folk-lore then develops: each program should contain only one READ statement for each input file. It follows that the program must be structured as an iteration of record processing, and the damage is done.

3.7

The data structure

is almost always wrong for a serial input file. It prevents us from expressing any relationships among the records, and relationships among records are almost always crucial to the problem to be solved. Suppose, for example, in Problem 4 we start from the structure

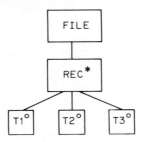

How are we to express the arrangement of the cards in batches? If there is no data component corresponding to a batch, there will be no program component "process one batch". Where , then, are we to allocate the operation "add 1 to count of batches"?

It is not enough that the data structure should be true. The structure given above for the file in Problem 4 is certainly true: the file does consist of records, and each record is either a T1, a T2 or a T3: but it is not true enough. We must express in the data structure all of the relationships which are relevant to the program.

EXERCISE 3.1 (b)

Write schematic logic for Problem 4 (Counting Batches).

EXERCISE 3.2 (b)

Code a COBOL program for Problem 4 from your schematic logic, using
PERFORM statements in the style of the COBOL coding shown for Problem
5 (Stores Movements Summary).

EXERCISE 3.3 (b)

Recode Problem 5 without using PERFORM statements, in the style of
the coding given for Problem 4.

EXERCISE 3.4 (b)

Examine the schematic logic given for Problem 3 (Cantor's Enumeration of
Rationals). Show how the solution can be optimized by using the variable S
both in its own role and in the role of Z. You will find it helpful to annotate the
schematic logic with statements about the values of S and T in terms of Z at
each point in the text: for example, at the end of **PZIGBODY** $T = 1 + 1$
$(2*Z - 1) = 2*Z$; the assignment statement $T := 2*Z$ in **PROCZAG** is
therefore not required.

QUESTION 3.1

Suppose that you have a machine in which numeric variables are always unsigned; the subtract operation specifies a branch address, the branch being taken when the result of the operation is negative. A subtract statement is therefore of the form

SUBTRACT A FROM B GIVING C,
ON NEGATIVE-RESULT GO TO BRANCH-ADDRESS.

Establish some general rules for writing programs involving signed arithmetic.

QUESTION 3.2

In Problem 3 (Cantor's Enumeration of Rationals) we were required to stop printing immediately after printing the number 100/1. Why was this so convenient? How would you design the program to stop after printing the number 99/2? How would you design the program to stop after printing an arbitrary number m/n? Can you write schematic logic for these designs? What are the difficulties?

QUESTION 3.3

Look at the COBOL coding given for Problem 4 (Counting Batches). What are the rules by which it has been derived from the schematic logic?

QUESTION 3.4

The COBOL coding given for Problem 5 (Stores Movements Summary) includes the statement

PERFORM PMVTREC UNTIL EOF-SMF OR
(PART-NUMBER NOT = PARTNO).

What does your COBOL language specification say about the generated code? Can you be certain that the test for PART-NUMBER NOT = PARTNO will be bypassed if EOF-SMF is true? Why might it matter? What change could you make to the COBOL program to ensure that it will never matter?

4. MULTIPLE DATA STRUCTURES

4.1 Structural Correspondence

So far, we have considered only problems which are concerned with a single file structure. More accurately, we have ignored all but one of the file structures in each program: the printed output in Problems 3, 4 and 5 was handled by DISPLAY statements, and we treated the DISPLAY as an elementary operation to be allocated in stage 3 of the design, taking no account of any structure the printed output might have.

This is not strictly permissible. The program structure must correspond to all of the data structures processed; if any structure is ignored we are liable to find that there are operations associated with that structure which cannot be allocated correctly in the program structure. We must therefore take all of the data structures into account when we form the program structure.

Consider, for example, the data structures of Problem 5, the Stores Movements Summary. There is a data structure for the input file, SMF, and a data structure for the printed report. Diagramming these side by side we have:

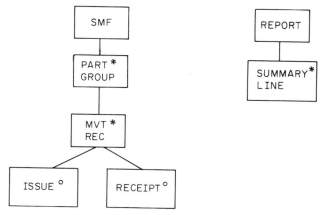

Our purpose is to form a program structure which corresponds simultaneously to both of these data structures. We begin by identifying the correspondences between the data structures themselves. Clearly, SMF corresponds to REPORT: when we run the program it will process one instance of SMF and produce one instance of REPORT. Similarly, PART GROUP corresponds to SUMMARY LINE: there is the same number of each, and the program produces one SUMMARY LINE from one PART GROUP. The reader may find it helpful to draw a line connecting SMF and REPORT, and another connecting PART GROUP and SUMMARY LINE in the diagrams above. We may then form the first two levels of the program structure:

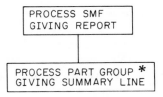

The second level component cannot itself be an iteration, as it is in the SMF data structure, because there is only one SUMMARY LINE. We therefore decide that it should be a sequence, and we complete the program structure:

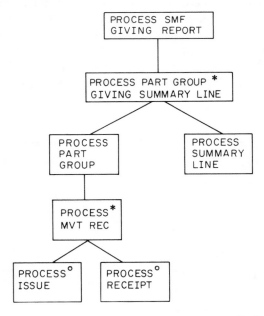

This structure now corresponds correctly to both of the data structures. A more substantial example is provided by the following problem.

PROBLEM 6—CUSTOMER PAYMENTS

Version 1

A transaction file contains details of payments made by customers. The file is stored by customer-number. Each payment record contains the customer-number and the date and amount of payment, and a record-type code having the value 1. An edited copy of the file is to be made, containing records of three types. The first, record type 1, is a copy of the input payment record, but with the date and amount fields in an edited format. The second, record type 2, is a total for each customer, containing the customer-number, the total amount and the record-type code, value 2. The third, record type 3, is a total for the whole file, containing only the total and the record-type code, value 3.

Version 2

In addition to producing the edited copy of the input file, the program must update a customer master file on tape. The customer master file contains a record for each customer, containing the customer-number and debt field. The debt field is to be reduced by the total of the payments made by the customer.

Version 2 of this problem is discussed below. For Version 1 the data structures are:

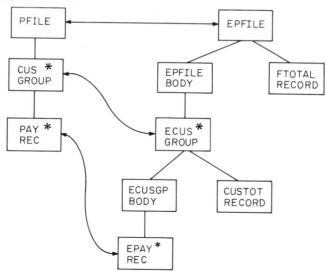

The lines drawn between the two structures show the correspondences. PFILE corresponds to EPFILE. CUS GROUP corresponds to ECUS GROUP; there is the same number of each, and they correspond pairwise. PAY REC corresponds to EPAY REC; within a CUS GROUP–ECUS GROUP pair, there is the same number of PAY RECs as of EPAY RECs, and again they correspond pairwise. So the required program structure for Version 1 is:

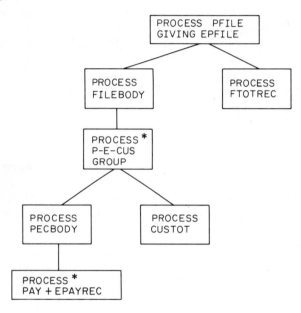

4.2   Collating

The above examples are concerned with correspondences between input and output files. An important class of problem is concerned with correspondences between two or more input files. Such problems are often referred to as "collating" or "matching" problems. Here is one.

PROBLEM 7—THE MAGIC MAILING COMPANY

The Magic Mailing Company has just sent out nearly 10 000 letters containing an unrepeatable and irresistible offer, each letter accompanied by a returnable acceptance card. The letters and cards are individually numbered from 1 to 9999. Not all of the letters were actually sent, because some were spoilt in the addressing process. Not all of the people who received letters returned the reply card. The marketing manager, who is a suspicious fellow, thinks that his staff may have stolen some of the reply cards for the letters which were not sent, and returned the cards so that they could benefit from the offer.

The letters sent have been recorded on a file; there is one record per letter sent, containing the letter-number and other information which does not concern us. The reply cards are machine readable, and have been copied to tape; each reply card returned gives rise to one record containing the letter-number and some other information which again does not concern us. Both the letter file and the reply file have been sorted into letter-number order.

A program is needed to report on the current state of the offer. Each line of the report corresponds to a letter-number; there are four types of line, each containing the letter-number, a code and a message. The four types of line are:

NNNNN   1   LETTER SENT AND REPLY RECEIVED

NNNNN   2   LETTER SENT, NO REPLY RECEIVED

NNNNN   3   NO LETTER SENT, REPLY RECEIVED

NNNNN   4   NO LETTER SENT, NO REPLY RECEIVED

There are three files to process: the letter file, the reply file and the report file. Data structures are:

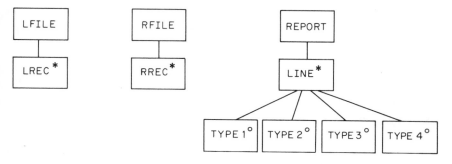

There is a perfect correspondence at the top level: each time the program is run it processes one LFILE and one RFILE and produces one REPORT. But there is no such correspondence at the next level. A given letter-number may appear on both LFILE and RFILE, on either, or on neither.

We may elaborate the input file structures in various ways in order to obtain the correspondences we need. For example, we may distinguish between matched and unmatched records, as in:

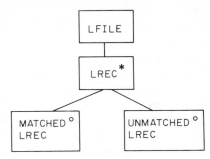

or we may distinguish between actual records and missing records, as in:

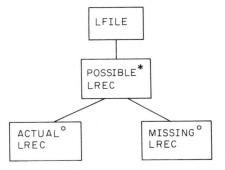

or we may use both of these distinctions, as in:

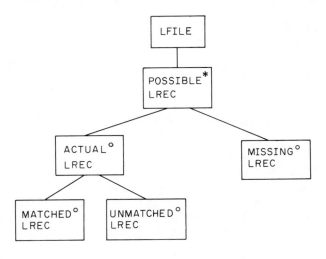

Analogous structures may be drawn for RFILE. However, whatever we do to achieve correspondence, we will be unable to escape from two constraints:

neither LFILE nor RFILE can be correctly interpreted by the program without reference to the other file

the program structure cannot contain a component "process lrec" or a component "process rrec".

Both of these constraints are due to the essential nature of any collating problem: none of the collated input files can be interpreted in isolation; there cannot be a unique program component to process each record of an input file because the records have various meanings according to the presence or absence of matching records on the other files.

Choosing the simplest of the data structures, distinguishing between matched and unmatched records on each file, we have the following correspondences:

LFILE, RFILE and REPORT correspond;

MATCHED LREC, MATCHED RREC and TYPE1 correspond;

UNMATCHED LREC corresponds to TYPE2;

UNMATCHED RREC corresponds to TYPE3;

nothing in the input files corresponds to TYPE4.

Listing and allocating the executable operations is straightforward, and we arrive at the following program:

```
PMAGIC    seq
          open LFILE; read LFILE;
          open RFILE; read RFILE;
          N:=1;
PMBODY    iter until N > 9999
   PROCNUM    select LNO = N = RNO
              write typel;
              read LFILE;
              read RFILE;
```

```
PROCNUM   or LNO = N ≠ RNO
          write type2;
          read LFILE;
PROCNUM   or LNO ≠ N = RNO
          write type3;
          read RFILE;
PROCNUM   or LNO ≠ N ≠ RNO
          write type4;
PROCNUM   end
          N:=N+1;
PMBODY   end
         close LFILE;
         close RFILE
PMAGIC   end
```

To avoid an irrelevant complication we have assumed that LNO is set to a value greater than 9999 at the end of LFILE, and that RNO is similarly set at the end of RFILE.

This program may be regarded as the standard form for all collating problems. It consists of an iteration which runs through all of the key values to be processed; the iterated part is a selection whose parts correspond to the possible matching cases on the input files. If we had three input files instead of two, the program would be unchanged except that PROCNUM would have 8 parts, there being 8 possible matching cases for three files.

4.3

Although we may regard PMAGIC as a standard form, most collating programs have a very different appearance.

Usually the fourth matching case—type4—is not required; if a key value is missing from all of the input files, then that key value is not to be processed. We may change the program PMAGIC appropriately by simply deleting the statement "write type4". The program then runs through the same set of key values as before, but processing of the fourth matching case, when the key value is absent from both of the input files, is now null. This change, however, is not usually sufficient. Usually the key values present in the input files are a very small subset of the set of all possible key values, and that set is very large. For example, if the key is an 8-character field, and each character has 8 bits, there are 2^{64} possible key values; even if the null fourth case can be processed in one microsecond, the program will spend tens of thou-

sand of years processing null cases. It is therefore essential to arrange that the
iteration PMBODY should run only through those values of the key which
are present in the input files.

We therefore modify the program components which assign the first and
and next values to N. Instead of the statements

$N := 1;$ and $N := N+1;$

we write

$N := \min(LNO, RNO);$

that is, we take the first and next values of N from the lesser of the two input
key values. We may now drop the fourth part of PROCNUM completely:
it can never be selected.

The program is now:

```
PMAGIC   seq
             open LFILE; read LFILE;
             open RFILE; read RFILE;
             N:=min(LNO,RNO);
PMBODY   iter until N > 2⁶⁴
         PROCNUM   select LNO = N = RNO
                       write type1;
                       read LFILE;
                       read RFILE
         PROCNUM   or LNO = N ≠ RNO
                       write type2;
                       read LFILE;
         PROCNUM   or LNO ≠ N = RNO
                       write type3;
                       read RFILE
         PROCNUM   end
                   N:=min(LNO,RNO);
PMBODY   end
             close LFILE;
             close RFILE;
PMAGIC   end
```

in which we have assumed that LNO is set to a value greater than 2^{64} at the
end of LFILE, and that RNO is set similarly.

This program is easy to write in schematic logic, but it is a little awkward
in COBOL. The assignment to N contains coding which compares the values

of LNO and RNO, and similar comparisons must be made to evaluate the conditions on the selection PROCNUM. If we cannot set LNO and RNO to a value greater than 2^{64}, as assumed in the schematic logic, we may find ourselves coding for the assignment to N

```
IF   EOF-L
     IF EOF-R
        MOVE TWO64PLUS1 TO N
     ELSE MOVE RNO TO N
ELSE IF EOF-R
        MOVE LNO TO N
     ELSE IF LNO > RNO
        MOVE RNO TO N
     ELSE MOVE LNO TO N.
```

and we still have to code for the first selection condition

IF (NOT EOF-L) AND (NOT EOF-R) AND LNO = N AND
$$\text{RNO} = \text{N}$$

with similar complications for the second condition.

The best solution for this difficulty is to avoid it. We are suffering from the fact that the contents of the record area become unavailable at end of file; we are forced to test for end-of-file before referring to the values of the keys in the record areas. We may conveniently abandon the effort to examine the keys in the record areas and use instead a composite key in working storage in which the record key is concatenated with the end-of-file flag. We declare

```
01   LKEY.
     02   L-EOF PIC X, VALUE SPACE.
          88   EOF-L VALUE "E".
     02   L-REC-KEY PIC X(8).
```

with a similar item for RKEY. The READ operation takes the form

```
READ LFILE AT END MOVE "E" TO L-EOF.
IF NOT EOF-L MOVE LNO TO L-REC-KEY.
```

and we may now regard the key of the next record in LFILE as given by LKEY. Declaring N as

```
01   N.
   02   FILLER PIC X.
   02   FILLER PIC X(8).
```

we may write the assignment to N as

```
IF LKEY < RKEY
   MOVE LKEY TO N
ELSE MOVE RKEY TO N.
```

and the conditions on the selection become

```
IF LKEY = N AND RKEY = N
```

and

```
IF LKEY = N and RKEY NOT = N ...
```

The condition on the iteration PMBODY is:

```
UNTIL N NOT LESS THAN "E" ...
```

This solution avoids the manipulative difficulties, and gives an efficient and intelligible program. However, a different solution is often adopted: the variable N is eliminated, giving the program:

```
PMAGIC    seq
              open LFILE; read LFILE;
              open RFILE; read RFILE;
       PMBODY    iter until EOF-L and EOF-R
           PROCNUM    select LNO = RNO
                      write type1;
                      read LFILE;
                      read RFILE;
           PROCNUM    or LNO < RNO
                      write type2;
                      read LFILE;
           PROCNUM    or LNO > RNO
                      write type3;
                      read RFILE;
```

E

```
        PROCNUM   end
    PMBODY   end
        close LFILE;
        close RFILE;
PMAGIC   end
```

This program is less intelligible. PMBODY is an iteration which runs through some set of keys, but there is no variable to identify the key being processed on each occurrence of the iterated part of PMBODY. If, for example, we wish to produce another output file containing the values of the keys processed, we would be in difficulty: we would need either to re-introduce N or to insert coding into each part of PROCNUM.

4.4

The standard form of the collating program may also be distorted by con-flating parts of the selection: instead of keeping the matching cases separate, we use the same program component to process two or more cases.

Consider Version 2 of Problem 6, in which the payments file must be collated with the customer master file. Eliminating the fourth matching case, we have the program structure shown opposite.

This is the standard form of the program, and allows us to handle any specification. For example, we may specify that unmatched payment groups are to be treated in the same way as matched groups, or that they are to be deleted from the edited payments file and a diagnostic message written, or that a special header record for each unmatched group is to be written to the edited payments file or that a diagnostic message is to be written for each individual unmatched payment record, or that a dummy customer master record is to be created, or anything else we please. None of these specifications will cause difficulty. Because the program structure distinguishes between matched and unmatched groups we have complete freedom to define distinct processing.

However, if we specify identical, or nearly identical, processing for matched and unmatched groups, we are tempted to use the same program component for both. The justification is, of course, reduction of the length of the program text: in a word, optimization.

One method is to define a program component "PROCESS PAYMENT GROUP" which can be invoked from both the first and the third parts of the selection PCNO GROUP. The structure is shown on p. 80.

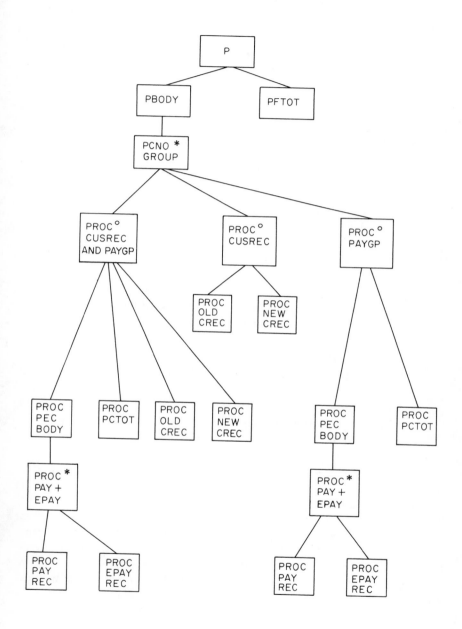

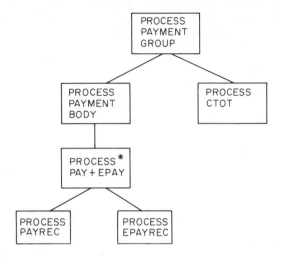

PCNO GROUP would then have the form:

PCNOGROUP	**select** CNO = PCNO = PNO
	do PROCESSPAYMENTGROUP;
	process old crec;
	process new crec;
PCNOGROUP	**or** CNO = PCNO ≠ PNO
	process old crec;
	process new crec;
PCNOGROUP	**or** CNO ≠ PCNO = PNO
	do PROCESSPAYMENTGROUP;
PCNOGROUP	**end**

The program is then very vulnerable to changes in the specification. If, for example, we specify that unmatched edited payment records are to be marked with a special code, we must distinguish in **PROCESS EPAYREC** between matched and unmatched edited payment records. If we specify that the customer total is to be similarly marked, we must make the same distinction again in **PROCESS CUSTOT**. Eventually, after several such changes, the program becomes impossibly difficult to understand and to maintain. The original decision to use a common component to process both matched and unmatched payment groups was wrong: the similarity between their processing was fortuitous.

Another method is to define a common component at a higher level. By generalizing the idea of a customer master record to include both actual and dummy (missing) records, we can use the same program component for both **PROCESS PAYGROUP** and **PROCESS CUSREC AND PAY-GROUP**. This gives the program structure:

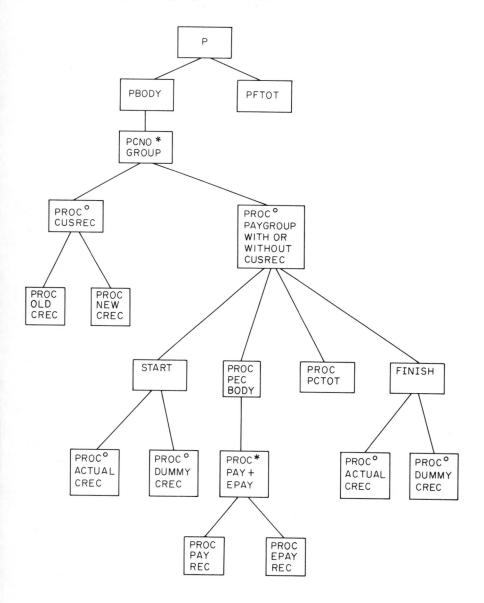

This structure is, of course, vulnerable to changes in the specification just as the preceding structure is. Such vulnerability is the inevitable price of optimization.

4.5

Sometimes the physical representation of the files makes a collating problem difficult to understand, and obscures the relevance of the standard solution. Here is such a problem.

PROBLEM 8—SOURCE STATEMENT LIBRARY

A program is to be written which will create a file of source text input for the COBOL compiler. The program reads a card file, which may be either:

a complete COBOL program in source text form, or

a request to retrieve a COBOL program from the source-statement library, together with any number of insertions and deletions to be made.

If the card file is a COBOL program, it should be copied without change to the file of source text for the COBOL compiler. Otherwise, the requested member should be retrieved from the source statement library and copied to the file of source text, insertions and deletions taking effect on the copied text but not on the source statement library.

The source statement library consists of a number of members, each member containing a COBOL program in card-image form. The card images carry sequence numbers in columns 1–6 and are stored in ascending order by sequence number within each member. The library is to be accessed by invoking a procedure which is already available. This procedure requires an OPEN command to make the library ready, then a FIND command to access an individual book; card images are read serially by a READ command, which may return the result "end-of-member"; a CLOSE command is required for the member, and another for the library. The FIND command may return the result "not found".

The card file, if it is not a COBOL program, consists of the following:

BASIS card.   "BASIS" in columns 1–5, and the name of the requested member in columns 7–14. Must be the first card of the file; only one library member can be accessed in any one run.

INSERT card.   "INSERT" in columns 1–6, sequence number in columns 7–12. May be followed by any number of COBOL text cards which are to be inserted following the source statement library card image with the specified sequence number.

DELETE card.   "DELETE" in columns 1–6, followed by one or more sequence-number pairs in columns 7–18, 19–30, etc. Each pair designates a range of source statement library card images to be deleted. If the second sequence number of the pair is blank, only one card image is to be deleted; if both are blank, there are no further pairs on the card. May be followed by any number of COBOL text cards which are to be inserted following the last card image deleted.

The insert and delete cards should be in ascending order by sequence number, and so should the pairs within a delete card.

An example of card input is:

```
BASIS PRGM1
INSERT000100
000101          MOVE A TO B.
DELETE000500000650001200
001200          ADD X TO Y.
001205          IF X=0,
/*
```

There are three data structures to consider. The first, the text file for the COBOL compiler, is trivial: we may regard it as a simple iteration of text records:

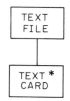

The source library and the card file are less simple. Their structures appear to be:

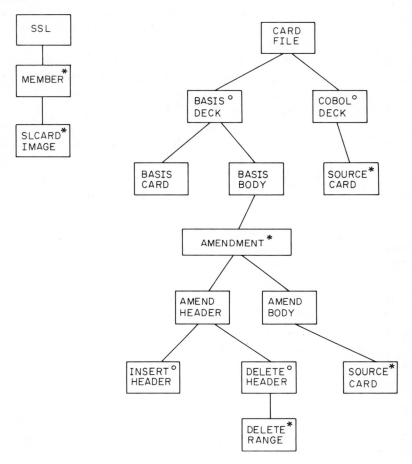

(Note that the SSL is described as an iteration of members: we should really describe it as an unordered set of members, since access to a member is direct. But we have no non-sequential construct, and must use iteration.)

There is no difficulty in putting these structures together at the higher levels as shown opposite (top diagram).

The difficulties begin when we come to consider the collation of the source-statement library with the body of the basis deck. What are we supposed to be collating? Card images? Groups of card-images? Amendments? None of these offers an obvious solution.

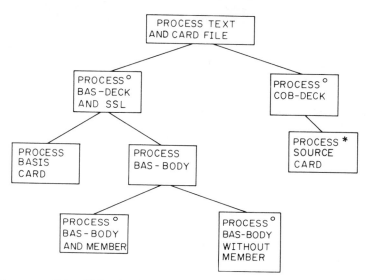

The root of the difficulty is the physical representation of the card file. We may imagine a very primitive version of the card file which is subject to this strong restriction: each delete card may delete only one source library card image. Clearly this restriction makes the program inconvenient to use—instead of the one card

DELETE000150000265000380000480

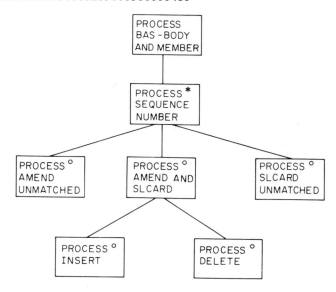

we would now need 217 cards, one for each card image to be deleted. However, if we suppose the restriction to apply, we can see that a unique sequence number is now associated with each amendment, and that the amendments can therefore easily be collated with the library card images. The required structure for **PROCESS BAS-BODY AND MEMBER** is shown at the bottom of p. 85.

From this point we can proceed quite simply. First, we relax the restriction to allow each delete card to contain a sequence number pair. A pair defines a group of consecutive cards in the library member, so we may treat the member as having the structure:

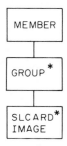

The collation is now between amendments and groups. The idea of a group needs careful definition. We may say that a group is either.

a group of consecutive cards in the library member corresponding to a sequence number pair in a delete card, or

a single card in the library member whose sequence number appears in an insert card, or

a single card in the library member whose sequence number does not appear on any amendment header card, or within the range of a sequence number pair.

Instead of the last of these we could specify:

a group of consecutive cards in the library member none of whose sequence numbers appear on any amendment header or within the range of a sequence number pair.

Taking the latter choice, we have the program structure:

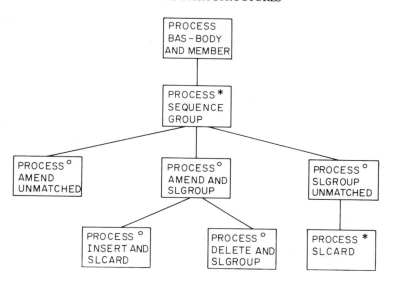

The next step in recovering the original specification is to relax the restriction that only one sequence number pair may appear in a delete card. This is more difficult than the previous step. There are two reasonable ways of proceeding:

we may construct a "read next card" procedure which decomposes each delete card into cards containing only one pair each—effectively restoring the restriction from the point of view of the program though not from the point of view of the user, or

we may define a "supergroup" in the library member, where a supergroup is a set of consecutive cards of which the first and last sequence numbers are the first and last sequence numbers in a delete card.

Obviously the first of these two ways is simpler. The second will involve us in a lower-level collation process within the program component **PROCESS DELETE AND SUPERGROUP**. We may also observe that the idea of a supergroup has no obvious meaning for the user of the program. A supergroup is an arbitrary concept derived from the physical arrangement of the cards: if the cards had 96 columns instead of 80 we would, in general, have a different dissection into supergroups.

It is important to understand that the foregoing discussion about data structures is, in essence, a discussion about the nature of the problem as seen by the user. Suppose, for example, that we were asked to count the amendments in each run of the program. What should we count? Any of these is reasonable:

> one library card deleted;

> one sequence number pair;

> one set of consecutive delete cards containing no blank sequence number pair except in the last or only card.

Our uncertainty about the answer reflects the uncertainty in the specification. The specification is an uneasy compromise between the logical and the physical structures of the card file: hence our difficulty in understanding and designing the collation process.

4.6 Serial and Direct Files

Some problems seem superficially to involve collating when deeper examination shows that they do not.

Consider again Version 2 of Problem 6 (Customer Payments). We will ignore the edited payments file, concentrating our attention on the payments file and the customer master file. We may define three tasks to be carried out by the program.

> 1. update the customer debt field from the total of payments made;

> 2. mark as delinquent those customers who have made no payments;

> 3. diagnose as errors those payments for which there is no customer master record.

For completeness, we add a fourth task:

> 4. list the customer numbers appearing on neither file.

Suppose now that we wish to write a version of the program which carries out only tasks 1 and 3. Suppose, further, that the customer file is a direct-access file which cannot be read sequentially: the read operation is:

> read cfile (key);

in which the key of the required record must be specified; a possible result of this operation is "not found", which, of course, happens when there is no record on the file with the required key. We would be forced to structure this program as:

```
PROG13    seq
              open pfile; read pfile;
              open cfile;
    P13BODY    iter until eof-pfile
        PPGROUP    seq
                       read cfile (pno);
              PPGBODY    select not found
                             process payments without cusrec;
                             do task 3;
              PPGBODY    or found
                             process payments with cusrec;
                             do task 1; write cfile (pno);
              PPGBODY    end
           PPGROUP    end
        P13BODY    end
              close pfile;
              close cfile;
    PROG13    end
```

in which the iteration P13BODY runs through only those key values which are present in the payments file. There is not way of accessing customer records whose keys are not present in the payments file (except by the ridiculously inefficient process of trying all possible key values).

Clearly this is not a collating program: it has only one serial input file, and the direct-access file does not affect the program structure. Consider, now, the program PROG12 which carries out only tasks 1 and 2. With the customer file in direct-access form this program cannot be written. To carry out task 2 we must be able to access all of the customer records irrespective of the key values in the payments file. So the customer file will be a serial file. Conversely, we may now store the payments in a direct-access file (assuming that the payment records for one customer may effectively be treated as a single record), because we no longer wish to carry out task 3.

The structure of PROG12 is:

```
PROG12    seq
              open cfile; read cfile;
              open pfile;
```

```
P12BODY   iter until eof-cfile
    PCGROUP   seq
                read pfile (cno);
        PCRECORD   select not found
                   process cusrec without payments;
                   do task 2;
        PCRECORD   or found
                   process cusrec with payments;
                   do task 1;
        PCRECORD   end
    PCGROUP   end
P12BODY   end
        close cfile;
        close pfile;
PROG12   end
```

With two input files, there are four possible matching cases for each key value. In principle, we may define 16 different programs to process these files, the programs differing in the subsets of the four tasks they can carry out. Using an obvious notation, we have PROG, PROG1, PROG2, PROG12, PROG3, PROG13, PROG23, PROG123, PROG4, PROG14, PROG24, PROG124, PROG34, PROG134, PROG234 and PROG1234.

Clearly, the last 8 of these, which carry out task 4, are not often required. The first, PROG, carries out no task at all, and is not useful. The remaining seven are practical possibilities.

We make the following observations about the 16 programs, the nature of the collating process and the use of serial and direct-access files:

all 16 programs are derivable from the standard form of collating program, provided that the input files are serially accessible.

all 16 programs require a logical transaction file. The logical transaction file provides the set of keys to be processed; it is necessarily serial, because it must allow the operation "get next key value".

for any program which carries out task 4, the logical transaction file is notional. The records of the file are the successive values of the key; the operation "get next key value" takes the form:

keyvalue: =keyvalue+1;

the logical transaction file may be a single real file, as in the case of the programs PROG12 and PROG13. This file must be serially accessible.

the logical transaction file may be formed from two or more real files, as in the case of program PROG123. These files must be serially accessible.

when the logical transaction file is formed from two or more real files, the standard collating program should be used, subject to the minimum necessary changes to obtain acceptable efficiency.

any real file which does not form a part of the logical transaction file may be treated as a direct-access file. Even if it is physically serial, a procedure may be designed which makes it appear to the program as a direct-access file.

EXERCISE 4.1 (b)

Complete the design of a program to solve the Magic Mailing Company problem (Problem 7), carrying it through to coding. Regarding this program as P1234, in the convention used in Section 4.6 above, specify in detail the coding changes needed to produce programs P, P1, P2, P12, etc.

EXERCISE 4.2 (b)

Design and code a complete solution to Problem 8 (Source-statement Library).

EXERCISE 4.3 (c)

Suppose that your are writing PROG13 for Version 2 of Problem 6 (Customer Payments). You wish to treat the customer file as if it were a direct-access file, although in fact it is held on magnetic tape. Design and code a procedure, in the form of a COBOL sub-program, to access the file in this way. Take advantage of the fact that PROG13 is known to access the customer records in ascending order of customer number.

EXERCISE 4.4 (a)

Write down the schematic logic for the standard collating program to handle three input files.

QUESTION 4.1

Why is it important that the program structure should correspond to all of the data structures?

QUESTION 4.2

Why was it possible to ignore the structure of the output file in Problem 4 (Counting Batches)?

QUESTION 4.3

Why are the data structures given above for the card file in Problem 8 (Source-statement Library) inadequate? What errors might occur in the card file? What should be done to handle them?

5. ERRORS AND INVALIDITY

5.1 Error Data

Error processing accounts for a high proportion of the program code in a data processing system. Some programs, often called "data vetting" programs, have no function other than the detection and elimination of erroneous input: typical errors are non-numeric information in numeric fields, wrong combinations of field values, wrong record sequences and wrong identifiers. Transaction processing in an on-line system often consists largely of dialogue in which the transaction program diagnoses input errors and the user resubmits corrected input. Errors also occur, especially in batch-processing systems, at later stages: a master file updating program must detect such errors as transactions for which no master record is present or transactions which are inapplicable to the corresponding master records.

We will use the term "error data" for data containing errors of this kind, and we will contrast error data with "good data". The distinction between error data and good data is meaningful to the user of a system: broadly, good data is what he tries to present to the system; error data is what he presents when he makes a mistake. But no such distinction is meaningful to the system itself. From the point of view of the system and its programs, both error data and good data require processing, and the processing must be correct according to the specifications. There is no difference in principle between writing a record on an error diagnostic file and writing a record on a vetted transactions file, or between a dialogue in which the user is correcting an error and a dialogue in which he is submitting new information.

Because error data must be processed correctly, just as good data must, we must design our programs to take account of error data. And this means that the data structures, on which the program design is based, must also take account of errors. It would be wrong to design a program to handle only good data, hoping to fit the error processing into a structure determined solely by the good data. The result would be a partially designed program—partially correct, partially intelligible and partially maintainable.

5.2

Here is a simple example of error processing. Suppose that we are designing a program to process the following card file:

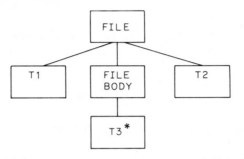

The file is created by keypunching the cards and submitting them directly to the program. Errors may occur through mispunching or through mishandling the deck, and the program must take account, somehow, of these errors. We must therefore devise a data structure which accommodates the errors. For example:

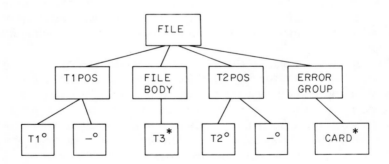

We have elaborated the structure to accommodate the errors. The file now consists of a possible T1 (which is either a T1 or null), the file body (which is an iteration of T3's), a possible T2 (which is either a T2 or null) and an errorgroup, which is an iteration of intermediate cards. A good file will be interpreted as before:

T1   interpreted as T1
T3   interpreted as T3 ⎫
T3   interpreted as T3 ⎬ interpreted as filebody
T2   interpreted as T2

but any error file whatsoever can be interpreted:

TX ⎤ all interpreted as cards of errorgroup; T1pos
T1 ⎬ is null; filebody consists of zero T3's; T2pos
T3 ⎥ is null.
T2 ⎦

T1   interpreted as T1
TX   interpreted as card of errorgroup; filebody consists of zero T3's;
      T2pos is null.

T3   interpreted as T3 ⎤ interpreted as filebody;
T3   interpreted as T3 ⎦ T1pos is null;
T2   interpreted as T2.

Diagnosis and processing of the errors takes place in the null parts of T1pos
and T2pos and in card of errorgroup.

There are two important points to be noted. First, the presence of errors
affects the processing of good cards: in the first of the three error examples
above, the presence of TX as the first card of the file causes the remaining
cards to be interpreted as cards of errorgroup. Second, there are many
different ways of elaborating the data structure to accommodate the errors.
For example, instead of the structure given above we might have used the
structure:

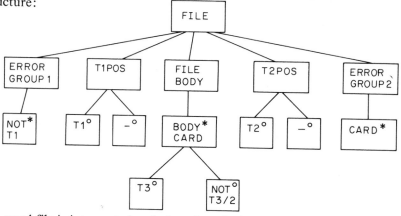

A good file is interpreted as before, but the interpretation of an error file
may be different. In the first of the three error examples above, TX as the
first card of the file is interpreted as a notT1 in errorgroup1; the remaining
cards are interpreted as if they were a good file.

Another simple example of error processing is a sequence checking problem. We have an input card file of transactions; each transaction carries a part-number, and the file should have been sorted into ascending order by part-number; there may be several transactions for each part-number. We need to design a program which will copy the file, diagnosing and dropping any cards which are out of sequence. The data structure of a good file is:

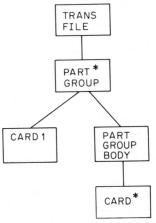

in which each card in the part group body contains the same part-number as card1 of that part group. To handle the sequence errors we may use a data structure:

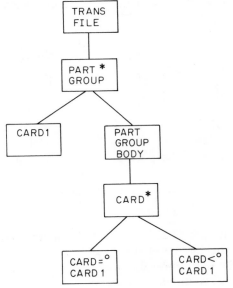

This structure would cause us to reject individual cards whose part-number is less than the part-number on the last accepted card1. Thus processing might be:

PART-NO 5   accepted as card1;
        5   accepted as card=;
        4   rejected as card<;
        5   accepted as card=;
        6   accepted as card1;
            etc., etc.

But we might instead have used the structure:

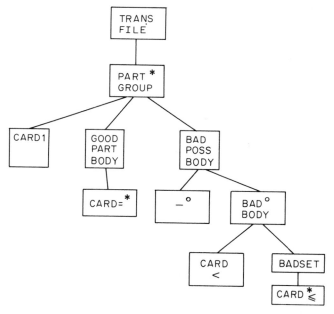

This structure would cause us to accept only unbroken sequences of cards beginning with an acceptable card1 and all containing the same part-number. Processing for the fragment shown above would therefore be:

PART-NO 5   accepted as card1;
        5   accepted as card=;
        4   rejected as card<;
        5   rejected as card ≤ in badset;
        6   accepted as card1;
            etc., etc.

A further example is to be found in Problem 8 (Source Statement Library). The data structures discussed in Chapter 4 took no account of errors. Even if we ignore the possibility of sequence number errors—and there is no reason why we should—we may still find errors of the following kind:

BASIS PROGM2
INSXRT000250
000255   ADD P TO Q.
      *

in which the word "insert" has been mispunched. It is clear that such an input file cannot be interpreted according to the structure

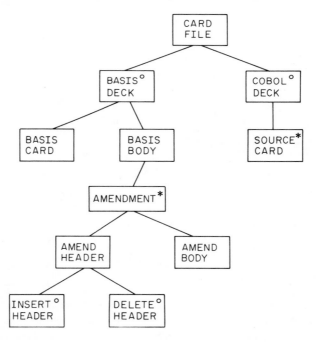

The file is clearly a basis deck; there is clearly at least one amendment; but the first card of that amendment is neither an insert header nor a delete header. To handle such errors we need to elaborate the structure of card file. Noting that the error in question can occur only once, at the beginning of the basis deck, we choose the structure shown opposite in which cards following the basis card but preceding the first amendment header card are treated as constituting an error group.

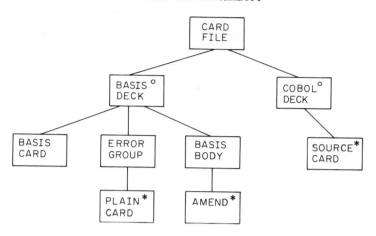

5.3

Design of data structures which accommodate errors is not easy. We have to make choices which affect both the kinds of errors that can be distinguished and the processing of good data in the presence of errors. These choices are properly the concern of a specialist in man-machine interfaces: they depend heavily on how often the various errors are likely to occur and how easily the user can correct them. But as programmers we may set ourselves the following objectives.

Because the data structure reflects the model of the problem, it should be known to the user. He should therefore be aware of the complete data structure, including the handling of errors. Most, perhaps all, programming language manuals err in this respect: they contain a careful and precise specification of the structure of a good program, but no clear description of the structure imposed on a program containing errors. One suspects that no such description exists, even in the design documentation for the compiler: certainly this would explain the arbitrary and perverse treatment of errors which many compilers provide.

Diagnosis of errors should be related to the data structure. The user should receive a clear indication of the interpretation placed on his data.

So far as possible, the data structure should be designed so that error data does not interfere with the processing of good data.

This last objective, that error data should not interfere with the processing of good data, can be very difficult to attain. Consider, for example, the good data structure

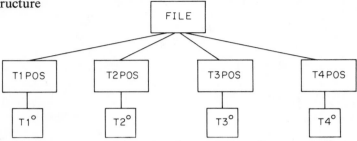

The file consists of up to four records. They are T1, T2, T3 and T4; any or none may be present, but those that are present must appear in the order given. We can easily devise a structure to take account of all possible errors:

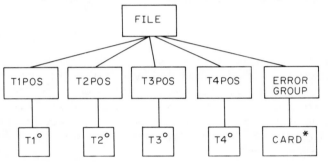

but this structure has the unfortunate effect that any error causes the remainder of the file to be treated as error data. We need instead to use some structure such as:

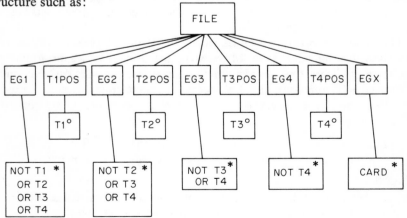

This structure is simple, but cumbersome and repetitive. Structures which take account of errors are often so.

5.4 Invalidity

We have drawn a distinction between good and error data. There is another, quite different, distinction to be drawn: between valid and invalid data.

We will say that data is valid for a program component if the operation of the component is specified for the data; conversely, data is invalid if operation of the component is not specified. It follows immediately that both good and error data are valid, because operation of the program component is specified for both. Indeed, when we elaborate a data structure to take account or error data, we are extending the definition of valid data for the program component in question. We must do so, because we want operation to be specified for error data just as it is for good data.

As an illustration, consider the following (simplified) specification of the COBOL divide instruction.

> DIVIDE item-1 INTO item-2
> ON SIZE ERROR imperative-statement.

"The value of item-1 is divided into the value of item-2. The value of the dividend (item-2) is replaced by the value of the quotient.

Item-1 and item-2 must both be elementary numeric items.

Division by zero results in a size error condition."

The first of the three paragraphs describes the operation; the second describes the valid data; the third describes a particular possible error. If we try to divide by zero, that is an error; operation is specified, namely the raising of a size error condition. But if we try to divide a non-numeric item, or to divide by a non-numeric item, that is invalid, and operation is not specified.

If a program component has no formal written specification, we cannot, in general, determine what data is valid for that component; in fact, it is unclear whether any useful sense can be attached to the notion of validity for such a component. Sometimes we will be able to show that certain data will cause the component to invoke a lower-level component with data which is invalid for that lower-level component, and we may then perhaps say that such data is invalid for the invoking component. What we must not do is to confuse the question whether operation of a component is specified with the question whether operation is predictable. We can almost always predict operation by reading the program coding, although sometimes the operation will prove to depend on chance factors, such as physical storage location of the loaded object program. But predictability is irrelevant: what matters is specification.

Suppose, for example, that we specify a program to process the file

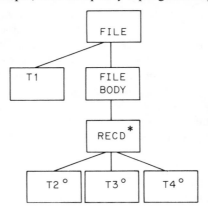

where a T1 record has the value 1 in position 1, a T2 record has the value 2, and so on. By defining the data structure shown, we are asserting that data which does not conform to that structure is invalid for the program. We might legitimately produce the following COBOL coding:

```
...
PF.   OPEN INPUT FILE-F.
      READ FILE-F AT END MOVE "E" TO F-EOF.
      PERFORM PROCESS-1.
      READ FILE-F AT END MOVE "E" TO F-EOF.
      PERFORM PROCESS-FBREC UNTIL EOF-F.
      CLOSE FILE-F.
      STOP RUN.
PROCESS-FBREC.
      IF REC-POS = 2
         PERFORM PROCESS-2
      ELSE IF REC-POS = 3
              PERFORM PROCESS-3
              ELSE PERFORM PROCESS-4.
      READ FILE-F AT END MOVE "E" TO F-EOF.
```

Operation of this program is predictable for any input file whatsoever, except perhaps for a file consisting of zero records. But operation is specified, we are supposing, only for input files conforming to the data structure given. We might therefore, equally legitimately, produce a quite different COBOL program: for instance, after a heavy bout of unrestrained optimization we might produce:

```
...
PF.   OPEN INPUT FILE-F.
      READ FILE-F AT END MOVE "E" TO F-EOF.
      PERFORM PROCESS-REC UNTIL EOF-F.
      CLOSE FILE-F.
      STOP RUN.
PROCESS-REC SECTION.
PR.   GO TO P1, P2, P3, P4, DEPENDING ON REC-POS.
P1.   ...   process-1   ...
      GO TO PX.
P2.   ...   process-2   ...
      GO TO PX.
P3.   ...   process-3   ...
      GO TO PX.
P4.   ...   process-4   ...
PX.   EXIT.
```

Both of these programs conform to the specifications: they process valid data identically. For invalid data, the operation of both programs is predictable, but it is not identical. For example, we can predict for a file containing records T3, T2, T1, T5, in that order:

Record	First Program	Second Program
T3	process-1	process-3
T2	process-2	process-2
T1	process-4	process-1
T5	process-4	process-1

while for a file of zero records we can predict that the second program will do nothing and that the first program will do process-1, possibly failing with an illegal program-check condition.

The predictability is valueless, depending as it does on the details of the coding. It is wrong in principle to enquire into the operation of a program when the data is invalid: we must be satisfied to say that operation is unspecified.

5.5

But should we not try to ensure that operation is always specified? Is it not a principle of good design that every program component should check the validity of its input? Surely the programmer should update the specification to reflect the code he has written?

The short answer is no, no and no again.

Certainly, any component which receives its input data directly from a human agent, or from an unreliable machine source, should be designed so that all input data is valid and hence operation is always specified. It would be very inconvenient for an on-line system to be vulnerable to a trivial error on the part of a terminal user. But components which receive their input data from other components of the same system must be able to rely on the correct functioning of those other components.

Suppose, for example, that we wish to calculate overtime pay as part of a payroll system. The inputs are an employee record from the employee master file and a time, expressed in hours and minutes. Calculation is specified for times not exceeding 11 hours 59 minutes. The result is a data item overtime-pay. If we cannot rely on the values of the hours and minutes in the input data, we may reasonably write:

> If HOURS > 11 OR MINUTES > 59
>   PERFORM ERROR-ROUTINE
> ELSE CALL "CALC" USING HOURS, MINUTES, EMP-REC,
>   OTIME.

The structure of this component is:

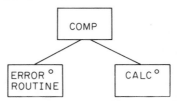

and CALC is relying on the correct functioning of COMP to ensure the validity of the hours and minutes values. If we insist that CALC's operation must be specified irrespective of the values of hours and minutes, we must structure CALC as

> IF HOURS > 11 OR MINUTES > 59
>   PERFORM BADCALC
> ELSE PERFORM GOODCALC.

giving the complete structure

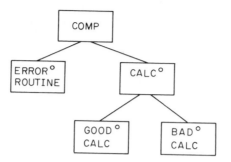

Now, of course, GOODCALC is relying on the correct functioning of CALC, just as CALC itself had previously been relying on the correct functioning of COMP. To avoid that reliance we must structure GOODCALC as . . . and so on, in an endless proliferation of futile code. If we are ever to write the program we must eventually reconcile ourselves to the idea that it will contain components whose operation is unspecified for certain data inputs.

That reconciliation should come at the earliest possible moment. Some data processing systems have been built on the avowed, though self-contradictory, principle that every component should check its input data fully. Because the principle is self-contradictory it cannot be observed consistently. Usually the result is that some of the checking is done twice or more, some is done once and some is not done at all. This is inevitable, because there is no consistent rule for allocating the responsibility for checking. The only consistent rule is:

every component specification must define precisely what data is valid for the component;

every component must be designed and coded on the assumption that its data is valid;

if component B is a part of component A, then A is responsible for ensuring that the data passed to B is valid for B.

Finally, we observe that it is a capital error for a programmer to update a component specification to reflect his code. If the original specification is imprecise, he should clarify it before starting to design and code; if it is precise, he should leave it alone.

EXERCISE 5.1 (b)

An input card file should have the following structure:

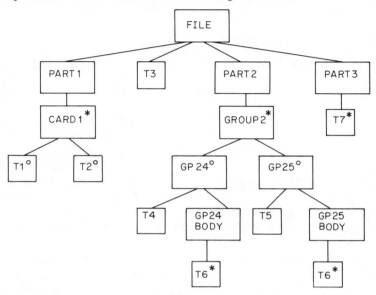

Write down ten different card sequences which do not conform to this structure. Elaborate the structure to take account of the errors exemplified in your ten sequences. Elaborate it again differently, but still taking account of your errors. Finally, elaborate it to take account of all possible errors.

EXERCISE 5.2 (b)

A file of cards contains dates punched in the form

Monday, 15th July, 1974

one date being punched on each card. No date should be earlier than 15th July, 1974.

Design a program to print out the cards with diagnostics of errors. Consider both format errors (such as "PQth June") and date errors (such as "31st February").

QUESTION 5.1

Choose a simple statement in a programming language which you known well
and use regularly. For example, you might choose the MOVE statement in
COBOL. Draw a data structure diagram of the syntax of this statement, as
described in your language specification manual. Now elaborate this data
structure to accommodate all possible syntax errors. Write down ten
examples of erroneous syntax. Present them to your compiler, and examine
the resulting diagnostics. What data structure do you think the compiler
writer used to handle the errors? Does it seem to be the same as your data
structure? If not, is it better or worse?

QUESTION 5.2

Here is part of a system flow diagram.

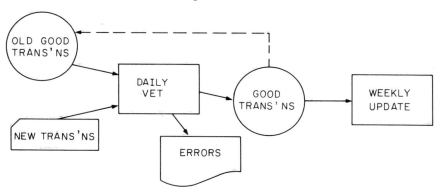

The vetting program is run every day for a week. On the second and subsequent days there is an old good transactions file to be merged with the new
transactions. At the end of the week, the resulting good transactions file is
used by the update program.

    Which component of the system is responsible for ensuring that the new
good transactions file is valid for the update? Which language is that
component written in? In what sense is the update program a part of it?

F

6. BACKTRACKING

6.1

We use forms of iteration and selection in which the condition test precedes execution of a part. And we use the technique of reading ahead to handle serial input files. The result is that our programs are very simple and very easily understood. For example, to process the file

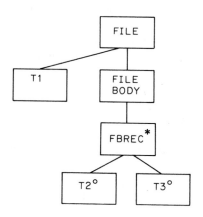

we write the program

```
PROCFILE    seq
                open file; read file;
                process T1;
                read file;
      PROCBODY    iter until eof (not T2 and not T3)
          PROCFBREC    select T2
                          process T2;
          PROCFBREC    or T3
                          process T3;
```

111

```
        PROCFBREC   end
                      read file;
        PROCBODY   end
                      close file;
                      stop;
    PROCFILE   end
```

The simplicity of this program depends largely on the fact that no component can be executed unless the appropriate data is present. PROCFBREC cannot be executed unless either a T2 or a T3 is present: that is assured by the condition test at the head of PROCBODY. Process T2 cannot be executed unless a T2 is present: that is assured by the condition test at the head of PROCFBREC. Similarly process T3 cannot be executed unless a T3 is present. The read ahead technique ensures that the necessary data is available in main storage for the condition tests to be made. We cannot ever find ourselves engaged in executing a component for which the appropriate data is not present.

This is all very obvious and straightforward. Indeed, the reader may well be wondering how one could ever construct a program lacking in this simplicity.

6.2 Multiple Read Ahead

Sometimes it is not enough to read ahead one record only. Consider the file

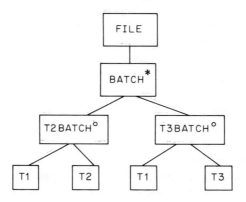

If we read ahead only one record, then at the beginning of each batch we will always find that the next record is a T1, and there will be no way of

determining whether the batch is a T2BATCH or a T3BATCH. Clearly, we can overcome the difficulty by reading ahead two records. We arrive at the program

```
PROCFILE   seq
                open file; read next; read next+1;
          PROCBODY   iter until eof (next is not T1)
                PROCBATCH   select next is T1 and next+1 is T2
                      PT2BATCH   seq
                                process T1 (next);
                                process T2 (next+1);
                                read new next;
                                read new next+1;
                      PT2BATCH   end
                PROCBATCH   or next is T1 and next+1 is T3
                      PT3BATCH   seq
                                process T1 (next);
                                process T3 (next+1);
                                read new next;
                                read new text+1;
                      PT3BATCH   end
                PROCBATCH   end
          PROCBODY   end
                close file;
                stop;
PROCFILE   end
```

The placing of the read statements is a little awkward here. Should we, perhaps, have written

```
process T1 (next);
read new next;
process T2 (next+1);
read new next+1;
```

etc? Is there not something slightly uncomfortable about having two different read statements? Should we have put the read statements at the end of PROCBATCH? But what would we then do if the T3batch had the structure shown on p. 114 so that we would need to read twice after a T1 batch but three times after a T3batch? And what if the file is empty?

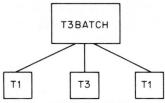

Some of these questions cannot be answered simply; they touch on points which form the substance of this chapter. But we can do something to tidy up the technique of multiple reading ahead.

Suppose, to be definite, that we want to read ahead three records. That is, at any point in the program we want to be able to examine the next record, the next plus 1 and the next plus 2. We declare three record areas:

    01   RA1.
    01   RA2.
    01   RA3.

At any point in the program RA1 will contain the next record; RA2 will contain the next plus 1; RA3 will contain the next plus 2. Because we think of the end-of-file flag as an extension to the record, we will need an end-of-file flag for each record area ·

    01   RA1.
       02   EF1 PIC X.
       02   DATA1 PIC X(n).
    01   RA2.
       02   EF2 PIC X.
       02   DATA2 PIC X(n).
    01   RA3.
       02   EF3 PIC X.
       02   DATA3 PIC X(n).

The general form of a single read operation must be:

    RA1: =RA2; (next+1 record to next-area)
    RA2: =RA3; (next+2 record to next+1-area)
    read file into RA3; (new record to next+2-area).

Taking account of the possibility that end of file has already been reached, we construct the paragraph:

    SREAD.   MOVE RA2 TO RA1.
                MOVE RA3 TO RA2.

```
        IF NOT END-FILE-3
            READ FILE INTO DATA3
            AT END MOVE "E" TO EF3.
```

It remains only to consider what must be done at the time the file is opened. We must initialize EF3, to ensure that we have the condition "not end-file-3" before the first read, and we must execute three single read operations:

```
OPEN INPUT FILEF.
MOVE SPACE TO EF3.
PERFORM SREAD 3 TIMES.
```

Just as it does no harm to read ahead one record unnecessarily, so it does no harm to read ahead three when two is enough. So we may return to our original problem described at the beginning of this section and code the program as follows:

```
    ...
01  RA1.
    ...
PROCEDURE DIVISION.
PROCFILE.
        OPEN INPUT FILEF.
        MOVE SPACE TO EF3.
        PERFORM SREAD 3 TIMES.
        PERFORM PROCBATCH UNTIL END-FILE-1.
        CLOSE FILEF.
        STOP RUN.
PROCBATCH.
        IF DATA2-POSITION-1=2
            CALL "PT12" USING DATA1
            PERFORM SREAD
            CALL "PT2" USING DATA1
            PERFORM SREAD
        ELSE CALL "PT13" USING DATA1
            PERFORM SREAD
            CALL "PT3" USING DATA1
            PERFORM SREAD.
SREAD.
        MOVE RA2 TO RA1.
    ...
```

Note that the principle of placing the read statements is virtually unchanged from the single read-ahead technique: we read three records at the open, and subsequently read one whenever a record has been processed.

The coding suggested above is exceptionally unsophisticated: there is really no need to move whole record areas around in main storage. In PL/I the record area would naturally be declared as a based variable; even in COBOL we can do something similar, and there is an exercise about it at the end of this chapter.

6.3

Multiple reading ahead will solve some problems, but not all. Consider, for example, the file

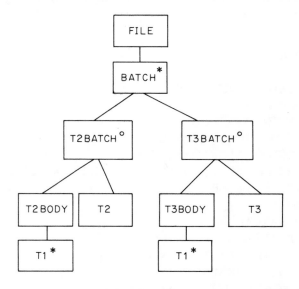

We cannot process this file by reading any fixed number of records ahead. However many we choose to read, and the number must be limited by the availability of storage space, we may still encounter a file with a batch containing more T1 records than we can accommodate. This is a very common problem in batch processing systems. The file may consist of control batches, each terminated by a batch control card; if the hash total of the detail cards agrees with the hash total in the batch control card, the batch is good, and must be written to the output file; if the hash totals do not agree, the batch is bad, and must be rejected.

Of course, it is not impossible to solve such problems by finding an *ad hoc* solution for each one individually. But we seek a more general solution.

Another type of difficulty which cannot be solved by multiple reading ahead appears in the following problem.

PROBLEM 9—A DAISY CHAIN

A program component is to be written to process a single card.

The card contains three fields—F1, F2 and F3. F1 should be numeric in the range 1 through 99 and if so, it can be used to retrieve an entry from a table. The entry contains two limit values and a multiplier. If F2 is within the limits, it can be multiplied by the multiplier to give a disk address. The record at the disk address contains a character string. F3 should be equal to a substring of this character string. If so, its prefix in the string is to be printed.

We therefore have the following situation. Each of the fields F1, F2 and F3 may be good data or error data. There are three processes, P1, P2 and P3, which may be carried out on F1, F2 and F3 respectively:

P1 retrieves the entry from the table:

P2 accesses the disk record;

P3 prints the prefix of F3 in the character string.

The program component should carry out the following operation:

if all of the fields are good, print the prefix of F3, otherwise execute the error routine PX.

Note the constraints which apply:

if Fn is not good, then process Pn cannot be executed (n = 1, 2, 3);

if Pn-1 has not been executed, it is not possible to evaluate whether Fn is good (n = 2, 3).

We may solve this problem with the following program:

```
PCARD    select good F1
         do P1;
  PF2    select good F2
         do P2;
```

```
       PF3    select good F3
              do P3;
       PF3    or error F3
              do PX;
       PF3    end
  PF2    or error F2
         do PX;
  PF2    end
PCARD    or error F1
         do PX;
PCARD    end
```

Within the constraints of the problem we cannot achieve a more elegant solution in well-formed schematic logic. Certainly multiple reading ahead will not help us. But we do need help: the present solution is unsatisfactory. The statement "do PX" appears three times, at levels two, four and six of the program structure; if the daisy chain were lengthened by a factor of ten, i.e. if there were thirty fields instead of three then the statement "do PX" would appear thirty times in a structure sixty levels deep. This is obviously intolerable. The problem is not deeply nested in this way: nor, then, should our program be.

We can see the source of the difficulty in the data structure on which, presumably, the schematic logic was based. We did not, in fact, start from the data structure on this occasion, but if we had, the structure would have been:

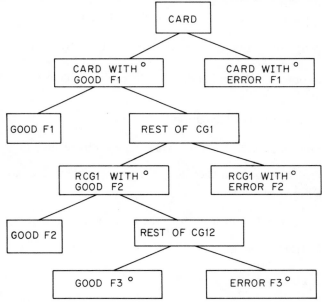

Because the question whether F2 is good can be meaningfully asked only in the context of a good F1, and similarly for F3 and F2, we are forced to adopt this disagreeable nested structure. We find ourselves, therefore, distinguishing the three possible error cases: error in F1; good F1 but error in F2; good F1 and F2 but error in F3. These three cases give rise to the three "do PX" statements in the schematic logic. We would prefer to make no such distinction and to content ourselves with a single "do PX" statement: the distinction, after all, was not in the problem specification.

6.4

The data structure which fits the problem most naturally is:

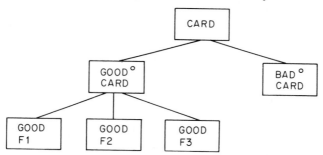

The card is either a good card or a bad card. If it is a bad card, we are not interested in its contents; we shall merely execute PX. If it is a good card, it consists of a good F1 (on which we shall carry out P1), followed by a good F2 (on which we shall carry out P2), followed by a good F3 (on which we shall carry out P3). The data structure is perfect; the operations are faultlessly allocated; the program is beautifully simple and self-evidently correct. But it does not work. There is no way in which we can determine on entry to the selection CARD whether we have a good card or a bad card: only the processing will answer the question, and we are demanding an answer before the processing begins.

We need a new form of selection. We need a form in which the condition test does not necessarily come at the head of the selection, at the entry point. Before looking in detail at what this means, let us look first at an analogy.

A MORAL TALE

Rashly, in the hope of financial gain beyond the dreams of programmers, you have enlisted in Big Louie's mob. As a result, you find yourself one hot summer's afternoon running along a country road, on your way to a rendez-vous with Big Louie. You are carrying a small but heavy bag containing the proceeds of the mob's latest enterprise. You pause at a fork in the road then check over your instructions: Louie is very hot on documentation.

> "100 yards after the fork, the road goes over a stream, and after a further 150 yards it goes under a railway line. Bury the bag just by the bridge, and chalk a cross on the bridge so that the boys will know you've made it OK. 200 yards on is the haunted house. I'll meet you there. Louie.

> PS. Bring a four-leaf clover with you, for luck. This is very important."

Thoughtfully, Louie has drawn a map:

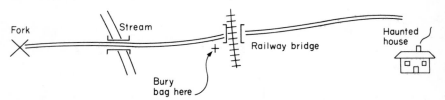

The instructions are fine—except that you don't know whether to go left or right at the fork: Louie forgot to say.

It's a very hot day, so you sit down for a moment while you think it out. After a short pause, you realize that a small man with pointed ears and a white beard is standing in front of you. "I am the friendly demon" he says in a business-like tone. "You know the rules: you are allowed to ask me one question, and I am allowed to answer 'yes' or 'no'." For an instant you think it's one of those tricky ones, where you have to ask him what his brother would say if you asked his brother what he would say—or something like that. But he doesn't appear to have a brother, and it's too hot for that kind of thing. So you come straight to the point. "Should I go left?" you ask. "Yes," he says, and immediately vanishes into a door in a nearby toad-stool.

So you set off along the left road. Sure enough, after 100 yards you cross a stream, and after another 150 you come to a railway bridge. You bury the bag of jewels, chalk the cross, and carry on. A little later you happen to see a four-leaf clover by the roadside, which you pick carefully and put in your pocket. But there is no sign of the haunted house, although you have gone a full 200 yards from the bridge. What now? Keeping as calm as you can under these very trying circumstances, you sit down to think it out again.

Here is your reasoning:

I'm glad I met the demon; I could have stayed at the fork for a very long time, wondering what to do. He certainly got me going in some direction, which is certainly better than none.

But I'm not sure that he was altogether reliable. I have been assuming that the left road is correct, because that's what the demon said. But Louie's map says that there is a haunted house at this point on the correct road: there is no haunted house on this road; ergo, this cannot be the correct road. Now that I come to think of it, I would also have known I was on the wrong road if I hadn't seen the stream and the railway; Louie's maps are never wrong. I had better go back to the fork and take the right road this time. It does occur to me that I might be able to cut across country by following the railway line. But if fate is feeling unkind, the lie of the land might be.

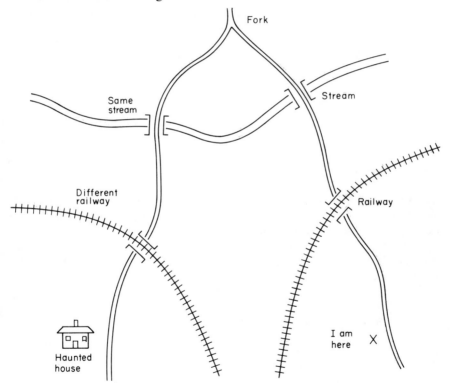

Yes, I will definitely go back to the fork. That way I'm safe.

One last thing. I musn't forget to dig up the bag of jewels. That's really important. The chalked cross I'm not so sure about: it won't do any harm, and I've got plenty of chalk to spare. The four-leaf clover I'll certainly keep: it would be crazy to throw it away—I would only have to find another one, and they aren't so plentiful hereabouts.

So back you go, digging up the bag of jewels on the way. The right road does turn out to be correct—it had to, because there were only two roads, and the left one was wrong—and you rendezvous successfully with Big Louie in the haunted house. When you tell him your advantures, he says something about programmers making the best robbers, and he gives you an extra ruby or two in appreciation.

6.5

We return to Problem 9. We had decided that the data structure we want to use is:

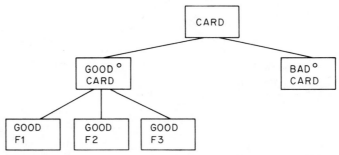

The difficulty is that the condition on the selection cannot be evaluated. We do not known whether to take the left path or the right path. So we tackle the problem in three stages.

At Stage 1 we rely on the friendly demon to tell us which way to go. The problem is therefore a trivially simple selection, and we may write down the solution directly:

```
PCARD   select good card
    PGOOD   seq
                do P1;
                do P2;
                do P3;
    PGOOD   end
PCARD   or bad card
            do PX;
PCARD   end
```

This solution is perfect, provided we can evaluate the selection condition: and we can, because we ask the demon "is this a good card?" and he says "yes" or "no". Anyone who feels that a friendly demon is out of place in programming may suppose that a preceding program has kindly punched an "X" in column 80 of each bad card; we will not enquire into the design of that preceding program.

At Stage 2 we recognize that the friendly demon is unreliable. We must therefore adopt a more sceptical attitude to the processing of a good card, asking ourselves at every opportunity whether perhaps it has turned out to be a bad card after all. The data structure diagram for a good card provides us with the map we need: we must check off each landmark as we go along. So we now write:

```
PCARD    posit good card
    PGOOD    seq
                quit PCARD if error F1;
                do P1;
                quit PCARD if error F2;
                do P2;
                quit PCARD if error F3;
                do P3;
    PGOOD    end
PCARD    admit
                do PX;
PCARD    end
```

We have made two changes. First, we have used the words **posit** and **admit** in place of the words **select** and **or**. To **posit** is to lay down a hypothesis: we are laying down the hypothesis that the card is a good card; if it turns out that our hypothesis is wrong, we will **admit** that the card is a bad card after all. Second, we have introduced the statements "**quit** PCARD **if** error F1", etc. These are executable statements, placed at each point in the data structure of a good card where the hypothesis that the card is good could be falsified by the facts. Thus "**quit** PCARD **if** error F1" means "if this is not a good F1. then, according to my data structure, the card cannot be a good card, and I must accordingly admit that my hypothesis is false". Possible COBOL coding for this program is:

```
    ...
PCARDPOSIT.
    NOTE POSIT CARD IS GOOD.
PGOODSEQ.
```

```
        IF ERROR-F1 GO TO PCARDADMIT. NOTE QUIT IF E1.
        PERFORM P1.
        IF ERROR-F2 GO TO PCARDADMIT. NOTE QUIT IF E2.
        PERFORM P2.
        IF ERROR-F3 GO TO PCARDADMIT. NOTE QUIT IF E3.
        PERFORM P3.
    PGOODEND.
        GO TO PCARDEND.
    PCARDADMIT.
        PERFORM PX.
    PCARDEND.
        ...
```

Stage 3 is the final stage, when we consider the side-effects. We may classify the side-effects as intolerable, neutral and beneficent:

an intolerable side-effect must be undone; if we have buried the bag of jewels we must dig it up again; if we have printed a line on the line printer we must backspace and erase it; if we have read a card we must backspace the card reader; if we have incremented a variable we must restore it to its original value;

a neutral side-effect may, but need not, be undone; if we have chalked a cross on the bridge we may erase it or leave it; if we have read a disk record into main storage we may leave it there or overwrite the buffer, whichever is more convenient; if we have set a value in a variable we may preserve it or overwrite it;

a beneficient side-effect is one which does us good; we would be foolish to throw away the four-leaf clover, so we keep it.

In Problem 9 we may perhaps regard all of the side effects as neutral: it does not matter, when we come to execute the **admit** part of the **posit**, whether or not we have retrieved the entry from the table and whether or not we have accessed the disk record. So we have no significant work to do at Stage 3.

6.6

More often, side-effects present a serious problem. It is instructive to examine how they arise in backtracking problems and to consider in general what methods we may use to deal with them. We will use the following trivial program for purposes of illustration:

```
A      select condition-b
  B        seq
             x:=x+5;
             y:=x/4;
             x:=x+y;
             x:=x+7;
  B        end
A      or condition-c
           x:=x-3;
A      end
```

Denoting by X the value of x on entry to component A, we may rewrite the program adding, in parentheses, certain assertions which we know to be true at various points in the text:

```
                              (x=X; condition-b or condition-c;)
A       select condition-b
                              (x=X; condition-b;)
  B         seq
              x:=x+5;
                              (x=X+5; condition-b;)
              y:=x/4;
                              (x=X+5; y=(X+5)/4; condition-b;)
              x:=x+y;
                              (x=(X+5)+((X+5)/4); y=(X+5)/4;
                                                       condition-b;)
              x:=x+7;
                              (x=(X+5)+((X+5)/4)+7; y=(X+5)/4;
                                                       condition-b;)
  B         end
A       or condition-c
                              (x=X; condition-c;)
              x:=x-3;
                              (x=X-3; condition-c;)
A       end
```

The assertion made at the entry to the second part of A is

x=X; condition-c;

That is to say, x has the same value as it has at the entry to the first part of A, and also condition-c is true. The values which x may take during execution of component B are of no interest· on entry to the second part of A B has not been executed.

Suppose now that condition-b cannot be evaluated on entry to A, and that we are forced to write A in the form of a **posit** component. Then at Stage 2 of the design of A, before dealing with the side-effects, we have:

```
A     posit condition-b
   B      seq
          x:=x+5;
          quit A if not b-1;
          y:=x/4;
          quit A if not b-2;
          x:=x+y;
          quit A if not b-3;
          x:=x+7;
          quit A if not b-4;
   B      end
A     admit condition-c
      x:=x-3;
A     end
```

The assertion we may now make at the entry to the second part of A is:

condition-c; x=X+5 or x=X+5 and y=(X+5)/4 or . . .;

The problem of handling the side-effects is the problem of restoring the truth of the original assertion

x=X; condition-c;

which has been destroyed by complete or partial execution of B. Not all of the executable statements of B give rise to side-effects: the variable y is local to B; it is not used in the second part of A, nor do we wish to make any assertion about its value on entry to the second part of A; the assignment statement

y:=x/4;

may therefore be ignored in our consideration of side-effects. The other assignments in B are all assignments to x, and we cannot ignore them.

One method of handling side-effects is to treat each **quit** statement separately.

After determining that the **quit** is to be executed, but before actually doing so, we undo the particular set of side-effects currently obtaining. For example, we might write for Stage 3:

```
A       posit condition-b
   B      seq
            x:=x+5;
            QA1    select not b-1
                      x:=x−5;
                      quit A;
            QA1    end
            y:=x/4;
            QA2    select not b-2
                      x:=x−5;
                      quit A;
            QA2    end
            x:=x+y;
            QA3    select not b-3
                      x:=x−y;
                      x:=x−5;
                      quit A;
            QA3    end
            x:=x+7;
            QA4    select not b-4
                      x:=x−7;
                      x:=x−y;
                      x:=x−5;
                      quit A;
            QA4    end
   B      end
A       admit condition-c
         x:=x−3;
A       end
```

Evidently, this is an unattractive method. It depends upon the reversibility of the individual side-effects, and it produces an unnecessarily long program text. We may overcome the second disadvantage by optimization, using the technique of common action tails discussed in Chapter 12. The first disadvantage is more serious, and the method is in any case inefficient in execution time. We will therefore not consider it further.

More general methods allow us to avoid detailed examination of the contexts of the individual quit statements. For instance, we may arrange

to remember the statement of the computation on entry to A and to restore
that state unconditionally on entry to the second part of A.

> A   **posit** condition-b
>   z:=x;   (x × X; condition-b or condition-c;)
>   (z=X; condition-b or condition-c;)
>
>   B   **seq**
>   x:=x+5;
>   (x=X+5;)
>   **quit** A **if** not b-1;
>   y:=x/4;
>   **quit** A **if** not b-2;
>   x:=x+y;
>   **quit** A **if** not b-3;
>   x:=x+7;
>   **quit** A **if** not b-4;
>   B   **end**
> A   **admit** condition-c
>   (z=X; condition-c;)
>   x:=z;
>   (x=X; condition-c;)
>   x:=x−3;
> A   **end**

In this trivial example, the only part of the state of the computation which
concerns us is the value of x; we have therefore remembered that state by
executing

    z:=x;

on entry to A, and restored it by executing

    x:=z;

on entry to the second part of A.

A different method is to avoid altogether the creation of side-effects in B.
Instead of operating on variables which are known outside B, we may
restrict operation of B to local variables. We must initialize appropriate local
variables on entry to B, and at the very end of B, after operation on the local
variables is complete, we must assign the new values of the local variables
to the variables known outside B. Thus we would write:

> A   **posit** condition-b
>   (x=X; condition-b or condition-c;)
>
>   B   **seq**
>   w:=x;

$$(x=X; \text{condition-b or condition-c};)$$

$$w:=w+5;$$

$$(x=X; \text{condition-b or condition-c};)$$

quit A **if** not b-1w;

$$y:=w/4;$$

$$(x=X; \text{condition-b or condition-c};)$$

quit A **if** not b-2w;

$$w:=w+y;$$

quit A **if** not b-3w;

$$w:=w+7;$$

quit A **if** not b-4w;

$$(x=X; w=(X+5)+((X+5)/4)+7;$$
$$\text{condition-b};)$$

$$x:=w; \qquad (x=(X+5)+((X+5)/4+7; \text{condition-b};)$$

   B   **end**

A   **admit** condition-c

$$(x=X; \text{condition-c};)$$

$$x:=x-3;$$

A   **end**

As before, the only non-local variable which concerns us is x; the equivalent local variable is w. Note that if the conditions b-1, etc., involve the value of x, they must now be implemented so that they refer instead to the value of w.

Serial input–output devices may be handled in an analogous way. We may either:

remember the state of the device on entry to the **posit** component and restore that state unconditionally on entry to the **admit** part; use of this technique implies availability of an input–output procedure capable of remembering and restoring the device state; or

restrict operation within the first part of the **posit** component so that the state of the device itself remains unchanged; for an output device we may build in main storage a queue of records to be output; for an input device we may use the read-ahead technique, executing no read operations but referring as necessary to the next-plus-one record, the next-plus-two record, etc.

6.7

Here is a bactracking problem.

PROBLEM 10—DELIMITED STRINGS

A program component is to be designed which will analyse a character string, recognizing and printing two substrings, S1 and S2. S1 is terminated by a character "@", and S2 by a character "&"; the complete string is terminated by a character "%".

On entry to the component two items of input data are available: the complete string, and a pointer or subscript which points to a current location in the string. S1 is defined to be the substring whose first character is the character pointed at and whose last character is the terminating "@"; S2 has as its first character the character following the terminating "@" of S1, and its last character is its terminating "&". Either or both strings may be empty of non-terminating characters.

It is known that the complete string is terminated (ie a "%" occurs) within 100 characters of the current location on entry: this fact can, and should, be relied on. However, it is not known that correct substrings S1 and S2 are present. If both are present and correct, a report should be printed in the form

GOOD STRING
S1=xxxxxxxxx@
S2=yyyyyy&

otherwise the string should be printed from the current location up to the terminator, in the form

BAD STRING
CHAR-001=f
CHAR-002=g
...
CHAR-nnn=%

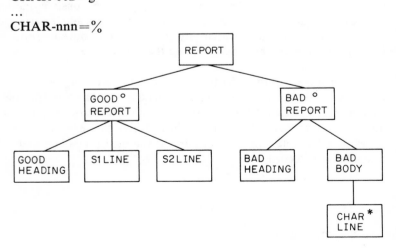

In either case the pointer should be left pointing one character past the terminating "%".

The data structure of the output report is shown opposite.

To achieve correspondence we will need to structure the string also as a selection. Relying on the friendly demon, we write boldly:

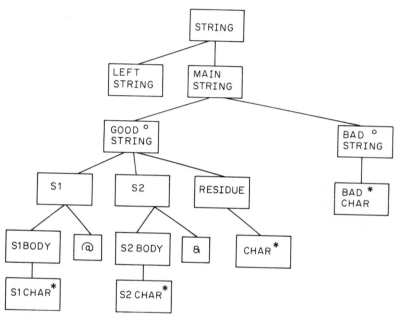

Refinement of these structures, creation of the program structure and listing and allocating executable operations are all left as exercises for the reader. The following is the Stage 1 solution:

```
PSTRING   seq
     MAINST   select good string
                write "GOOD STRING";
                clear printstring;
                ps:=1;
          PS1BDY   iter until schar (ss) = "@"
                      pchar(ps):=schar(ss); ps:=ps+1; ss:=ss+1;
          PS1BDY   end
                pchar(ps):=schar(ss); ps:=ps+1; ss:=ss+1;
                write "S1=" printstring;
```

```
                clear printstring;
                ps:=1;
     PS2BDY   iter until schar(ss) = "&"
                pchar(ps):=schar(ss); ps:=ps+1; ss:=ss+1;
     PS2BDY   end
                pchar(ps):=schar(ss); ps:=ps+1; ss:=ss+1;
                write "S2=" printstring;
     PRESID   iter until schar(ss) = "%"
                ss:=ss+1;
     PRESID   end
                ss:=ss+1;
   MAINST   or bad string
                write "BAD STRING";
                ch:=001;
     BADBDY   iter until schar(ss) = "%"
                  write "CHAR-" ch"=" schar (ss);
                  ss:=ss+1; ch:=ch+1;
     BADBDY   end
                write "CHAR-" ch"=" schar(ss);
                ss:=ss+1; ch:=ch+1;
   MAINST   end
 PSTRING   end
```

The pointer to the string is the variable ss; the current location (i.e. the next character to process) is schar(ss). The variable ps is used as a pointer to the string to be printed for S1 and S2.

At Stage 1 we have the friendly demon to tell us whether the string is good or bad. We therefore know, within the first part of MAINST, that the string is good and that we will encounter an "@" and an "&", in that order, before reaching the end of the string. In Stage 2, however, we no longer have the demon, and we must examine critically our hypothesis that the string is good. The hypothesis can be refuted only when we encounter a "%" before S1 and S2 have been completely processed. We therefore insert a **quit** statement into each of PS1BDY and PS2BDY, to check for a possible "%". The Stage 2 solution is therefore:

```
   PSTRING   seq
     MAINST   posit good string
                write "GOOD STRING";
                clear printstring;
                ps:=1;
       PS1BDY   iter until schar(ss) = "@"
```

```
                    quit MAINST if schar(ss) = "%";
                    pchar(ps): =schar(ss); ps: =ps+1; ss: =ss+1;
    PS1BDY    end
                  pchar(ps): =schar(ss); ps: =ps+1; ss: =ss+1;
                  write "S1=" printstring;
                  clear printstring;
                  ps: =1;
    PS2BDY    iter until schar(ss) = "&"
                    quit MAINST if schar(ss) = "%";
                    pchar(ps): =schar(ss); ps: =ps+1; ss: =ss+1;
    PS2BDY    end
                  pchar(ps): =schar(ss); ps: =ps+1; ss: =ss+1;
                  write "S2=" printstring;
    PRESID    iter until schar(ss) = "%"
                    ss: =ss+1;
    PRESID    end
                  ss: =ss+1;
MAINST    admit bad string
                  write "BAD STRING";
                  ch: =001;
    BADBDY    iter until schar(ss) = "%"
                    write "CHAR−" ch"=" schar(ss);
                    ss: =ss+1; ch: =ch+1;
    BADBDY    end
                  write "CHAR−" ch"=" schar(ss);
                  ss: =ss+1; ch: =ch+1;
    MAINST    end
PSTRING    end
```

We are now ready to consider the side-effects. Since printstring and ps are local to the first part of MAINST, we are concerned only with the assignments to ss and the statements which output the lines of the good report. The former may be handled most conveniently by remembering and restoring the original value of ss. Unless we have an appropriate output procedure available we cannot handle the line printer in the same way, but must arrange to write to local variables in main storage. The resulting program, on completion of Stage 3, is:

```
PSTRING    seq
    MAINST    posit good string
                  xs: =ss;
                  line-1: ="GOOD STRING";
```

```
                    clear printstring;
                    ps:=1;
        PS1BDY   iter until schar(ss) = "@"
                    quit MAINST if schar(ss) = "%";
                    pchar(ps):=schar(ss); ps:=ps+1; ss:=ss+1;
        PS1BDY   end
                    pchar(ps):=schar(ss); ps:=ps+1; ss:=ss+1;
                    line-2:="S1=" printstring;
                    clear printstring;
                    ps:=1;
        PS2BDY   iter until schar(ss) = "&"
                    quit MAINST if schar(ss) = "%";
                    pchar(ps):=schar(ss); ps:=ps+1; ss:=ss+1;
        PS2BDY   end
                    pchar(ps):=schar(ss); ps:=ps+1; ss:=ss+1;
                    line-3:="S2=" printstring;
        PRESID   iter until schar(ss) = "%"
                    ss:=ss+1;
        PRESID   end
                    ss:=ss+1;
                    write line-1;
                    write line-2;
                    write line-3;
  MAINST      admit bad string
                    ss:=xs;
                    write "BAD STRING";
                    ch:=001;
        BADBDY   iter until schar(ss) = "%"
                    write "CHAR-" ch "=" schar(ss);
                    ss:=ss+1; ch:=ch+1;
        BADBDY   end
                    write "CHAR-" ch "=" schar(ss);
                    ss:=ss+1; ch:=ch+1;
  MAINST      end
 PSTRING   end
```

Some readers may well feel that this program is perversely inefficient.
Various possibilities for optimizing it are discussed in Chapter 12. For the
moment we remark only that the storage needed for the output lines can be
reduced by the following expedient:

delete the statement "line-1:='GOOD STRING';"

delete the three "write" statements;

replace the statement "line-3 := 'S2 =' printstring;" by the statements

> write "GOOD STRING";
> write line-2;
> write "S2 =" printstring;

The storage areas for line-1 and line-3 are not then required.

6.8

We will use the following problem to illustrate the difference between the two suggested methods for handling side-effects in input–output operations.

PROBLEM 11—GOOD AND BAD BRANCHES

A tape file contains sorted card-images. Each card carries a branch-number and a card-type indicator, together with some other information. A program must be designed to purge this file of error data, producing a file of good data and an error listing. Detailed diagnosis of errors is not required. If the data for a branch is good, according to the criteria given below, it is written to the file of good data; otherwise a line is written in the error listing in the form:

ERROR DATA FOR BRANCH-NUMBER nnnnnn

followed by a listing of the card-images for the branch in error.

Data for a branch is good if, and only if, it satisfies all of the following criteria:

> there must be exactly two cards for the branch, a T1 and a T2, in that order;

> the field F1 in the T1 card and the field F2 in the T2 card must be numeric;

> the value of F1 in the T1 card must be strictly greater than the value of the F2 field in the T2 card.

The card-images have been sorted into ascending order by card-type within branch-number.

The basic steps in design are left as an exercise for the reader. The Stage 1 program is:

```
PURGE   seq
            open files;
            read cardfile;
        PFBODY   iter until eof-cardfile
                    bn:=branch number (from next card-image);
            PBRANCH   select good branch
                        write T1 to goodfile;
                        read cardfile;
                        write T2 to goodfile;
                        read cardfile;
            PBRANCH   or bad branch
                        write "ERROR DATA FOR BRANCH-
                                        NUMBER" bn;
                PBADBDY   iter until eof-cardfile or branch-
                                        number ≠ bn
                            write card-image;
                            read cardfile;
                PBADBDY   end
            PBRANCH   end
        PFBODY   end
            close files;
            stop;
PURGE   end
```

With the help of the friendly demon we have no need of tests to determine whether a branch is good or bad. Nor need we consider the possibility that end-of-file will come up at an inconvenient moment: once we embark on a good branch we know certainly that it must contain two cards—otherwise it would not be a good branch.

The **quit** statements required for Stage 2 are obvious: they are all but enumerated in the specification. We must check:

first card is T1 and F1 is numeric;

second card belongs to same branch, is T2, F2 is numeric and less than F1 in first card;

no third card is present for the branch.

We will consider more than one version of Stage 3. For the first version, we will suppose that we have available a backspaceable input file reader and a backspaceable output writer for the goodfile. In addition to the normal operations on these files, we can also execute the operations:

note; when a note operation is executed, the state of the file, including for an input file the contents of the last record read, is remembered by the input–output procedure;

restore; when a restore operation is executed, the file is restored to its state at the preceding note; for an input file this includes restoring the contents of the last record read (which may be in a user area, whose name must then be specified in the restore statement).

Thus the sequence of operations

```
open goodfile;
write record-1;
note goodfile;
write record-2;
write record-3;
restore goodfile;
write record-4;
close goodfile;
```

will cause only the records record-1 and record-4 to be written to the file.

It is not a small task to implement backspaceable files in a completely satisfactory form. However, assuming that this task has been carried out, we have the following simple Stage 3 program:

```
PURGE   seq
            open files;
            read cardfile;
PFBODY      iter until eof-cardfile;
                bn: = branch-number (from next card-image)
        PBRANCH     posit good branch
                    note cardfile;
                    note goodfile;
                    quit PBRANCH if not T1;
                    quit PBRANCH if F1 not numeric;
                    XF1: = F1;
                    write T1 to goodfile;
```

```
                    read cardfile;
                    quit PBRANCH if eof-cardfile;
                    quit PBRANCH if branch-number ≠ bn;
                    quit PBRANCH if not T2;
                    quit PBRANCH if F2 not numeric;
                    quit PBRANCH if F2 not less than XF1;
                    write T2 to goodfile;
                    read cardfile;
                    quit PBRANCH if (not eof-cardfile) and
                                              branch-number = bn;
       PBRANCH    admit bad branch
                    restore cardfile;
                    restore goodfile;
                    write "ERROR DATA FOR BRANCH-
                                              NUMBER" bn;
         PBADBDY    iter until eof-cardfile or branch-
                                              number ≠ bn
                    write card-image;
                    read cardfile;
         PBADBDY    end
       PBRANCH    end
    PFBODY    end
                    close files;
                    stop;
    PURGE    end
```

The only side-effects of the first part of PBRANCH are the operations on cardfile and goodfile; the restore statements ensure than any such side-effects are nullified on entry to the admit part.

For the second version of Stage 3 we will adopt the technique of multiple reading ahead. At any point in the program after the three initial read operations have been executed, the next card-image is available in card-1, the next-plus-one in card-2 and the next-plus-two in card-3. Tests for end-of-file must be made on a specific card, as, for instance,

        ...   if eof-card-2

meaning

        ...   if the next-plus-one card-image is eof.

All other references to card-images must be similarly specific, and will be written with suffixes to indicate which card-image is referred to. The program, in this second Stage 3 version, is:

```
PURGE   seq
            open files;
            read cardfile; read cardfile; read cardfile;
     PFBODY   iter until eof-cardfile-1
                bn: =branch-number-1;
           PBRANCH   posit good branch
                       quit PBRANCH if not T1-1;
                       quit PBRANCH if F1-1 not numeric;
                       quit PBRANCH if eof-card-2;
                       quit PBRANCH if branch-number-2 ≠ bn;
                       quit PBRANCH if not T2-2;
                       quit PBRANCH if F2-2 not numeric;
                       quit PBRANCH if F2-2 not less than F1-1;
                       quit PBRANCH if (not eof-card-3) and
                                          branch-number-3 = bn;
                       write T1-1 to goodfile;
                       write T2-2 to goodfile;
                       read cardfile;
                       read cardfile;
           PBRANCH   admit bad branch
                       write "ERROR DATA FOR BRANCH-
                                         NUMBER" bn;
                  PBADBDY   iter until eof-card-1 or branch-
                                         number-1 ≠ bn
                              write card-image-1;
                              read cardfile;
                  PBADBDY   end
           PBRANCH   end
     PFBODY   end
            close files;
            stop;
PURGE   end
```

The card-1 and card-2 areas have been used both for the read ahead and for storing the records to be written to the goodfile. This would not always be possible: it is possible in this program because the output records are direct transcriptions of the input records. Conceptually, the write statements at the end of the first part of PBRANCH are:

write stored-output-record-1;
write stored-output-record-2;

It would be wrong, therefore, to order the statements as:

write T1-1 to goodfile;
read cardfile;
write T2-1 to goodfile;
read cardfile;

implying that the correspondence between the pairs of input and output records holds good in general rather than merely for this particular problem.

6.9

We have so far encountered only neutral and intolerable side-effects—except, of course, for the four-leaf clover. Here is a problem in which a beneficent side-effect occurs. The problem is also interesting because it is not commonly treated as a problem in backtracking.

PROBLEM 12—SERIAL LOOK-UP

A table in main storage has the format:

```
01   TABLE.
   02   ENUM PIC S9(4) COMP.
   02   TBODY.
      03   ENTRY OCCURS 500.
      04   EKEY PIC X(5).
      04   EVAL PIC X(11).
```

There are 500 locations available for holding entries, but at any moment only the locations ENTRY (1), ENTRY (2), . . . ENTRY (ENUM) are occupied. The value of ENUM is always non-negative, but may be zero.

A program component is required which will look up a given argument in this table. That is, given an argument SKEY, in the form

```
01   SKEY PIC X(5).
```

the table is to be searched for an entry ENTRY (S) such that EKEY (S) = SKEY and S $\leqslant$ ENUM.

If the argument is in the table, the component must set RESULT, which is

   01   RESULT PIC X(11).

to the value of EVAL (S); otherwise, RESULT should be set to spaces and a diagnostic routine PX performed.

The data structure of the output is evidently:

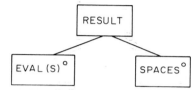

The structure of the table is:

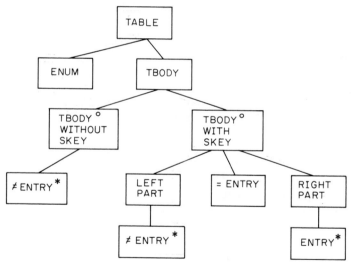

We will assume that the table is to be searched from left to right, that is, from low to high values of S, and that the first matching entry found is to be used.

The Stage 1 program is:

```
PTABLE   seq
            s:=1;
         PTBODY   select without skey
```

```
              result: =spaces;
              do PX;
     PTBODY   or with skey
        PLEFTP   iter until ekey(s)=skey
                 s: =s+1;
        PLEFTP   end
           result: =eval(s);
     PTBODY   end
  PTABLE   end
```

If the friendly demon tells us that the SKEY is absent, we ignore the table altogether; if he tells us it is present, we need only find our way through the left part to the equal entry. There is no need to test the value of S against the value of ENUM: if we know that the SKEY is present, we are certain to encounter the equal entry before S > ENUM.

The Stage 2 program requires that we examine the entries in tbody without skey; clearly the assumption that the skey is absent can be falsified only by discovering its presence. We must therefore examine every entry in the table, quitting if it proves to be an equal rather than an unequal entry.

```
  PTABLE   seq
           s: =1;
     PTBODY   posit without skey
        PWITHOUT   iter until S > ENUM
                   quit PTBODY if ekey(s) = skey;
                   s: =s+1;
        PWITHOUT   end
              result: =spaces;
              do PX;
     PTBODY   admit with skey
        PLEFTP   iter until ekey(s) = skey
                 s: =s+1;
        PLEFTP   end
           result: =eval(s);
     PTBODY   end
  PTABLE   end
```

The side-effects are the assignment to s in PWITHOUT, the assignment to result and the execution of PX. We may ignore the last two, because the program structure shows clearly that neither can precede a quit. The first, however, is significant.

The **admit** part of PTBODY has been written on the assumption tha' s=1 on entry; this assumption is destroyed by the assignment of new values to s in PWITHOUT.

Examination of the program text shows that:

there is only one quit statement; execution of the admit part of PTBODY must therefore follow immediately after execution of this quit;

when the quit is executed we have ekey(s) = skey, and this condition must therefore hold on entry to the admit part of PTBODY;

the effect, indeed the purpose, of the component PLEFTP is to set s so that ekey(s) = skey.

We can therefore deal with the assignment of a new value to s in PWITHOUT by regarding it as a beneficent side-effect. We have found the four-leaf clover, albeit while travelling the wrong path; we therefore need not seek it when we travel the right path. We delete the component PLEFTP, giving the final Stage 3 program:

```
PTABLE    seq
              s:=1;
          PTBODY    posit without skey
              PWITHOUT    iter until S > ENUM
                          quit PTBODY if ekey(s) = skey;
                          s:=s+1;
              PWITHOUT    end
                          result:=spaces;
                          do PX;
          PTBODY    admit with skey
                          result:=eval(s);
          PTBODY    end
PTABLE  end
```

6.10

Backtracking may occur in iteration no less than in selection, and for the same reason. In an iteration we are constrained to test the condition on entry, before beginning to execute each instance of the iterated part. This arrangement ensures that we execute the iterated part an integral number of times, and that we never attempt to execute it in the absence of valid data.

Sometimes, however, this arrangement is inadequate. It may be that the condition for terminating the iteration can occur at several points within the iterated part; they cannot all correspond to the beginning. Consider, for example, Problem 3 (Cantor's Enumeration of Rationals). In the version specified in Chapter 3, it was conveniently required that the program should stop after executing an integral number of zigzags. But this requirement is unrealistic, and we would wish to write the program in such a manner that it could stop after (or before) printing any arbitrarily chosen number.

Essentially, the program is:

```
PNSET    seq
            z:=1;
     PSBODY    iter until z > 50
                  s:=2*z−1;
                  t:=1;
            PZIGBODY    iter until s < 1
                           display s/t;
                           s:=s−1;
                           t:=t×1;
            PZIGBODY    end
                  s:=1;
                  t:=2*z:
            PZAGBODY    iter until t < 1
                           display s/t;
                           s:=s+1;
                           t:=t−1;
            PZAGBODY    end
                  z:=z+1;
     PSBODY    end
            stop;
PNSET    end
```

The program stops after 50 zigzags. If we wish to stop after printing an arbitrary number, we must take into account the fact that the number may occur within either zigbody or zagbody: there is no way of reordering the statements of the program so that the test at the head of the iteration PSBODY is executed for each number printed.

We therefore introduce a "**quit**" statement into iterations: the format of the statement is the same as the format in a selection or **posit** component; the effect is to transfer control to the exit from the iteration. We could rewrite our program for Problem 3 as:

```
PNSET    seq
            read endnumber;
```

```
              z: = 1
       PSBODY   iter
                   s: = 2*z−1;
                   t: = 1;
              PZIGBODY   iter until s < 1
                            display s/t;
                            quit PSBODY if s/t = endnumber;
                            s: = s−1;
                            t: = t+1;
              PZIGBODY   end
                   s: = 1;
                   t: = 2*z;
              PZAGBODY   iter until t < 1
                            display s/t;
                            quit PSBODY if s/t = endnumber;
                            s: = s+1;
                            t: = t−1;
              PZAGBODY   end
                   z: = z+1;
       PSBODY   end
              stop;
   PNSET   end
```

and the program will now stop immediately after printing the rational endnumber. Observe that there is now no condition test at the head of PSBODY: the iteration can be terminated only by execution of a **quit** statement.

It is important to recognize that use of the **quit** in iteration does involve backtracking. There may be side-effects from the final, partial, execution of the iterated part. In principle, we ought perhaps to treat an iteration in a visibly different way when it incorporates **quit** statements. For example, we might write it in the form:

```
   A     posit integral number of C's
      B      iter
          C     seq
                . . .
                quit A if . . .
                . . .
          C     end
      B     end
   A     admit non-integral number of C's
          . . .
   A     end
```

in which the iteration is enclosed in a **posit** component, and the **quit** statements refer to the **posit**. Or we might write:

```
A     iter until no more C's
   B      posit this C is complete
      C      seq
                . . .
             quit B if . . .
                . . .
             quit B if . . .
                . . .
      C      end
   B      admit this C is incomplete
                . . .
                . . .
             quit A;
   B      end
A      end
```

in which component B takes care of any side-effects from an incomplete C and also terminates A when the last C is incomplete: if the last C is complete, A is terminated by the condition test at its head.

In practice, it seems permissible to use the quit statement directly in a simple iteration, as shown above in the program for Problem 3.

EXERCISE 6.1 (b)

The technique for multiple reading ahead suggested in Section 6.2 above is very crude. Devise instead a technique which achieves a similar effect but avoids the need to move record areas in storage.

EXERCISE 6.2 (b)

Write COBOL coding for the program to solve Problem 10 (Delimited Strings).

EXERCISE 6.3 (c)

Design a suitable interface for a card-read procedure which permits back-spacing. Do the same for a tape-write procedure.

EXERCISE 6.4 (b)

Write COBOL coding for the two solutions given to Problem 11 (Good and Bad Branches). In the first version (using "note" and "restore") assume the availability of the procedures you specified in Exercise 6.3.

EXERCISE 6.5 (c)

Two tables are given, in the form described in Problem 12 (Serial Look-up). Design a program component which will determine whether there are at least two entries appearing in both tables—that is, whether there are four entries EA1, EA2, EB1 and EB2 such that:

> the key of EA1 is the same as the key of EB1, and the key of EA2 is the same as the key of EB2;
> EA1 and EA2 are distinct entries of table-A, and EB1 and EB2 are distinct entries of table-B.

EXERCISE 6.6 (b)

A file is to be processed which should have the structure:

    FILE   iter
        REGION   seq

```
              region-header record;
      REGBODY   iter
          BRANCH   seq
                  T1 record;
                  T2 record;
          BRANCH   end
      REGBODY   end
              region-trailer record;
   REGION   end
FILE   end
```

The records within each region carry the region-number; the records within each branch carry the branch-number in addition to the region-number and the type-code; the region-header and region-trailer records are of type T0 and T9 respectively.

Some of the branches are in error, because some records have been dropped from the file; for the same reason, some of the regions are in error. There is no other source of error.

Design a program to analyse the file, producing this report:

```
FILE ANALYSIS
NUMBER OF KNOWN REGIONS   nnn
NUMBER OF ERROR REGIONS   mmm

NUMBER OF KNOWN BRANCHES   bbbb
NUMBER OF ERROR BRANCHES   cccc
```

where an error region is one for which either the region-header or the region-trailer record is missing, and an error branch is one for which either the T1 or the T2 record is missing. A known region is one for which any record at all is present (possibly only a T1 or a T2 belonging to a branch of the region); a known branch is one for which any record at all is present (either a T1 or a T2). There are no duplicate region-numbers or branch-numbers.

QUESTION 6.1

When we code the schematic logic

  A   **iter until** condition-1
    B   **seq**
           . . .
    B   **end**
  A   **end**

in COBOL in the form

  AITER.
      IF CONDITION-1 GO TO AEND.
  BSEQ.
       . . .
       . . .
  BEND.
      GO TO AITER.
  AEND.

there is an important sense in which the COBOL GO TO statements are "not really GO TO statements": they are really hand-compiled machine instructions, implementing the schematic logic iteration component.

Can we say similarly that the **quit** statement is not really a GO TO statement? What is the difference? Why are GO TO statements considered undesirable?

QUESTION 6.2

In Problem 12 (Serial Look-up) the data structure for the table was given as:

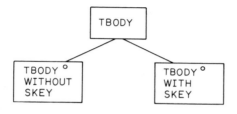

Redesign the program, going through the three stages carefully, using the structure:

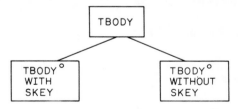

You will need to pay special attention to the second stage, which is now much more difficult. It is easy to place the quit statements wrongly, or to place too few of them. Why?

QUESTION 6.3

In Problem 11 (Good and Bad Branches) the data structure for a branch was taken to be:

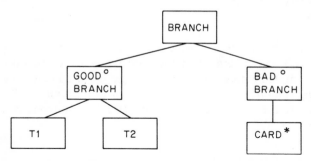

The structure of a bad branch, as shown, includes the structure of a good branch as a special case: that is, any instance of good branch is inevitably also an instance of bad branch. Does this matter? How does it affect the order of the parts in the selection? Redesign the structure for bad branch so that it explicitly excludes all instances of good branch. Is the redesigned structure better than the original?

QUESTION 6.4

Look at the second Stage 3 version of the solution to Problem 11, given in Section 6.8 above. All of the **quit** statements appear at the beginning of the **posit** component PFBRANCH. Does this mean that PFBRANCH is now just an ordinary **select** component?

7. STRUCTURE CLASHES

7.1

The structure of a program must be based on the structures of all of the data it processes. Each executable operation is associated with some component of some data structure; we wish to allocate that operation to an appropriate program component, and we must therefore find a program component which corresponds, in its place in the program structure, to the data component within the data structure.

For example, in Problem 5 (Stores Movements Summary) there is an operation "add quantity to net movement". This operation is associated with a receipt record in the input file; we cannot allocate it correctly in the program structure unless the program structure contains a component "process receipt record". Similarly, there is an operation "print net movement line". This operation is associated with a net movement line in the printed summary; we cannot allocate it correctly unless the program structure contains a component "process net movement line".

To be sure of being able to allocate the operations correctly, we must fit the data structures together by identifying the 1–1 correspondences between them: only then can the program structure correspond to different data structures at the same time.

This chapter is about structure clashes. That is, it is about problems in which the data structures cannot be fitted together in the way we would like, in which the necessary 1–1 correspondences cannot be found. In this chapter we explore the nature of the difficulty caused by a structure clash, and give some examples of clashes: the technique of solution is suggested, but is not fully developed until Chapters 8 and 9.

7.2

Consider first the following problem. We have a card file, containing a matrix. Each card contains the elements of one row of the matrix. We wish to write a program which will print out the matrix by columns: each line of

151

print-out should contain the elements of one column of the matrix. The data structures are:

There is, of course, a correspondence at the top level. The print file is derived from the card file. But there is no correspondence at the lower levels. Row does not correspond to column: the printed output for one column is not derived from the input data for one row; in general, there will not be the same number of rows as of columns. Nor does row-element correspond to column-element: there must be the same number of both, but they are differently ordered. Because we cannot identify the necessary correspondences we cannot form the data structures into a single program structure: there is a structure clash between the card file and the print file. We may call this type of clash an "ordering clash".

The practical implication is obvious: we must construct the program as two structures, not as one. For this particular problem, there are two ways of proceeding. The first way is to redraw the system flow diagram to include a sort between input and output:

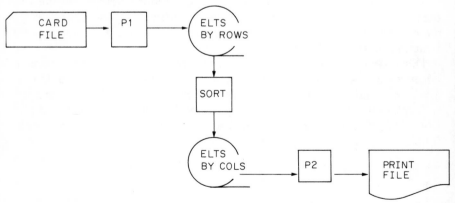

Program P1 writes a file of element records; each record carries the row and column number of the element. The sort reorders this file into ascending sequence by column number, retaining the row ordering within each column.

Program P2 reads the output file from the sort, and prints the matrix as required.

The second way can be used if there is enough main storage to hold the whole of the matrix. We structure the program as follows:

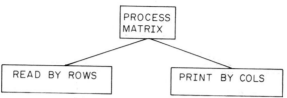

The program is a sequence of two components: first the matrix is read into main storage by rows, then it is printed out by columns. The fact that access to main storage is direct and not sequential makes the sorting step unnecessary. But, just as in the first method, the whole of the matrix must be read before printing can begin; reading and printing are handled by separate program components.

7.3

We have already seen a hidden example of another type of clash in Problem 8 (Source Statement Library). This problem was specified as the construction of a program to build a tape file for input to the COBOL compiler:

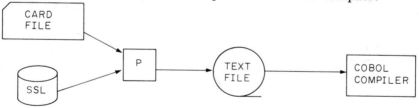

The true, original specification of the problem was quite different. Originally the requirement was for a COBOL compiler capable of accepting its input in the form specified for the input to P:

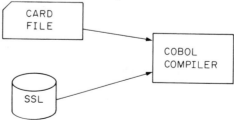

Consider the problem of constructing such a compiler. Without delving too deeply we can see that the compiler must deal with the structure of the card file and the structure of the source-statement library, and must also deal with the structure of the syntax of a COBOL program. There are other data structures involved, naturally, but we can see immediately that there is a clash between the structure of the card file and the structure of COBOL syntax:

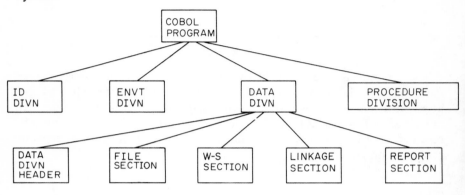

Now, taking the card file and the source statement library member together, it is clear that they must define a proper COBOL program in which the various components—ID Division, Environment Division, Data Division, etc.—appear in their proper order. But there is no way of knowing where the boundaries between the divisions and sections will come in relation to the structure of the card file and library member. For instance, the Data Division header may come from the library member, or from the card file as part of an insertion, or as part of a deletion, or from the card file without any reference to the library at all. We cannot therefore find correspondences between the COBOL syntax structure and the structure of the card file.

We cannot therefore form a single program structure to process both the data structures. The form of the program specified in Problem 8 presupposes an obvious solution: the compiler is split into two programs, one of which, P, produces the text file from the card file and the library, while the other is the COBOL compiler proper. Only program P needs to know about the structure of the card file, and only the compiler proper needs to know about the structure of COBOL syntax.

We may call this type of clash a "boundary clash". There is no difficulty about ordering: everything is in an appropriate order already. But there is still a clash between the structures which completely prevents them from being handled by a single program structure. There is no need for a sort; but there is an inescapable need for at least two program structures.

The solution we have considered is inefficient. Since P must produce the whole of the text file before compilation can begin, we have greatly increased the minimum elapsed time for a complete compilation. We can use various techniques to overcome this inefficiency: for the moment we are chiefly concerned with the recognition and resolution of the structure clash.

7.4

Here is another example of a boundary clash. The problem was suggested by a paper on structured programming ("An Experiment in Structured Programming", P. Henderson and R. Snowdon, BIT 12 (1972), pp 38–53). The authors discuss a similar, though not identical, problem, and show how easy it is to introduce bugs into even an apparently simple program. They conclude, appropriately, that

"Data structures should be explicitly stated and a data concept should be elaborated in the same manner as any other concept . . ."

PROBLEM 13—TELEGRAMS ANALYSIS

An input file on paper tape contains the texts of a number of telegrams. The tape is accessed by a "read block" instruction, which reads into main storage a variable-length character string delimited by a terminal EOB character: the size of a block cannot exceed 100 characters, excluding the EOB. Each block contains a number of words, separated by space characters; there may be one or more spaces between adjacent words, and at the beginning and end of a block there may (but need not) be one or more additional spaces. Each telegram consists of a number of words followed by the special word "ZZZZ"; the file is terminated by a special end-file block, whose first character is EOF. In addition, there is always a null telegram at the end of the file, in the block preceding the special end-file block: this null telegram consists only of the word "ZZZZ". Except for the fact that the null telegram always appears at the end of the file, there is no particular relationship between blocks and telegrams: a telegram may begin and end anywhere within a block, and may span several blocks; several telegrams may share a block.

The processing required is an analysis of the telegrams. A report is to be produced showing for each telegram the number of words it contains and the number of those words which are oversize (more than 12 characters). For purposes of the report, "ZZZZ" does not count as a word, nor does the null telegram count as a telegram. The format of the report is:

TELEGRAMS ANALYSIS
TELEGRAM 1
    15 WORDS OF WHICH 2 OVERSIZE
TELEGRAM 2
    106 WORDS OF WHICH 13 OVERSIZE
TELEGRAM 3
    42 WORDS OF WHICH 0 OVERSIZE
. . .

. . .
END ANALYSIS

No attention need be paid to the provision of page headings, skipping over the perforations in the paper, or any other details of page formatting.

The data structure of the printed report is straightforward:

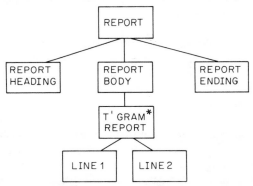

The structure of the input file is less obvious. But we will not be able to do much better than that shown opposite.

In a sense, this structure is the result of some optimization; the point is discussed in Chapter 12. The point which concerns us now is the correspondence, or absence of correspondence, between the two data structures.

There is a correspondence between report and ptape: the report is derived from the ptape. The heading-body-ending structure of the report causes no difficulty. But there is a boundary clash between block and telegram report: the words of the blocks are the words of the telegrams, and they appear in the same order in both; but the components block and telegram themselves cannot be fitted together. We cannot say that a block consists of an integral number of telegrams, nor can we say that a telegram consists of an integral number of blocks; we cannot say that a block is followed by a telegram, or vice versa; we cannot say there is a component X which is either a block or a telegram. Effectively, this exhausts our repertoire of possible ways to fit the two components together, and we have recognized a clash.

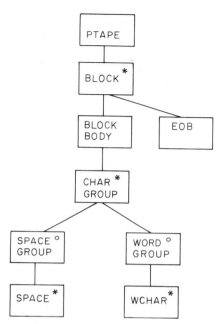

A very important point arises here. This boundary clash is, like the house-maid's baby, only a small one. Perhaps if we ignore it everything will turn out all right. The clash in the Source Statement Library problem was impossible to ignore, but surely this one is different? Perhaps a well-judged first-time switch will solve it?

Resist this satanic temptation. If the clash can be easily solved, we shall solve it easily by our methods. But only after we have understood it thoroughly. And there is a clash to be understood. When we come to write the program we will certainly need an instruction "read block"; we had better put it in a program component which is executed once per block. We will also need an instruction "add 1 to count of telegrams"; that must go into a program component which is executed once per telegram. So our program structure must contain a component which is executed once per block and another which is executed once per telegram. These components cannot both appear in one structure, so we will need at least two.

We will restructure the system as:

P1 will create an intermediate file from the paper tape input; P2 will produce the report from the intermediate file. Our purpose is to overcome the structure clash, so we must ensure that only P1 need have a component "process block" and only P2 need have a component "process telegram". What, then, should be the intermediate file? It must be something which can be constructed without knowledge of telegrams—for P1 knows nothing of telegrams—and which can be rebuilt into the report by a program component which knows nothing about paper tape blocks—for P2 knows nothing of blocks.

Greatly simplifying the two data structures, we may regard them as:

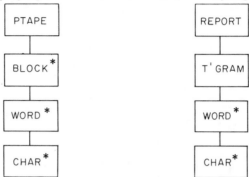

There is a good correspondence between every pair of components on the same level except for the block-telegram pair. We may therefore solve the structure clash by choosing to write as a single record of the intermediate file either:

> the complete paper tape, or
> one word, or
> one character.

To write the whole of the paper tape file as a single record of the intermediate file we would read the whole paper tape into main storage, replace each EOB character by a space character, and write the resulting string. This would overcome the structure clash, because all evidence of the blocks would have been removed and there would be no further need for any instructions concerned with blocks. But, of course, it is hopelessly impractical: we would not be able to fit the whole of the paper tape file into main storage.

The best choice is to write a record of the intermediate file for each word in the paper tape file. This is the best choice because a word is the largest component which corresponds in the two structures and can also be held in main storage. If we choose to write a record for each character, we are put to the unnecessary trouble of dissecting words into characters and then reconstituting the characters into words in P2.

We therefore decide that each record of the intermediate file will be a word of the paper tape file. It seems reasonable to include with each word a count of the number of characters it contains, since P1 must generate such a count as a byproduct of scanning for the end of the word. The format of each record in the intermediate file will be then:

```
01   WORD.
  02   CCT PIC 999.
  02   WORDBODY.
    03   WCH PIC X OCCURS 100.
```

There is no need to retain the delimiter of the word: the character count is sufficient.

The structure of the intermediate file, as seen by P1, is:

The structure of the same file, as seen by P2, is:

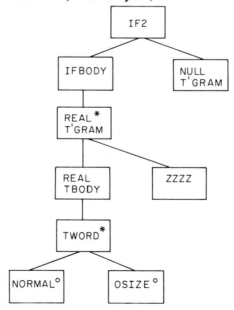

The first of these structures fits with the structure of the paper tape file; the second fits with the structure of the report. So the clash is resolved. We have only to design the two programs P1 and P2. Again, there is a reduction of efficiency: elapsed time for execution is roughly doubled. But, as we shall discover in the next chapter, this is not a problem.

7.5

Here is another problem involving a structure clash.

PROBLEM 14—SYSTEM LOG

This problem, like Problem 13, was suggested to me by Dr Peter Henderson. I have changed many details, and arranged the problem in two versions.

A time-sharing system collects information about system usage. This information consists of records, one for each log-on, log-off, program-load and program-unload. When a user of the system logs on, he is allocated a unique job-number for that session: one user would receive two different job-numbers if he logged on on two different occasions. The system ensures that no user can log on unless the terminal is free (that is, no other session is in progress at that terminal), and that he cannot log off unless he has previously logged on. Further, he is allowed only one active program at any one time: he must unload that program before he can load another or load the same program again.

The collected information is written to magnetic tape. The records contain the following information:

log-on record: code "N"; job-number; time of logging on;

log-off record: code "F"; job-number; time of logging off;

program-load record: code "L"; job-number; program-id; time of loading;

program-unload: code "U"; job-number; program-id; time of unloading.

The records are written in strict chronological sequence.

Version 1

The tape is to be analysed, and a report produced in the format:

SYSTEM USAGE REPORT

NUMBER OF JOBS = nnnn   AVERAGE TIME = tttt
NUMBER OF PGMS = pppp   AVERAGE TIME = uuuu

where the average time for jobs is the average of the difference between the time in the log-on record and the time in the log-off record, and the average time for programs is similarly calculated.

Version 2

The system component which writes the tape has a low priority. The tape is written in blocks, many records in each block, and if channel time is not available a complete block may be lost. As a result, the tape may contain incomplete information about some jobs and some programs: there may be a log-on record with no matching log-off, or vice versa; there may be a program-load record with no matching program-unload, or vice versa. The report should reflect these possibilities.

SYSTEM USAGE REPORT

NUMBER OF COMPLETE JOBS = nnnn
                        AVERAGE TIME = tttt
NUMBER OF KNOWN JOBS = mmmm
NUMBER OF COMPLETE PGMS = pppp
                        AVERAGE TIME = uuuu
NUMBER OF KNOWN PGMS = qqqq

A complete job is a job for which both the log-on and the log-off records are present on the tape; a complete program is one for which both the load and the unload records are present. A complete job may contain incomplete programs. A job is known if its job-number appears anywhere on the tape; a program is known if either the load or the unload record is present.

Initially, we consider only Version 1. The structure of the report is:

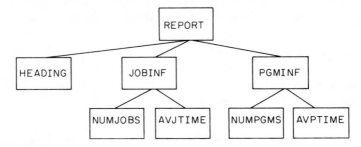

The structure of the input file, the system log tape, is:

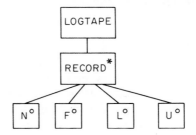

Superficially, we may fit these structures together as:

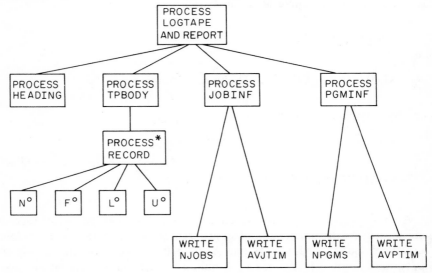

That is, we must process the details before we can write the summary report. However, when we come to allocate the executable operations, we realise the inadequacy of this program structure. There must be an operation "add 1 to number of jobs", and this operation must be executed once per job. Where is the program component which is executed once per job? Perhaps we could use the component which processes a record "N"? But what about the operation "subtract log-on time from log-off time"? This must be part of a component which processes both the log-on and the log-off records for a job:

```
PROCESSJOB    seq
              remember log-on time;
              . . .
              subtract log-on time from log-off time;
              add result to total time for jobs;
              . . .
PROCESSJOB    end
```

And, of course, there is a similar difficulty for program-loads and unloads.

The resourceful and ingenious reader may well be ahead of me here. We can evade all of these difficulties. We write the component "process record" as:

```
PROCREC    select log-on
           njobs: = njobs + 1;
           totjobtime: = totjobtime − logontime;
PROCREC    or log-off
           totjobtime: = totjobtime + logofftime;
PROCREC    or program-load
           nprogs: = nprogs + 1;
           totprogtime: = totprogtime − loadtime;
PROCREC    or program-unload
           totprogtime: = totprogtime + unloadtime
PROCREC    end
```

There is no need to bring together the log-on and log-off for each job, or the load and unload for each program.

Is this a good solution? It works, and it is cheap and easy. But if we have any aspirations to solve Version 2 of the problem, or to make even minor enhancements to Version 1, it is quite wrong. The concept of a job and the concept of a program are central to the problem: we cannot hope to solve the problem correctly without components "process job" and "process program" in our solution. An obvious and likely enhancement to Version 1 would be to produce additional lines in the report:

SHORTEST JOB TIME = ssss   LONGEST JOB TIME = xxxx
SHORTEST PGM TIME = yyyy   LONGEST PGM TIME = zzzz

The ingenious solution mentioned above cannot be changed to provide this enhancement: effectively we must start again.

One way of looking at the problem is to consider it as an ordering clash, like the matrix printing problem. There is an ordering clash between the structures:

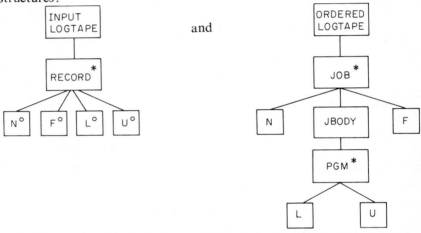

We can resolve this clash by sorting the input logtape before processing. But the problem has certain special features: the records of each job, taken alone, are already ordered in the input tape (the matrix problem, too, has this feature); and we are not interested in ordering the jobs, merely in separating them (the matrix problem does not have this feature). We will call this a "multi-threading clash".

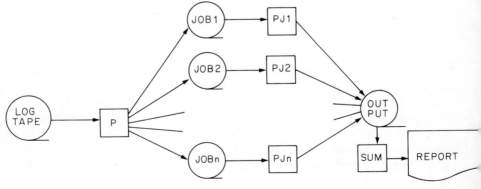

A multi-threading clash can be resolved by separating out the individual threads into distinct files as shown at the bottom of p. 164.

The program P reads the logtape and writes a distinct file for each job. The n programs PJ1, PJ2, . . . PJn are then run: each reads its jobtape and writes a record on the output tape, the record containing information about the job. The output tape is finally processed by a program SUM which calculates averages and totals and prints the report. Clearly the solution is impractical in this form: the techniques necessary to make it practical and efficient are discussed in the next chapter.

The structure of each jobtape is:

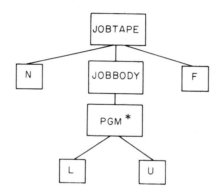

and the structure of the output tape is:

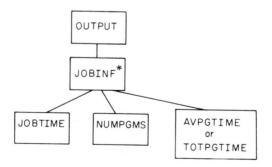

Ignoring the practical obstacles, we may easily design and construct the programs P, PJ1, PJ2, . . . PJn and SUM. For Version 2, we will need a more elaborate structure for the jobtape, involving backtracking at two levels: readers who have already solved Exercise 6.6 will find nothing new here. We will also need to incorporate more information in each jobinf record of the output tape.

7.6

At the heart of any structure clash is a synchronization problem. The program is required to execute two or more processes simultaneously, and the processes cannot be synchronized. But synchronization is essential for a healthy hierarchical program structure: the program has only one linear text, and only one location counter; the current place in the text must correspond to the current place in the data structure being processed; if there are two data structures the same location counter must serve to point to the current place in both.

The technique we have used to resolve clashes allows the program to ignore structures which cannot be synchronized. In Problem 13 (Telegrams Analysis) the first program, P1, ignores the report structure: it busies itself with the structure of the paper tape, and cannot simultaneously be concerned with telegrams. Because its view of the intermediate file is

it can write each word it finds without asking where that word fits into the structure of the report or where it fits into the current telegram.

In Section 3.7 above we observed that the structure

is almost invariably wrong for a serial input file, because it precludes expression of any relationship among the records. The same structure is invaluable when we come to handle a structure clash. Precisely because it precludes expression of relationships among records we want to use it as an output file structure: we want to avoid knowing anything about those relationships; any necessary structure can be imposed by some other program when the file is read.

EXERCISE 7.1 (b)

Design and write Programs P1 and P2 for Problem 13 (Telegrams Analysis).

EXERCISE 7.2 (b)

Design and write the programs P, PJ1, ... and SUM for Problem 14 (System Log). Naturally, since the programs PJ1, PJ2, ... PJn are identical, only one of them need be written.

EXERCISE 7.3 (b)

Show how Problem 3 (Cantor's Enumeration of Rationals) can be solved without backtracking for an arbitrary stopping point. You should assume that the arbitrary stopping point must lie within the first 1000 zigzags.

QUESTION 7.1

Design a data structure for the paper tape file in Problem 13 (Telegrams Analysis) which is perfectly explicit and unambiguous and free from optimization.

QUESTION 7.2

Suppose that in Problem 5 (Stores Movements Summary) the input file were unsorted. Suppose also that there cannot be more than 50 different part-numbers, although there is no limit on the number of movements for each part-number. Show that the problem can be treated as a structure clash or, alternatively, by the obvious method of holding 50 accumulators in main storage. What is the essential difference between these methods? How is one derivable from the other?

QUESTION 7.3

Show how to treat the matrix printing problem (Section 7.2) in the same way as Problem 14 (System Log).

QUESTION 7.4

How could we solve Problem 14 if we knew definitely that there are too few tape drives to hold the files JT1, JT2, . . . JTn? Elaborate your answer into a simple design for a sort program.

QUESTION 7.5

What methods can you think of for eliminating the inefficiency of the solutions proposed for structure clashes? What do you have to do to get rid of the intermediate tape files?

8. PROGRAM INVERSION

8.1

All of our solutions to structure clash problems have depended on introducing intermediate files. In Problem 8 (Source Statement Library) we introduce the text file between program P and the COBOL compiler; in Problem 13 (Telegrams Analysis) we introduce the word file between programs P1 and P2; in Problem 14 (System Log) we introduce many job files between program P and the output program SUM.

These intermediate files solve the structure clashes perfectly: the problems are reduced to simple processing of structures between which satisfactory correspondences exist. But the inefficiencies are inconvenient and sometimes intolerable. We are compelled to write the whole of a serial file before we can read any part of it, a constraint which is often inherent not in the problem but only in our method of solution. In the Telegrams Analysis problem there is no reason in principle why we should not begin printing the report at the same time as we begin to read the paper tape; as we come to the end of each telegram in the paper tape we can print the associated lines in the report. But the presence of the intermediate word file forces us to process all of the paper tape before we can start on the report. In the System Log problem the inefficiency is much worse: we have to provide a tape drive, or, equivalently, a disk area, for each job represented in the log tape; the number of drives needed will certainly be greater than the number we can conveniently provide. In the Source Statement Library problem we are forced to write the intermediate text file even if it proves to be no more than a copy of the card input file: we have added a pass to the compiler, and sometimes that pass will be entirely useless.

One way of eliminating the intermediate files is to run the programs under the control of a multi-programming supervisor. Each successive record of the file is then written into an area of main storage by the first program and retrieved directly from main storage by the second program; no physical tape file is necessary. We may picture this scheme as shown on p. 170.

Taking the Telegrams Analysis problem as our illustration, we have the two programs P1 and P2. P1 writes the word file which is read by P2. The

169

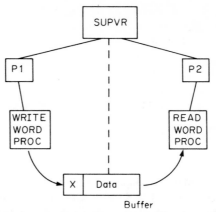

Buffer

area of main storage (the "buffer") consists of a data item and a flag X: the flag X indicates whether the buffer is full or empty. The "write word" and "read word" procedures of P1 and P2 respectively have been replaced by instructions which write to and read from the buffer. Operation is as follows:

the supervisor sets the flag X to indicate that the buffer is empty; it then passes control to one of the programs, which begins execution;

when a "write word" operation in P1 is executed, the effect is:

```
WW    seq
        WAIT until buffer is empty;
        move word to buffer;
        SET buffer-flag = full;
WW    end
```

the WAIT instruction returns control to the supervisor; control cannot return to the "move word" instruction until the buffer is empty;

when a "read word" operation in P2 is executed, the effect is:

```
RW    seq
        WAIT until buffer is full;
        move data to word;
        SET buffer-flag = empty;
RW    end
```

the WAIT instruction returns control to the supervisor; control cannot return to the "move data" instruction until the buffer is full;

when either program is waiting, the supervisor passes or returns control to the other (which cannot be waiting, since the buffer must be either full or empty);

when either program completes execution, it returns control to the supervisor finally.

A realistic multi-programming system is more elaborate than this, but not different in principle.

P1 and P2 are synchronized by the buffer. At no point can P2 have read more words than P1 has written; nor can P1 have written more than one word more than P2 has read. The second of these constraints can be relaxed by introducing additional buffers: if we have n buffers we can allow P1 to write n words more than P2 has read. But the total number of records written by P1 must be the same as the total number read by P2: otherwise one of the programs will complete execution leaving the other waiting for an event which will never happen.

8.2 Program Inversion

Multi-programming is expensive in system resources. Unless we have an unusually favourable environment we will not wish to use the sledgehammer of multi-programming to crack the nut of a small structure clash. So we seek a cheaper solution. Instead of running P1 and P2 in parallel, we convert one so that it can run as a subroutine of the other.

We will call the conversion process "program inversion". It is concerned with the coding of the inverted program, not with its basic design. Keeping to the Telegrams Analysis problem as our illustration, we have the system flow diagram:

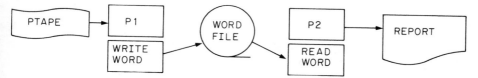

in which "write word" and "read word" are assumed to be existing subroutines or procedures of P1 and P2 respectively. If we choose to invert P1 we will code it in such a manner that it can be used as a replacement for the "read word" subroutine of P2. This is shown at the top of p. 172. P1W is P1 coded in this manner. We will say that it is "P1 inverted with respect to the word file". When P2 requires a word from the word file, it invokes

P1W; P1W then returns to P2 the next word which P1, in its original form, would have written to the word file. Provided that P2 reads all the words of the word file, its successive invocations of P1W will cause P1W to read all the blocks of the paper tape.

Alternatively, we may choose to invert P2 with respect to the word file. We then have:

P2W is a replacement for the "write word" subroutine of P1. When P1 requires to write a word to the word file, it invokes P2W; P2W then disposes of the word, using it to contribute to the report, and returns to P1. Provided that P1 writes all the words of the word file, its successive invocations of P2W will cause P2W to produce the complete report.

8.3

We will illustrate the basic technique of coding by inverting P2, thus creating P2W. Schematic logic for P2 is:

```
P2      seq
        open IF2; read word;
        write "TELEGRAMS ANALYSIS";
        telno: =1;
PRPTBODY   iter until word = ZZZZ
        PTELGRAM   seq
                   write "TELEGRAM" telno;
                   wordcount: =0;
                   osizecount: =0;
          PTELBODY   iter until word = ZZZZ
          PWOSIZE   select cct > 12
                    osizecount: =osizecount+1;
          PWOSIZE   end
```

```
                          wordcount: = wordcount + 1;
                          read word;
          PTELBODY   end
                      read word;
                      write wordcount "WORDS OF WHICH"
                            osizecount "OVERSIZE";
          PTELGRAM   end
                      telno: = telno + 1;
       PRPTBODY   end
          write "END ANALYSIS";
          read word;
          close IF2;
   P2     end
```

Note the final "read word" statement: it reads one record beyond the ZZZZ of the null telegram, thus reading the end-of-file marker in the word file.

Here is COBOL coding for P2:

```
   ...
   ENVIRONMENT DIVISION
   ...
        SELECT IF2 ASSIGN TO...
   ...
   DATA DIVISION.
   FILE SECTION.
   FD   IF2 DATA RECORDS ARE WORD.
   01   WORD.
      02   CCT PIC 999.
      02   WORDBODY.
         03   WCH PIC X OCCURS 100.
      02   WORDTEST REDEFINES WORDBODY.
         03   ZWORD PIC XXXX.
         03   FILLER PIC X(96).
   WORKING-STORAGE SECTION.
   77   IF2-EOF PIC X VALUE SPACE.
   77   TELNO PIC 9(8).
   77   WRDCT PIC 9(8).
   77   OSZCT PIC 9(8).
   PROCEDURE DIVISION.
   P2SEQ.
        OPEN INPUT IF2.
        READ IF2 AT END MOVE "E" TO IF2-EOF.
```

H

```
        DISPLAY "TELEGRAMS ANALYSIS".
        MOVE 1 TO TELNO.
    PRPTBODYITER.
        IF CCT = 4 AND ZWORD = "ZZZZ" GO TO PRPTBODYEND.
    PTELGRAMSEQ.
        DISPLAY "TELEGRAM" TELNO.
        MOVE 0 TO WRDCT, OSZCT.
    PTELBODYITER.
        IF CCT = 4 AND ZWORD = "ZZZZ" GO TO PTELBODYEND.
        IF CCT GREATER THAN 12
            ADD 1 TO OSZCT.
        ADD 1 TO WRDCT.
        READ IF2 AT END MOVE "E" TO IF2-EOF.
        GO TO PTELBODYITER.
    PTELBODYEND.
        READ IF2 AT END MOVE "E" TO IF2-EOF.
        DISPLAY WRDCT "WORDS OF WHICH" OSZCT
                                            "OVERSIZE".
    PTELGRAMEND.
        ADD 1 TO TELNO.
        GO TO PRPTBODYITER.
    PRPTBODYEND.
        DISPLAY "END ANALYSIS".
        READ IF2 AT END MOVE "E" TO IF2-EOF.
        CLOSE IF2.
        STOP RUN.
    P2END
```

The style of coding used is designed specifically to avoid PERFORM statements, for a reason which is explained later. Effectively, it is a direct transcription of the schematic logic.

We now wish to invert P2 with respect to the word file, to create a replacement for the "write word" subroutine of P1. We will assume that P1 invokes P2W by the statement

    CALL "P2W" USING WORD.

passing on each invocation the next word to be processed. The first call of P2W passes the word which is read by the "READ IF2" statement immediately following the "OPEN IF2" in P2; the last call passes the ZZZZ word of the null telegram.

The changes needed in P2 to convert it into P2W are:

remove the SELECT sentence, the FD entry, the OPEN and CLOSE for IF2; these are all concerned with handling the physical file, which is no longer present;

provide an ENTRY statement to match the CALL:

ENTRY "P2W" USING WORD.

and place the description of the record WORD in LINKAGE SECTION;

recode the READ statements to reflect the fact that P2W acquires records by returning to P1 and being invoked again.

Only the last change presents any difficulty. In general, we want to replace READ statements of P2 by coding which will have the effect:

return to P1 to acquire another record; resume operation of P2W at the point immediately following the replaced "READ".

But we must recognize that the first and last READ statements are special. On the first invocation of P2W we must begin execution at the point following the first READ: the first record is passed by P1 on the first invocation. The last READ statement in P2 causes the end-of-file marker to be read; P2W returns to P1 to read the end-of-file marker, but P1 never invokes P2W again.

Here is COBOL coding for P2W:

```
...
DATA DIVISION.
WORKING-STORAGE SECTION.
77   QS PIC 99 VALUE 1.
77   TELNO PIC 9(8).
77   WRDCT PIC 9(8).
77   OSZCT PIC 9(8).
LINKAGE SECTION.
01   WORD.
   02   CCT PIC 999.
   02   WORDBODY.
      03   WCH PIC X OCCURS 100.
   02   WORDTEST REDEFINES WORDBODY.
      03   ZWORD PIC XXXX.
      03   FILLER PIC X(96).
```

```
PROCEDURE DIVISION.
    ENTRY "P2W" USING WORD.
    GO TO Q1, Q2, Q3, Q4 DEPENDING ON QS
P2SEQ.
Q1.
    DISPLAY "TELEGRAMS ANALYSIS".
    MOVE 1 TO TELNO.
PRPTBODYITER.
    IF CCT = 4 AND ZWORD = "ZZZZ" GO TO PRPTBODYEND.
PTELGRAMSEQ.
    DISPLAY "TELEGRAM" TELNO.
    MOVE 0 TO WRDCT, OSZCT.
PTELBODYITER.
    IF CCT = 4 AND ZWORD = "ZZZZ" GO TO PTELBODYEND.
    IF CCT GREATER THAN 12
        ADD 1 TO OSZCT.
    ADD 1 TO WRDCT.
    MOVE 2 TO QS.      GOBACK.
Q2.
    GO TO PTELBODYITER.
PTELBODYEND.
    MOVE 3 TO QS.      GOBACK.
Q3.
    DISPLAY WRDCT "WORDS OF WHICH" OSZCT
                                        "OVERSIZE".
PTELGRAMEND.
    ADD 1 TO TELNO.
    GO TO PRPTBODYITER.
PRPTBODYEND.
    DISPLAY "END ANALYSIS".
    MOVE 4 TO QS.      GOBACK.
Q4.
P2END.
```

In this coding, QS plays the part of a return link address, and the GO TO
DEPENDING statement ensures that execution resumes at the point
specified by the link. This mechanism is a visible equivalent of the normally
invisible subroutine linkage mechanism. Its effect is:

MOVE n TO QS. Remember the return address. We are concerned
only with the READ statements of P2, so QS need remember only
which of the four READ statements is active.

GOBACK. Transfers control to the program component—in this case, P1—which will provide the service required.

GO TO DEPENDING... Picks up the return link and resumes execution at the point specified.

Qn. These labels are the identifiers of the various return addresses.

We will refer to the variable QS as the "state variable" of P2W. It records the state of the process which P2W is concerned with—that is, the point reached in the input word file and the point reached in producing the output report. The full state of P2W depends also on the values of TELNO, WRDCT and OSZCT. It will sometimes be useful to collect all these variables into a single item, as:

```
01   STATE-VECTOR.
     02   QS PIC 99 VALUE 1.
     02   TELNO PIC 9(8).
     02   WRDCT PIC 9(8).
     02   OSZCT PIC 9(8).
```

We will refer to such an item as the "state vector" of P2W. To predict with certainty what P2W will do on a particular invocation, we need to know only:

the program text of P2W;

the current value of the state vector of P2W;

the value of the record passed in the invocation.

8.4

The reader should compare the coding of P2W very carefully with the coding of P2, and be sure he understands it fully. The following points are especially important.

First, the coding sequence

```
     MOVE n TO QS.      GOBACK.
Qn.
```

is, conceptually, a "read" statement. Its effect is precisely to acquire the next record from the intermediate word file and to continue execution at the next sequential instruction. Once convinced of this, the programmer need pay no more attention to the details of the mechanism than he does to the mechanism of an ordinary subroutine call. Obviously, it would be more agreeable to hide the details in some macro-statement, writing, perhaps,

PSEUDO-CALL.   NOTE READ WORD.

and leaving the compiler to generate the necessary linkage coding. But the issue is one of program cosmetics, and beauty is in the eye of the beholder.

Second, apart from a few details in the handling of the word file and in the linkage mechanism, P2W is identical to P2. It has exactly the same structure and substantially the same coding. In particular, it would be quite wrong to think of P2W as having the structure of a selection:

P2W   **select** QS = 1
    ...
P2W   **or** QS = 2
    ...

P2W has the structure of a sequence, as shown in the schematic logic. The schematic logic for P2W is the schematic logic for P2; there is no provision in the schematic logic notation for representing the GO TO DEPENDING statement which is coded at the beginning of P2W.

Third, there is obviously no particular reason to regard either the inverted or the uninverted form as basic. We have presented the inverted form as a secondary, derived form purely for purposes of explanation. In practice, either form may be coded directly from the design as expressed in schematic logic.

Fourth, for the inverted form the avoidance of PERFORM statements is necessary. Consider the following coding, in which a PERFORM statement is used:

```
    ...
    ENTRY "P2W" USING WORD.
    GO TO Q1, Q2, Q3, Q4 DEPENDING ON QS.
P2SEQ.
Q1.
    ...

    ...
    PERFORM PTELGRAM UNTIL CCT = 4 AND
                            ZWORD = "ZZZZ".
```

```
      ...
      ...
      PTELGRAM SECTION.
      PTG1.
          DISPLAY "TELEGRAM" TELNO.
          ...
          ...
          MOVE 3 TO QS.     GOBACK.
      Q3.
          DISPLAY WRDCT "WORDS OF WHICH" OSZCT
                                          "OVERSIZE".
      PTGX.
          EXIT.
      ...
```

The PERFORM statement sets a return link address in the exit paragraph PTGX of PTELGRAM SECTION. This return link must be preserved across each complete execution of PTELGRAM, to ensure that control can return correctly to the condition test in the PERFORM statement. But the COBOL language specification does not guarantee that the return link will survive execution of the GOBACK. It would be foolish to rely on the fact that the link does survive in the code generated by this or that particular compiler: the compiler does not define the language.

In principle, the limitation to be observed is this. We are assuming that certain language constructs do, or may, give rise to an increase in the stacking level in the run-time environment: in COBOL there are few such constructs, but PERFORM and CALL are among them. We are assuming also that the operating environment for the language is incapable of maintaining multiple stacks. We must therefore code an inverted program in such a manner that the stacking level is always zero when an "inverted input–output statement" is executed. If the local variables for the inverted program are held in a stack, as they would be in PL/I or ALGOL, we must either push them up, to the level of the invoking component or above, or else "freeze" them, by declaring them as STATIC in PL/I or as own variables in ALGOL. The limitation, of course, does not apply to procedure code or variables which are never active when an inverted input–output statement is executed.

In practice, in COBOL, we will find it more convenient to adhere to the PERFORM-free style of coding throughout an inverted program. Similar conventions can be devised for other languages. Ideally, the compiler would tackle the whole problem for us; while we are waiting for such a COBOL compiler we are forced to carry out a part of its task by hand.

Fifth, operation of P2W is undefined if it is invoked when the value of

QS is 4. That invocation would happen only if the paper tape file contained another word following the "ZZZZ" word of the null telegram: the input file would then be invalid.

8.5

We have produced two versions of P2—P2W and P2 itself. Here are the two corresponding versions of P1—P1 and P1W. P1 may be used in conjunction with P2W, and P1W may be used in conjunction with a modified version of P2. The necessary modifications to P2 are concerned only with the intermediate word file by invoking P1W instead of by executing COBOL READ statements.

Here is COBOL coding for P1:

```
...
ENVIRONMENT DIVISION.
...
      SELECT PTAPE ASSIGN TO...
...
DATA DIVISION.
FILE SECTION.
FD   PTAPE DATA RECORDS ARE BLOCK.
01   BLOCK.
   02   BCH PIC X OCCURS 101.
WORKING-STORAGE SECTION.
77   PTAPE-EOF PIC X VALUE SPACE.
77   BS PIC 999.
77   WS PIC 999.
01   WORD.
   02   CCT PIC 999.
   02   WORDBODY.
      03   WCH PIC X OCCURS 100.
   02   WORDTEST REDEFINES WORDBODY.
      03   ZWORD PIC XXXX.
      03   FILLER PIC X(96).
PROCEDURE DIVISION.
P1SEQ.
      OPEN INPUT PTAPE.
      READ PTAPE AT END MOVE "E" TO PTAPE-EOF.
PTAPEBODYITER.
      IF PTAPE-EOF = "E" GO TO PTAPEBODYEND.
```

```
        MOVE 1 TO BS.
PBLOKBODYITER.
        IF BCH (BS) = EOB GO TO PBLOKBODYEND.
PCHGPSLCT.
        IF BCH (BS) NOT = SPACE GO TO PCHGPOR.
PSPCITER.
        IF BCH (BS) NOT = SPACE GO TO PSPCEND.
        ADD 1 TO BS.
        GO TO PSPCITER.
PSPCEND.
        GO TO PCHGPEND.
PCHGPOR.
        MOVE 1 TO WS.
        MOVE 0 TO CCT.
PWDBODYITER.
        IF BCH (BS) = SPACE OR BCH (BS) = EOB
        GO TO PWDBODYEND.
        MOVE BCH (BS) TO WCH (WS).
        ADD 1 TO BS.    ADD 1 TO WS.    ADD 1 TO CCT.
        GO TO PWDBODYITER.
PWDBODYEND.
        CALL "P2W" USING WORD.
PCHGPEND.
        GO TO PBLOKBODYITER.
PBLOKBODYEND.
        READ PTAPE AT END MOVE "E" TO PTAPE-EOF.
        GO TO PTAPEBODYITER.
PTAPEBODYEND.
        CLOSE PTAPE.
        STOP RUN.
P1END.
```

Here is COBOL coding for P1W:

```
...
ENVIRONMENT DIVISION.
...
        SELECT PTAPE ASSIGN TO...
...
DATA DIVISION.
FILE SECTION.
FD   PTAPE DATA RECORDS ARE BLOCK.
```

```
01   BLOCK.
   02   BCH PIC X OCCURS 101.
WORKING-STORAGE SECTION.
77   QS PIC 99 VALUE 1.
77   PTAPE-EOF PIC X VALUE SPACE.
77   BS PIC 99.
77   WS PIC 99.
LINKAGE SECTION.
01   WORD.
   02   CCT PIC 999.
   02   WORDBODY.
      03   WCH PIC X OCCURS  100.
   ...
PROCEDURE DIVISION.
     ENTRY "P1W" USING WORD.
     GO TO Q1, Q2, DEPENDING ON QS.
P1SEQ.
Q1.
     OPEN INPUT PTAPE.
     READ PTAPE AT END MOVE "E" TO PTAPE-EOF.
PTAPEBODYITER.
     IF PTAPE-EOF = "E" GO TO PTAPEBODYEND.
     MOVE 1 TO BS.
PBLOKBODYITER.
     IF BCH (BS) = EOB GO TO PBLOKBODYEND.
PCHGPSLCT.
     IF BCH (BS) NOT = SPACE GO TO PCHGPOR.
PSPCITER.
     IF BCH (BS) NOT = SPACE GO TO PSPCEND.
     ADD 1 TO BS.
     GO TO  PSPCITER.
PSPCEND.
     GO TO PCHGPEND.
PCHGPOR.
     MOVE 1 TO WS.
     MOVE 0 TO CCT.
PWDBODYITER.
     IF BCH (BS) = SPACE OR BCH (BS) = EOB
        GO TO PWDBODYEND.
     MOVE BCH (BS) TO WCH (WS).
     ADD 1 TO BS.     ADD 1 TO WS.     ADD 1 TO CCT.
     GO TO PWDBODYITER.
```

```
PWDBODYEND.
      MOVE 2 TO QS.      GOBACK.
Q2.
PCHGPEND.
      GO TO PBLOKBODYITER.
PBLOKBODYEND.
      READ PTAPE AT END MOVE "E" TO PTAPE-EOF.
      GO TO PTAPEBODYITER.
PTAPEBODYEND.
      CLOSE PTAPE.
      GOBACK.
P1END.
```

There is an apparent anomaly. The STOP RUN statement in P1 has been coded as a simple GOBACK in P1W, although we did not treat the STOP RUN statement in P2 in this way. The GOBACK in P1W corresponds to the last invocation of P1W by P2, namely the last read statement in P2, which reads the end-of-file marker in the word file. Because of this anomaly, and for other reasons also, we need a more careful treatment of the beginning and end of the intermediate file: it is not enough simply to remove the open and close statements from both programs. This topic is discussed in Chapter 9.

8.6

Here is another example of the use of program inversion. So far, we have approached program inversion as a technique for converting a main program, which processes a file, into a sub-program, which processes successive records of that file. This problem is posed as a problem in constructing a sub-program or, more generally, a closed subroutine. We tackle it by asking ourselves the question "what main program, when inverted, would become the required subroutine?" We then design that main program, and invert it to give the subroutine we want.

PROBLEM 15—GENERATING TEST DATA

A program is being constructed which will generate files of test data. Two components, X and Y, are already available to generate certain contributions of values; we require to design a component Z which will generate all the X combinations followed by all the Y combinations. Thus, for example, if the

X combinations are X1, X2, X3 and the Y combinations are Y1, Y2, Y3, and
Y4, in that order, then the component Z should generate X1, X2, X3, Y1, Y2,
Y3 and Y4, in that order.

The interface with the components X and Y, and with the new component
Z, consists of a data area and a flag. When a component is invoked, it returns
the next combination in the data area; the flag is set to 1 when the first combination is returned, and otherwise to 0.

It is to be assumed that the data areas for X, Y and Z are distinct and do not
overlap. It is also to be assumed that X and Y are never used, except by Z,
and that the first time each is invoked it will return its first combination. Z
should be capable of being invoked an arbitrary number of times; it may
therefore return its first combination more than once.

We may usefully think about this problem in the following form. We have
two input files, FX and FY. We wish to construct a program Z which reads
these files and writes an output file FZ. FX and FY consist of a infinite
number of groups GX and GY respectively; FZ consists of an infinite number
of groups GZ, where the nth GZ is formed by concatenating the nth GX and
the nth GY.

The reader should draw the data structures for FX and FY, and use them to
form the program structure for Z. The resulting schematic logic should be:

```
PROGZ    seq
            read FX;
            read FY;
         PZBODY   iter
            PGROUPZ   seq
                        flagZ: = 1;
                        write X;
                        read FX;
               PGXBODY   iter until flagX = 1
                           flagZ: = 0;
                           write X;
                           read FX;
               PGXBODY   end
                           flagZ: = 0;
                           write Y;
                           read FY;
               PGYBODY   iter until flagY = 1
                           flagZ: = 0;
                           write Y;
                           read FY;
```

> PGYBODY **end**
> PGROUPZ **end**
> PZBODY **end**
> PROGZ **end**

Making suitable assumptions about the form of the components X, Y and Z, namely that they are all COBOL sections, we may write down the inverted form of Z without further ado:

```
...
DATA DIVISION.
...
WORKING-STORAGE SECTION.
77   QS PIC 99 VALUE 1.
...
PROCEDURE DIVISION.
...
...
Z SECTION.
Z0.
     GO TO Q1, Q2, Q3, Q4, Q5 DEPENDING ON QS.
PROGZSEQ.
Q1.
     PERFORM X.
     PERFORM Y.
PZBODYITER.
PGROUPZSEQ.
     MOVE 1 TO FLAGZ.
     MOVE AREAX TO AREAZ.
     MOVE 2 TO QS.        GO TO ZX.
Q2.
     PERFORM X.
PGXBODYITER.
     IF FLAGX = 1 GO TO PGXBODYEND.
     MOVE 0 TO FLAGZ.
     MOVE AREAX TO AREAZ.
     MOVE 3 TO QS.        GO TO ZX.
Q3.
     PERFORM X.
     GO TO PGXBODYITER.
PGXBODYEND.
```

```
        MOVE 0 TO FLAGZ.
        MOVE AREAY TO AREAZ.
        MOVE 4 TO QS.    GO TO ZX.
    Q4.
        PERFORM Y.
    PGYBODYITER.
        IF FLAGY = 1 GO TO PGYBODYEND.
        MOVE 0 TO FLAGZ.
        MOVE AREAY TO AREAZ.
        MOVE 5 TO QS.    GO TO ZX.
    Q5.
        PERFORM Y.
        GO TO PGYBODYITER.
    PGYBODYEND.
    PGROUPZEND.
        GO TO PZBODYITER.
    PZBODYEND.
    PROGZEND.
    ZX.    EXIT.
```

Readers distressed by the evident lack of optimization in this program may take comfort from the discussion in Chapter 12.

8.7

Program inversion is very important. At a stroke it halves the techniques needed to deal with most of the problems we are likely to encounter. There is no difference between a file-processing main program and a record-processing sub-program—other than a trvial difference in the details of coding. Basically, we need only concern ourselves with main programs which process serial files: other forms of program, such as interrupt handling routines and transaction routines in on-line systems, can be derived from these main programs by the use of inversion.

We may characterize inverted programs as "variable-state" components. A main file-processing program is "fixed state" in the sense that it is always in the same state when invoked by the operating system: its action depends only upon the values of the inputs received in that one invocation, and not all on what happened in previous invocations. A variable-state component, by contrast, behaves on each invocation in a way which depends both on the values of the inputs passed in that invocation and on its internal state— that is, the value of the state variable QS and other items in the state vector.

This distinction is important, and is not destroyed by placing the state vector in the parameter list, thus creating a "re-entrant" or "pure procedure" component. The contents of the state vector are private to the component: they are truly "own variables" in the sense that no other component should be able to inspect or change them, or to take any cognizance of their formats and values.

Any system must contain such variable-state components. It matters greatly how we construct them, because they are potentially the most difficult to design. A traditional method of designing is to define a number of switches, each switch indicating some aspect of the component's state. For example, for Problem 15 (Generating Test Data) we might begin by defining these switches:

SW1: on if the component has not been previously invoked, otherwise off (the traditional "first-time switch");

SW2: on if the component is engaged in processing an X group, off if it it is processing a Y group;

SW3: on if X has been invoked at least once, otherwise off;

SW4: on if Y has been invoked at least once, otherwise off.

It is not clear that this is the right set of switches, even for this very simple problem: more or fewer or a different set altogether may be required. In a realistically larger problem, dozens of switches may be needed. However, even in the simple problem, we have an immediate difficulty. There are 4 binary switches. Together they define 16 possible states of the component. So it appears that we ought to construct a program containing 16 labels, each a possible starting point for some invocation of the component. But we can see at once that if switch 1 is off then switches 3 and 4 must also be off. So there are not more than 10 possible states. (Check that calculation!) And no doubt other similar arguments can be made. But the arguments, and the calculations, are very prone to error. In any case, they are not usually made explicitly. What usually happens is that the programmer informally and intuitively decides to treat certain states as possible and distinct, others as possible but arranged in groups of equivalent states, and others again as impossible. To do this correctly, especially by informal intuitive methods, is very hard. Resulting bugs may include, in a typical data processing program:

parts of the program can never be executed, whatever the inputs; states thought to be possible are in fact impossible;

a change of name and address is treated as a credit transaction; states thought to be equivalent are in fact distinct;

the last transaction is ignored if it is unmatched and has a key higher than the last master record; a state thought to be impossible is in fact possible.

By contrast, the integer-valued state variable QS is an explicit enumerator of the states considered possible. Its values are derived from an enumeration of the terminal nodes (the elementary components) of the data structure: each record in the file has a read or write statement associated with it, and each read or write gives a distinct value for QS. The correctness, or otherwise, of the data structure is open to ready inspection, and, with it, the correctness of the values of QS.

EXERCISE 8.1 (a)

Recode the COBOL solution to Problem 3 (Cantor's Enumeration of Rationals), inverting it with respect to the printer output file. Now write another program which reads this printer output file, line by line, displaying each line and stopping at an arbitrary number.

EXERCISE 8.2 (a)

Invert the COBOL solution to Problem 4 (Counting Batches) with respect to the card file. You now have an output procedure for records of the card file, which writes them to the line printer in the form of a summary. Make sure that the counts are not lost at the end.

EXERCISE 8.3 (a)

Modify the COBOL program given in Section 8.3 for P2 so that it invokes P1W to acquire records of the word file.

EXERCISE 8.4 (b)

Invert the COBOL program given in Section 8.5 for P1, with respect to the paper tape file. What might the resulting program be used for?

EXERCISE 8.5 (b)

Invert your solution to Problem 8 (Source Statement Library) with respect to the text file, giving a "read next card to be compiled" procedure.

EXERCISE 8.6 (b)

Design a program to solve Problem 13 (Telegrams Analysis) given that you must use both P1W and P2W in the solution.

QUESTION 8.1

It is usually considered bad practice to initialize variables at compile time. So, instead of writing

    77   FILE-EOF PIC X VALUE SPACES.

we ought to write

    77   FILE-EOF PIC X.
         ...

         OPEN INPUT FILE.
         MOVE SPACE TO FILE-EOF.
         ...

Can we do the same for QS?

QUESTION 8.2

Was it correct to eliminate the "open" and "close" statements for the intermediate word file when we inverted the two programs for Problem 13 (Telegrams Analysis)? What might we do to re-introduce them? What is the effect of a "close" operation for a serial output file?

QUESTION 8.3

It was suggested, in the introduction to Problem 15 (Generating Test Data) that a subroutine could be thought of as an inverted program. Is this true of all subroutines? If so, why do some subroutines have no state variable?

QUESTION 8.4

We could invert the program P in Problem 8 (Source Statement Library) with respect to the card file, and we would then have a routine which could be activated from a keyboard terminal on-line: we would key-in, in the simplest case

    BASIS PROGX
    /*

and PROGX would be retrieved from the library and written to a text file. Could we, instead, invert P with respect to the source library member, allowing us to key in the card-images of the member at the terminal?

QUESTION 8.5

Could we invert the solution to Problem 11 (Good and Bad Branches) with respect to the input file? If so, which of the two suggested solutions to the side-effects problem would be preferable, and why?

9. COMPLEX INVERSIONS

9.1

In Chapter 8, in our treatment of Problem 13 (Telegrams Analysis), we carefully avoided a potential source of difficulty. The paper tape file was terminated both by a null telegram and by a special end-of-file block. Both P1 and P2 were therefore able to recognize end of file without external help: for P1, end of file was indicated by the special block; for P2 it was indicated by the null telegram. Further, we specified that for a valid file these indications must agree: if there is no null telegram, or if it is followed by additional words, the file is invalid and we need not consider the problem of processing it.

These specifications allowed us to restrict the interface between P1 and P2W, or between P1W and P2, to a single operation type: every invocation of P2W is, in effect, a "write" command; every invocation of P1W is, in effect, a "read" command. That is why we were able to eliminate the "open" and "close" operations on the word file when we inverted P1 and P2.

But we cannot always eliminate them. An interface for general use with input–output procedures must include an operation code which can take various values: the function of the procedure must depend, in part, on the value of that code. We must also include in the interface an item to hold the result of the invocation: for a serial read operation, one possible result is "end of file" and we cannot, in general, indicate end of file in the record area. We will define the following interface for input–output operations:

CALL "IOPROC" USING COMM, RECAREA.

where COMM is a communications area and RECAREA is the area used to hold the data being transferred. A possible format of COMM is:

```
01   COMM.
   02   OPCODE PIC XX.
      88   OPEN-OP VALUE "OP".
      88   RD-NEXT VALUE "RN".
```

193

```
88   WT-NEXT VALUE "WN".
88   CLOSE-OP VALUE "CL".
02   RESULT PIC XX.
   88   OK VALUE "OK",
   88   EOF VALUE "EF".
```

Clearly, this is only a tentative suggestion. We have ignored direct-access operations entirely, and we have ignored such operations as "note" and "restore", which were discussed in Chapter 6. We have also assumed the simplest form of transmission of the data: data is physically transferred from one area of main storage to another ("move mode" in IBM terminology), whereas it is possible, and often far superior, to pass only a pointer to the record ("locate mode" in IBM terminology). However, this simple interface will suffice for our discussion here.

9.2

We begin by considering this system:

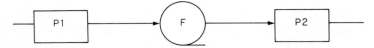

P1 writes a serial file F which is read by P2. The reader may wish to relate the discussion to Problem 13 (Telegrams Analysis): we will consider that problem specifically at a later stage in the discussion.

Consider first the structure of P1. P1 writes file F unconditionally: that is, there is no occasion on which P1 is executed but file F is not written. P1 must therefore have the structure:

```
P1   seq
     do X;
     open F;
     ...
     ...
     write F;
     ...
     ...
     write F;
     ...
     write F;
     ...
```

```
        ...
        do Y;
        close F;
        do Z;
P1   end
```

That is: the open operation for F must appear within the sequence P1 directly as a part of that sequence, and not enclosed in a selection or an iteration (although it could be enclosed in another sequence); the open operation must precede all the write operations, both in the text and in the order of execution; there is an indefinite number of write operations (but at least one) which must appear after the open, and may be enclosed in selections and iterations at any level; the close operation must appear after all of the write operations, both in the text and in the order of execution, and may not be enclosed in a selection or iteration. Any or all of the components X, Y and Z may be null.

The structure of P2 is similarly:

```
P2   seq
        do S;
        open F;
        do T;
        read F;
        ...
        ...
        read F;
        ...
        read F;
        ...
        ...
        ...
        read F;
        ...
        read F;
        ...
        ...
        do U;
        close F;
        do V;
P2   end
```

In P2 there must be an initial read operation, for the read ahead, which follows the open. It is good practice to place it immediately after the open in the text, but this is not strictly necessary: in the structure shown, component T intervenes.

The situation seems to be lacking in symmetry: if P2 must always have an initial read operation, should not P1 have something which corresponds? The answer can be found from a consideration of the number of read operations executed by P2 and the number of write operations executed by P1. If the file F contains r records, the P2 will execute $r+1$ read operations: the extra read returns the end-of-file marker. P1, however, will execute only r write operations. The extra write is embedded in the close: the effect of executing a close operation on a serial file must always be to write the end-of-file marker. So we do, after all, have symmetry: P1 has an extra (hidden) write at the end, and P2 has an extra (visible) read at the beginning.

Now let us suppose that P1 is to be inverted with respect to F. The operations in P2 will be coded as follows:

```
open: MOVE "OP" TO OPCODE.
      CALL "P1F" USING COMM, RECAREA.

read: MOVE "RN" TO OPCODE.
      CALL "P1F" USING COMM, RECAREA.

close: MOVE "CL" TO OPCODE.
       CALL "P1F" USING COMM, RECAREA.
```

and the condition test for end of file will be:

```
IF EOF...
```

Here, in skeleton form, is P1F. The usual definition of QS and the coding at the entry point are assumed.

```
      ...
      GO TO Q1, Q2, ... Qn DEPENDING ON QS.
P1SEQ.
Q1.
      PERFORM X.
      MOVE "OK" TO RESULT.
      MOVE 2 TO QS.      GOBACK.
Q2.
      ...
      ...
```

```
          MOVE RECORD TO RECAREA.
          MOVE "OK" TO RESULT.
          MOVE 3 TO QS.        GOBACK.
     Q3.
          ...
          ...

          ...
          PERFORM Y.
          MOVE "EF" TO RESULT.
          MOVE n TO QS.        GOBACK.
     Qn.
          PERFORM Z.
          GOBACK.
     P1END.
```

The treatment of the close is important. We have split it into two parts. The first part is a write operation, which writes the end-of-file marker by placing the value "EF" in the result field. This write operation in P1F is the response to whichever read operation in P2 happens to encounter the end of file. The second part is the response to the close operation in P2. It begins at Qn and terminates with the lone GOBACK. Observe that it would be quite wrong to code:

```
     Qn.
          MOVE p TO QS.        GOBACK.
     Qp.
          PERFORM Z.
     P1END.
```

because P2 will not invoke P1F again after it has executed its close operation. Execution of P1F would therefore never resume at Qp, and Z would never be performed.

We have chosen to return the result "OK" on the open, and to leave the result unspecified on the close. This is a question of the detailed specification of the interface. We must observe whatever conventions we adopt as a standard.

Note that if P2 does not read the end-of-file record, possibly because it is independently able to recognize end of file, then P1F will not operate correctly. The instructions

```
     PERFORM Y.
     MOVE "EF" TO RESULT.
     MOVE n TO QS.        GOBACK.
```

will be executed in response to the close invocation from P2, instead of in response to the last read invocation; the instruction

PERFORM Z.

will not be executed at all. Unless P1F is redesigned so that it, too, can recognize when it is being invoked for the last time, it will be left waiting for an invocation which never comes. One method of recognition is, of course, for P1F to examine the value of OPCODE: this creates some complications, which are discussed below. For the moment we are assuming that the value of OPCODE need never be examined in P1F: provided that the design of P2 is correctly co-ordinated with that of P1, and provided that P2 reads all of the records of F, including the end-of-file marker, then we know that OPCODE has the value "OP" at Q1, the value "CL" at Qn, and the value "RN" at all other times.

The inversion of P2, giving P2F, is left as an exercise for the reader.

9.3

We now return to Problem 13 (Telegrams Analysis), to consider in more detail the version in which P1 is inverted with respect to the word file.

First, we introduce the standard interface between P2 and P1W. P2 now invokes P1W with OPCODE values "OP", "RN" and "CL" to open, read and close the word file respectively. The coding for P1W given in Section 8.5 must therefore be amended to:

```
      ...
      ENTRY "P1W" USING COMM, WORD.
      GO TO Q1, Q2, Q3, Q4 DEPENDING ON QS.
P1SEQ.
Q1.
      OPEN INPUT PTAPE.
      READ PTAPE AT END MOVE "E" TO PTAPE-EOF.
      MOVE "OK" TO RESULT.
      MOVE 2 TO QS.      GOBACK.
Q2.
PTAPEBODYITER.
      IF PTAPE-EOF = "E"...
      ...
      ...
PWDBODYEND.
```

```
        MOVE "OK" TO RESULT.
        MOVE 3 TO QS.        GOBACK.
    Q3.
        ...

        ...
    PTAPEBODYEND.
        MOVE "EF" TO RESULT.
        MOVE 4 TO QS.        GOBACK.
    Q4.
        CLOSE PTAPE.
        GOBACK.
    P1END.
```

P1W now processes an OPEN invocation and a CLOSE invocation; also, it writes an end-of-file marker on the word file. Corresponding changes must, of course, be made to P2.

So far, we have merely brought our solution for Problem 13 up to date with the discussion in Sections 9.1 and 9.2 above. We now introduce a significant complication. Instead of assuming that P2 will always read through to the end of the word file, we will allow it to close the word file prematurely. For example, we may suppose that P2 processes the first 20 telegrams on the tape, or the whole tape if there are fewer than 20 telegrams present. P1W must now examine the value of OPCODE. Previously, P1W ignored the value of OPCODE, assuming that it had the value "OP" at Q1, "RN" at Q2 and Q3, and "CL" at Q4; effectively there was no flow of information from P2 to P1W. Now, we have a flow of information from P2 to P1W in the form of a file, FINV, of invocations:

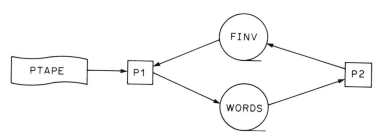

Of course, this file of invocations was always present: but we had previously ignored it. Now we must take it into account in our design of P1, and we must invert P1 with respect simultaneously to FINV and WORDS.

The structure of FINV is, evidently as shown at the top of p. 200. in which the number of RN records must not exceed $W + 1$, where W is the

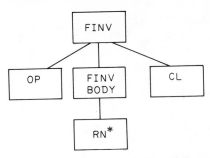

number of words on the paper tape. If there are $W+1$ RN records then P2 is reading the whole tape; otherwise the word file is prematurely closed.

To design the new version of P1W we must start by designing a new version of P1, in which we treat FINV as if it were a physical file. Taking account of the possibility of premature closing of the word file by P2, we have these data structures:

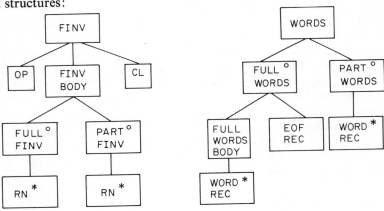

in which full finv consists of $W+1$ RN records, part finv consists of fewer than $W+1$ RN records, full words consists of W word records followed by the end marker, and part words consists of W or fewer word records, not followed by the end marker. The corresponding structure for the paper tape file is shown opposite.

The structure of part ptape has not been shown in detail for a reason which will become apparent later.

The correspondences required to form the program structure are:

finv body corresponds to words and to ptape

full finv corresponds to full words and to full ptape

part finv corresponds to part words and to part ptape

RN in full finv corresponds to word rec in full words body and to eof rec, and to word and eof block in full ptape.

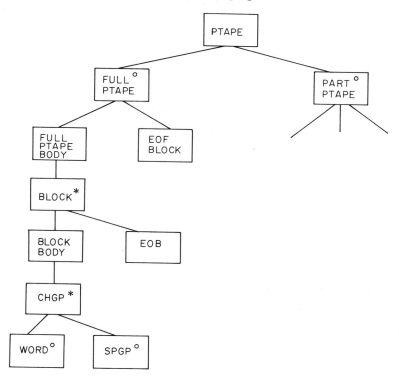

Since we cannot tell in advance whether we have a full finv or a part finv, we will structure the program body as a selection with backtracking. At the first stage of design, before introducing the quit statements or handling the side effects, we have:

P1   **seq**
        open finv;
        read finv (OP record);
        open words; ⎫
        open ptape; ⎬ (process OP record)
        read block; ⎭
        read finv (1st RN or CL record);

```
PBODY    select full
    PFULLBODY    iter until eof-ptape
                BS:=1;
        PBLOCKBODY    iter until EOB
            PCHARGROUP    select word
                          build word;        ⎫ (process RN
                          write word rec;    ⎬          record)
                                             ⎭
                          read finv (RN record);
            PCHARGROUP    or space group
                          process spaces;
            PCHARGROUP    end
        PBLOCKBODY    end
                    read block;
    PFULLBODY    end
            write eof-rec; (process RN record)
            read finv (CL record);
PBODY    or part
            ...
            ...
PBODY    end
        close ptape;    ⎫
        close words;    ⎬ (process CL record)
                        ⎭
        close finv;
P1       end
```

The parenthesized comments refer to the records of finv: thus, for example,

    read finv (RN record);

means that the result of the read operation must be a RN record of finv, and

    build word;   ⎫ (process RN record)
    write word rec;   ⎭

means that the build and write operations constitute the processing of an RN record of finv.

Clearly we will require two quit statements for the second stage of the backtracking design. PBODY will take the form:

```
PBODY    posit full
    PFULLBODY    iter until eof-ptape
                BS:=1;
```

```
     PBLOCKBODY   iter until EOB
          PCHARGROUP   select word
                         quit PBODY if not RN;
                         build word;
                         write word rec;
                         read finv;
          PCHARGROUP   or space group
                         process spaces;
          PCHARGROUP   end
     PBLOCKBODY   end
               read block;
   PFULLBODY   end
        quit PBODY if not RN;
        write eof-rec;
        read finv;
PBODY   admit part
          ...
          ...
PBODY   end
```

Note that the **quit** statements are placed where the finv records are processed, not where they are read. This has the effect at run time of causing the paper tape to be processed slightly further than is absolutely necessary: processing continues until the beginning of the first word to be ignored instead of stopping at the end of the last word to be written. If this slight inefficiency is important—and it is unlikely to be so—we could optimize by moving the quit statements so that they are executed at the earliest possible time, namely as soon as each record of finv is read. The resulting program would be:

```
PBODY   posit full
          quit PBODY if not RN;
   PFULLBODY   iter until eof-ptape
               BS:=1;
     PBLOCKBODY   iter until EOB
          PCHARGROUP   select word
                         build word:
                         write word rec;
                         read finv;
                         quit PBODY if not RN;
          PCHARGROUP   or space group
                         process spaces;
          PCHARGROUP   end
```

```
PBLOCBODY   end
              read block;
PFULLBODY   end
              write eof-rec;
              read finv;
PBODY   admit part
              ...

              ...
PBODY   end
```

We now come to consider the third stage, the handling of side effects. It is now apparent that all of the side effects are beneficent: when we **quit** PBODY we have processed exactly as much of the paper tape as we should, and we do not need to repeat that processing in the **admit** part of PBODY or to consider the side effects further. We must, however consider whether any processing is required for the residue of the part ptape. This residue may consists of the end-file block only or of the end-file block preceded by a number of ordinary blocks the first of which may be partly processed. In most realistic environments we may ignore this residue: it will not matter if we close the paper tape file without having read all of its blocks. However, to provide an illustration, we will suppose that all of the blocks must be read. The form of the second part of PBODY must then be:

```
PBODY   admit part
  PPARTBODY   iter until eof-ptape
                read block;
  PPARTBODY   end
PBODY   end
```

We now have a complete design for the new version of P1, and it remains only to invert it with respect to finv and the word file to give the required version of P1W. COBOL coding for P1W is shown below. The following points are worth noting:

the simultaneous inversion with respect to two files causes no difficulty because the "write word" statements are matched with "read finv" statements;

since the end-file marker has been treated explicitly as a record of the word file there is no need to write it when the word file is closed;

the open and close statements for finv are ignored in the inversion—we would otherwise be involved in an endless regression.

COBOL coding for P1W is:

...

```
        ENTRY "P1W" USING COMM, WORD.
        GO TO Q1, Q2, Q3, Q4 DEPENDING ON QS.
P1SEQ.
Q1.
        OPEN INPUT PTAPE.
        READ PTAPE AT END MOVE "E" TO PTAPE-EOF.
        MOVE "OK" TO RESULT.
        MOVE 2 TO QS.      GOBACK.
Q2.
PBODYPOSIT.
PFULLBODYITER.
        IF PTAPE-EOF = "E" GO TO PFULLBODYEND.
        MOVE 1 TO BS.
PBLOKBODYITER
        IF BCH (BS) = EOB GO TO PBLOKBODYEND.
PCHGPSLCT.
        IF BCH (BS) = SPACE GO TO PCHGPOR.
        IF NOT RD-NEXT GO TO PBODYADMIT.
        MOVE 1 TO WS.
        MOVE 0 TO CCT.
PWDBODYITER.
        IF BCH (BS) = SPACE OR BCH (BS) = EOB
           GO TO PWDBODYEND.
        MOVE BCH (BS) TO WCH (WS).
        ADD 1 TO BS.      ADD 1 TO WS.      ADD 1 TO CCT.
        GO TO PWDBODYITER.
PWDBODYEND.
        MOVE "OK" TO RESULT.
        MOVE 3 TO QS.      GOBACK.
Q3.
        GO TO PCHGPEND.
PCHGPOR.
PSPCITER.
        IF BCH (BS) NOT = SPACE GO TO PSPCEND.
        ADD 1 TO BS.
        GO TO PSPCITER.
PSPCEND.
PCHGPEND.
        GO TO PBLOKBODYITER.
PBLOKBODYEND.
```

I

```
    READ PTAPE AT END MOVE "E" TO PTAPE-EOF.
    GO TO PFULLBODYITER.
PFULLBODYEND.
    IF NOT RD-NEXT GO TO PBODYADMIT.
    MOVE "EF" TO RESULT.
    MOVE 4 TO QS.      GOBACK.
Q4.
    GO TO PBODYEND.
PBODYADMIT.
PPARTBODYITER.
    IF PTAPE-EOF = "E" GO TO PPARTBODYEND.
    READ PTAPE AT END MOVE "E" TO PTAPE-EOF.
    GO TO PPARTBODYITER.
PPARTBODYEND.
PBODYEND.
    CLOSE PTAPE.
    GOBACK.
P1END.
```

Some further elaborations of this problem are suggested in the exercises at the end of this chapter.

9.4

P1W was constructed by inverting P1 simultaneously with respect to finv and the word file. Clearly any input or output procedure which uses the standard interface and examines the opcode must be similarly inverted with respect to two files, one a data file and the other a file of invocations. Here is a problem in which inversion with respect to more than one data file is required.

PROBLEM 16—SORT EXIT

A transaction file contains records of the form:

```
01   RECORD.
   02   KEY PIC X(8).
   02   AMOUNT PIC S9(6).
   02   TYPE PIC X.
```

These records are to be sorted into ascending order of key value by a manufacturer's sort program. The output phase of this sort program provides a "user exit", to allow the sorted file to be modified while it is being written to the final output device.

It is required to design a "user exit routine" which will perform the following functions:

delete any record for which TYPE="X";

create a total record for each key group, of the form:

```
01  GPTOT.
   02  KEY PIC X(8).
   02  TOTAMT PIC S9(10).
   02  TYPE PIC X.
```

in which TOTAMT is the total of all of the amounts in the records of the key group, and TYPE has the fixed value "Z";

create a total record for the whole file, of the form:

```
01  FTOT.
   02  KEY PIC X(8).
   02  FTOTAMT PIC S9(16).
   02  TYPE PIC X.
```

in which FTOTAMT is the total of all of the amounts in the transaction records, KEY has the fixed value HIGH-VALUES, and TYPE has the fixed value "Z".

The user exit routine is invoked by the sort output phase by an instruction:

CALL "EXITRTN" USING CODE, RECORD.

where:

CODE may take the values 0, 1, 2 and 3;

RECORD contains a record of the file.

The sort output phase sets the value 0 in CODE to indicate end of file, otherwise it sets the value 1. The user exit routine should set the value of

CODE as follows:

0 to indicate that nothing further is to be written to the output file;

1 to indicate that the record is to be written to the output file and a further invocation made with a new record;

2 to indicate that the record is to be deleted (ie not written to the output file) and a further invocation made with a new record;

3 to indicate that the record is to be written to the output file and a further invocation made with no new record, thus providing the possibility of insertions

The GPTOT and FTOT records are to be written to the final output at the end of the key group and the end of the file respectively.

This problem may be treated in the same way as we treated Problem 15 (Generating Test Data). That is, we begin by asking ourselves "what main program, when inverted, would become the required routine?"; we then proceed to design that main program and code it in an inverted form to give the routine we want.

Clearly the appropriate main program is one which reads a serial input file of transactions and writes a serial output file of transactions together with the total records. The system flow diagram is:

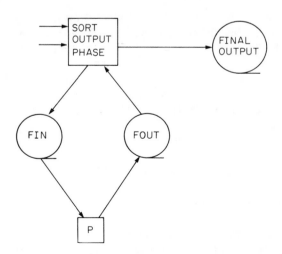

We will design P, and invert it with respect to the files fin and fout.
P itself is trivial. Schematic logic is:

```
P    seq
        open fin; read fin;
        open fout;
        ftotamt: =0;
        PBODY    iter until eof-fin
                    gpkey: =key;
                    totamt: =0;
                PGPBODY    iter until eof-fin or key ≠ gpkey
                            PTRANSREC    select type ≠ X
                                        ftotamt: =ftotamt+amount;
                                        totamt: =totamt+amount;
                                        write transaction rec;
                            PTRANSREC    end
                                read fin;
                PGPBODY    end
                    write gptot rec;
        PBODY    end
        write ftot rec;
        close fout;
        close fin;
P    end
```

in which we have assumed that a gptot record is to be written for every key
group, even if all of the transaction records of the group are of type "X",
and that neither totamt nor ftotamt should include amounts from type "X"
transactions.

To code P in a suitably inverted form, we must consider how the interface
provided by the sort program can be used to implement the necessary
input–output instructions for fin and fout. Taking the instructions in the
order in which they appear in the schematic logic:

open fin may be ignored in the inversion;

read fin is automatically implemented by the first invocation of the
routine;

open fout may be ignored in the inversion;

eof-fin may be tested by testing for code = 0;

write transaction rec may be implemented by setting code = 3 and returning to the sort program;

read fin may be implemented by setting code = 2 and returning to the sort program;

write gptot and write ftot may be implemented similarly to write transaction rec;

close fout may be implemented by setting code = 0 and returning to the sort program;

close fin may be ignored in the inversion.

These arrangements will work adequately. However, we are conspicuously avoiding the use of the value 1 in code. This value corresponds to a composite operation

write record to fout;   read fin;

and we have no such composite operation in our program. If we are anxious to make use of the composite operation, possibly because it is more efficient, we may do so by changing the schematic logic to:

```
...
PGPBODY    iter until eof-fin or key ≠ gpkey
    PTRANSREC    select type ≠ X
                 ftotamt: =ftotamt+amount;
                 totamt: =totamt+amount;
                 write transaction rec;
                 read fin;
    PTRANSREC    or type = X
                 read fin;
    PTRANSREC    end
PGPBODY    end
...
```

We must also consider the handling of the record area, which is common to fin and fout. A convenient and efficient method is to establish the general rule that it should contain the last fin record read; exceptions to the rule will occur when records are being written to fout which do not appear in fin.

The resulting COBOL coding is:

```
...
DATA DIVISION.
WORKING-STORAGE SECTION.
77   QS PIC 9 VALUE 1.
01   GPTOT.
  02   GPKEY PIC X(8).
  02   TOTAMT PIC S9(10).
  02   GPTYPE PIC X VALUE "Z".
01   FTOT.
  02   FTKEY PIC X(8) VALUE HIGH-VALUES.
  02   FTOTAMT PIC S9(16).
  02   FTYPE PIC X VALUE "Z".
01   STOREDCODE PIC 9.
01   STOREDREC.
  02   FILLER PIC X(8).
  02   FILLER PIC S9(6).
  02   FILLER PIC X.
LINKAGE SECTION.
01   CODE PIC 9.
01   RECORD.
  02   KEY PIC X(8).
  02   AMOUNT PIC S9(6).
  02   TYPE PIC X.
PROCEDURE DIVISION.
      ENTRY "EXITRTN" USING CODE, RECORD.
      GO TO Q1, Q2, Q3, Q4, Q5 DEPENDING ON QS.
PSEQ.
Q1.
      MOVE 0 TO FTOTAMT.
PBODYITER.
      IF CODE = 0 GO TO PBODYEND.
      MOVE KEY TO GPKEY.
      MOVE 0 TO TOTAMT.
PGPBODYITER.
      IF CODE = 0 OR (KEY NOT = GPKEY) GO TO
                                PGPBODYEND.
PTRANSRECSLCT.
      IF TYPE = "X" GO TO PTRANSRECOR.
      ADD AMOUNT TO FTOTAMT.
      ADD AMOUNT TO TOTAMT.
      MOVE 1 TO CODE.
      MOVE 2 TO QS.      GOBACK.
```

```
Q2.
    GO TO PTRANSRECEND.
PTRANSRECOR.
    MOVE 2 TO CODE.
    MOVE 3 TO QS.      GOBACK.
Q3.
PTRANSRECEND.
    GO TO PGPBODYITER.
PGPBODYEND.
    MOVE RECORD TO STOREDREC.
    MOVE CODE TO  STOREDCODE.
    MOVE GPTOT TO RECORD.
    MOVE 3 TO CODE.
    MOVE 4 TO QS.      GOBACK.
Q4.
    MOVE STOREDREC TO RECORD.
    MOVE STOREDCODE TO CODE.
    GO TO PBODYITER.
PBODYEND.
    MOVE FTOT TO RECORD.
    MOVE 3 TO CODE.
    MOVE 5 TO QS.      GOBACK.
Q5.
    MOVE 0 TO CODE.
    GOBACK.
PEND.
```

Note that it is necessary to store both the RECORD and the CODE when writing GPTOT: after a return with CODE = 3, the sort program will invoke the exit routine again without passing a new record; but there is no guarantee that it will pass the old record and the old value of CODE. When FTOT is written, it is known that the old value of CODE is 0, and the old value of RECORD is therefore undefined.

9.5

The technique so far described for coding inverted programs imposes a constraint. If a program is inverted with respect to a file F, then no input or output operation for F may appear within the scope of a PERFORM or CALL statement in that program. Usually, this constraint is acceptable: the PERFORM-free coding is not difficult to write, and the explicitly structured design allows us to write lengthy program texts without suffering the penalties of complexity. Sometimes, however, we will have good reasons for wishing to construct an inverted program as a set of two or more independently compiled modules, with input or output instructions appearing in more than one of the modules.

Consider, for example, Problem 4 (Counting Batches), described in Section 3.2. Let us suppose that we wish to create a solution which is inverted with respect to the input file, and which has a separately compiled module to process the batch part. Then the inverted program has the general form:

```
PROCCDIPT   seq
                ...
            process prepart;
            process first T1;
            process batchpart;
            process T2;
                ...
PROCCDIPT   end
```

in which "process batchpart" is to be implemented by suitable invocation of a separately compiled module.

The coding for the inverted program is:

```
    ...
    GO TO Q1, Q2, Q3, Q4 DEPENDING ON QS.
PROCCDIPTSEQ.
Q1.
    MOVE 0 TO CA.
PREPARTITER.
    IF T1 GO TO PREPARTEND.
    ADD 1 TO CA.
    MOVE 2 TO QS.     GOBACK.
Q2.
    GO TO PREPARTITER.
PREPARTEND.
    DISPLAY INCARD.
    MOVE 3 TO QS.     GOBACK.
Q3.
    MOVE 0 TO CB, CC, CD.
    process batchpart;
    DISPLAY INCARD.                  NOTE DISPLAY T2
    MOVE 4 TO QS.     GOBACK.        NOTE READ EOF.
```

Q4.
```
     DISPLAY CA, CB, CC, CD.
     GOBACK.
PROCCDIPTEND.
```

in which the coding for "process batchpart" remains to be written.

The separately compiled module is itself an inverted program, BP. It processes a file consisting of the batch part of the original input file; in inverted form, it processes one card of the batch part on each invocation. We must therefore arrange to invoke it once for each card of the batch part. Further, it must return an indication to the invoking program when the batch part is exhausted: it would be quite wrong to recognize the end of the batch part outside BP.

Suitable coding for BP is shown below. To avoid confusion, new names have been used for the state variable and for the counters, although this is not necessary.

```
. . .
DATA DIVISION.
WORKING-STORAGE SECTION.
77   BPQS PIC 9 VALUE 1.
LINKAGE SECTION.
01   BPCB PIC 9(6).
01   BPCC PIC 9(6).
01   BPCD PIC 9(6).
01   BPCARD.
   02   BPTYP PIC 9.
      88   BPT1 VALUE 1.
      88   BPT2 VALUE 2.
      88   BPT3 VALUE 3.
   02   FILLER PIC X(79).
01   BP-EOF PIC X.
PROCEDURE DIVISION.
     ENTRY "B" USING BPCB, BPCC, BPCD, BP-EOF,
     BPCARD.
     GO TO BPQ1, BPQ2, BPQ3 DEPENDING ON BPQS.
BPSEQ.
BPQ1.
PBPARTITER.
     IF (NOT BPT1) AND (NOT BPT3) GO TO PBPARTEND.
     ADD 1 TO BPCB.
PBBODYSLCT.
```

```
        IF NOT BPT1 GO TO PBBODYOR.
PT1BITER.
        IF NOT BPT1 GO TO PT1BEND.
        ADD 1 TO BPCC.
        MOVE SPACE TO BP-EOF.
        MOVE 2 TO BPQS. GOBACK.
BPQ2.
        GO TO PT1BITER.
PT1BEND.
        GO TO PBBODYEND.
PBBODYOR.
        ADD 1 TO BPCD.
PT3BITER.
        IF NOT BPT3 GO TO PT3BEND.
        MOVE SPACE TO BP-EOF.
        MOVE 3 TO BPQS. GOBACK.
BPQ3.
        GO TO PT3BITER.
PT3BEND.
PBBODYEND.
        GO TO PBPARTITER.
PBPARTEND.
        MOVE "E" TO BP-EOF.
        GOBACK.
BPEND.
```

We now recode PROCCDIPT so that it will invoke BP correctly, that is, once for each card of the batch part. Adjusting the values of QS so that they appear in ascending order in the text, we have:

```
. . .
DATA DIVISION.
WORKING-STORAGE SECTION.
77   END-INDIC PIC X.
. . .

. . .
PROCEDURE DIVISION.
        ENTRY . . .
        GO TO Q1, Q2, Q3, Q4, Q5 DEPENDING ON QS.
PROCCDIPTSEQ.
Q1.
        MOVE 0 TO CA.
```

```
PREPARTITER.
    IF T1 GO TO PREPARTEND.
    ADD 1 TO CA.
    MOVE 2 TO QS.        GOBACK.
Q2.
    GO TO PREPARTITER.
PREPARTEND.
    DISPLAY INCARD.
    MOVE 3 TO QS.        GOBACK.
Q3.
    MOVE 0 TO CB, CC, CD.
    CALL "BP" USING CB, CC, CD, END-INDIC, INCARD.
PBATCHPARTITER.
    IF END-INDIC = "E" GO TO PBATCHPARTEND.
    MOVE 4 TO QS.        GOBACK.
Q4.
    CALL "B" USING CB, CC, CD, END-INDIC, INCARD.
    GO TO PBATCHPARTITER.
PBATCHPARTEND.
    DISPLAY INCARD                      NOTE DISPLAY T2.
    MOVE 5 TO QS.        GOBACK.        NOTE READ EOF.
Q5.
    DISPLAY CA, CB, CC, CD.
    GOBACK.
PROCCDIPTEND.
```

EXERCISE 9.1 (a)

Invert the program P2 of Section 9.2, giving P2F.

EXERCISE 9.2 (b)

Redesign the solution to Problem 15 (Generating Test Data), given in Section 8.6, so that flagZ is set to the value 1 when the last (not the first) combination is returned. The components X and Y are unchanged.

EXERCISE 9.3 (b)

Design an inverted program to solve Problem 8 (Source Statement Library) in which the amendments are handled in a separately compiled module.

EXERCISE 9.4 (b)

Design an inverted program to solve Problem 8 (Source Statement Library) which permits the invoking program to close the text file without reading all of it.

EXERCISE 9.5 (b)

Design a solution to Problem 11 (Good and Bad Branches) which can operate as an exit routine for the sort. The input to the sort is the unsorted card file; the output required is the good data file; the exit routine has access to a line printer to allow it to produce the error listing.

QUESTION 9.1

The discussion of Problem 13 (Telegrams Analysis) in Section 9.3 may seem to be more complex than is really necessary. For example, we might solve the whole problem by taking the version shown at the beginning of that section and inserting the coding

```
IF OPEN-OP
    MOVE 1 TO QS
ELSE IF CLOSE-OP
    MOVE 4 TO QS.
```

after the ENTRY statement and before the GO TO DEPENDING. Is this solution generally applicable? Could we use the same technique to solve Exercise 9.4?

QUESTION 9.2

Why should we not use the OPCODE (Section 9.3) in the standard interface as the state variable for the invoked routine?

QUESTION 9.3

The file FINV (Section 9.3) for any input–output procedure may, in principle, contain error data. Give some examples of errors it might contain, and suggest alternative designs for handling them.

QUESTION 9.4

Identify a non-trivial input–output facility available in your installation (for example, IBM users might choose BSAM with the OUTIN option and NOTE and POINT). Try to determine from the specifications what are the valid instances of the file of invocations that the chosen facility can process. Why is it so difficult to find out?

QUESTION 9.5

Specify a standard input–output interface, along the lines of that suggested in Section 9.1, which is capable of handling all the logical file types you can think of. Exclude those operations (such as "retry error" and "truncate block") and those results (such as "more disk space needed") which are physical rather than logical.

10. MULTI-THREADING

10.1

In this chapter we return to Problem 14 (System Log), of which a preliminary discussion appears in Section 7.5 above. Before reading this chapter the reader should review the problem description and the preliminary discussion.

The system flow diagram to resolve the structure clash is:

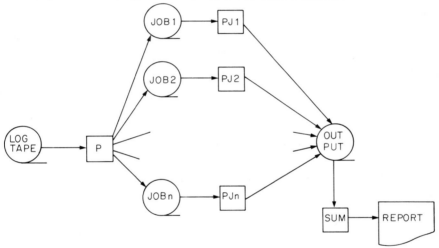

The data structures of the logtape and the jobtapes are:

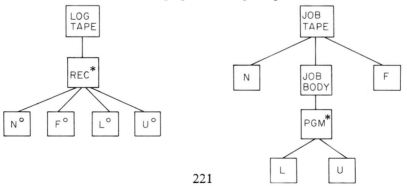

in which the structure of the jobtape is suitable only for Version 1 of the problem. Version 2 is discussed later in the chapter.

The structures of the output tape and the report are (again restricting ourselves to Version 1):

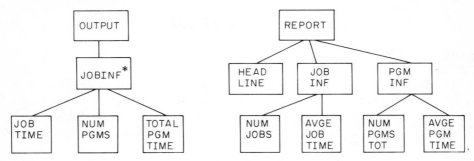

Each jobinf record of the output file is written by one of the programs PJ1, PJ2, ... PJn. The order of the jobinf records is not significant for the SUM program, which writes the report from the output file.

10.2

Our solution to the problem will be this:

Design program P, which will contain an instruction "write logtape record to jobtape JOBj, where j is the job-number in the record";

Design programs PJ1, PJ2, ... PJn, each of which will contain an instruction "write jobinf record to output file";

Invert the programs PJ1, PJ2, ... PJn with respect to their respective jobtapes;

Separate out the state vector of each of these programs, giving the state vectors SV1, SV2, ... SVn and a common program text PJ;

Implement the "write logtape record" instruction in P as a sequence:

find SVj;
invoke PJ, passing SVj and the record;
remember the new value of SVj;

Design the program SUM, and invert it with respect to the output file;

Implement the "write jobinf" instruction in PJ as an invocation of the inverted program SUM.

There are certain difficulties which we shall encounter (and overcome), all concerned essentially with opening and closing the jobtapes and the output file.

10.3

The basic design of program P is:

```
P     seq
          open logtape;
          read logtape;
      PB    iter until eof-logtape
              write record to jobtapej;
              read logtape;
      PB    end
          close logtape;
P     end
```

This program contains no statements to open or close jobtapej. It would be quite wrong to introduce these statements by writing

```
      . . .
PB        iter until eof-logtape
          POPEN    select record N
                       open jobtapej;
          POPEN    end
              write record to jobtapej;
          PCLOSE   select record F
                       close jobtapej;
          PCLOSE   end
              read logtape;
PB        end
      . . .
```

because the structure of a jobtape is, in principle, unknown to P. Certainly this solution would not work for Version 2 of the problem, in which the first record for a job may not be an N record, and the last may not be an F.

A possible solution is to write

```
P      seq
           open logtape;
           read logtape;
           open all jobtapes;
       PB   iter until eof-logtape
               write record to jobtapej;
               read logtape;
       PB   end
           close all jobtapes;
           close logtape;
P      end
```

but obviously this ignores the difficulty that we do not know how many
jobtapes there should be or what the job-numbers are.

The programs PJ1, PJ2, . . . PJn have the structure:

```
PJJ    seq
           open jobtapej;
           read jobtapej; (record N)
           numpgms: =0;
           totpgmtime: =0;
           x: =log-on time;
           read jobtapej;
       PJJB   iter until no more pgm records (L or U)
                   numpgms: =numpgms+1;
                   y: =pgm-load time;
                   read jobtapej;
                   totpgmtime: =totpgmtime + pgm-unload time − y;
                   read jobtapej;
       PJJB   end
           jobtime: =log-off time − x;
           read jobtapej; (eof-jobtapej)
           write jobinf record to output file;
           close jobtapej;
PJJ    end
```

Making certain assumptions, we may code PJJ, inverted with respect to
jobtapej, as:

```
    . . .
        ENTRY "PJJ" USING RECORD.
        GO TO Q1, Q2, Q3, Q4, Q5 DEPENDING ON QS.
```

```
PJJSEQ.
Q1.
       MOVE  0 TO NUMPGMS, TOTPGMTIME.
       SUBTRACT LOGONTIME FROM 0 GIVING X.
       MOVE 2 TO QS.       GOBACK.
Q2.
PJJBITER.
       IF (NOT L) AND (NOT U) GO TO PJJBEND.
       ADD 1 TO NUMPGMS.
       MOVE PGMLOADTIME TO Y.
       MOVE 3 TO QS.       GOBACK.
Q3.
       ADD PGMUNLOADTIME TO TOTPGMTIME.
       SUBTRACT Y FROM TOTPGMTIME.
       MOVE 4 TO QS.       GOBACK.
Q4.
       GO TO PJJBITER.
PJJBEND.
       SUBTRACT X FROM LOGOFFTIME GIVING JOBTIME.
       MOVE 5 TO QS.       GOBACK.
Q5.
       WRITE JOBINF.
       GOBACK.
PJJEND.
```

The assumptions we have made are that PJJ is not invoked with an "open" command, and that there is an end-file marker on jobtapej.

When the state vector is separated from the program coding, it will be passed as a parameter in the invocation of PJ. It will therefore appear, along with the record, in the linkage section of PJ. The procedure coding for PJ will be as shown above for PJJ, and the data division will be:

```
DATA DIVISION.
LINKAGE SECTION.
01   STATE-VECTOR.
     02   QS PIC 9.
     02   X PIC S9(6).
     02   Y PIC S9(6).
     02   JOBINF.
          03   NUMPGMS PIC 9(4).
          03   TOTPGMTIME PIC 9(6).
          03   JOBTIME PIC 9(6).
```

```
01   RECORD.
   02   . . .
```

The entry statement will be

ENTRY "PJ" USING STATE-VECTOR, RECORD.

Note that because the state vector is defined in the linkage section of PJ, it is impossible to write a VALUE clause for QS. We must find some other way of initializing the state variable QS at the beginning of each job.

10.4

The handling of the state vectors requires some thought. A very crude technique would be to define a complete set of state vectors for PJ in the working-storage of P:

```
DATA DIVISION.
WORKING-STORAGE SECTION.
01   SV-TABLE.
   02   SV OCCURS 1000.
      03   QS PIC 9.
      03   X PIC S9(6).
      . . .
      . . .
         04   JOBTIME PIC 9(6).
01   FILLER REDEFINES SV-TABLE.
   02   SV1.
      03   QS1 PIC 9 VALUE 1.
      03   X1 PIC S9(6).
      . . .
      . . .
         04   JOBTIME1 PIC 9(6).
   02   SV2.
      03   QS2 PIC 9 VALUE 1.
      . . .
      . . .
```

The invocation of PJ by P would then take the form

CALL "PJ" USING SV (JOB-NUMBER), RECORD.

in which the appropriate state vector is found by subscripting, and its new value automatically remembered because PJ would update it *in situ*.

The disadvantages of this technique are obvious. Apart from the cumbersome enumeration of the individual state vectors, due to a defect of the COBOL language, we have the disadvantages:

The number of jobs to be processed must be known at the time P is written;

There must be a simple one-to-one correspondence between the job-numbers and the integers;

Two jobs cannot share a state vector even if one of them is completed before the other begins;

All of the state vectors must be held in core storage;

The format of a state vector must be known in P, although the state vector is essentially private to PJ.

A better solution is to regard the state vectors as constituting a direct-access file. We will need an input–output procedure, HSV, to handle this file. HSV must be able to satisfy the following invocations:

Read sv (job-number); HSV returns the state vector for the specified job-number or, if there is no state vector for the specified job-number, returns a "not-found" result;

Insert sv (job-number); HSV inserts the state vector as a new record in the file, associating it with the specified job-number; there must be no state vector for the specified job-number already on the file;

Delete sv (job-number); HSV deletes the state vector for the specified job-number;

Update sv (job-number); HSV deletes the existing state vector and inserts the new state vector for the specified job-number.

From the point of view of the invoking program, HSV appears to be an ordinary input–output procedure. There is no reason, however, why we should not implement various versions of HSV, including one which stores the state vectors in main storage and another which stores them on disk:

these versions would be indistinguishable to the invoking program.

In addition to providing ourselves with the procedure HSV, we will modify the program PJ. We will add a communication area to the list of parameters:

CALL "PJ" USING STATE-VECTOR, COMM, RECORD.

which will allow P to issue distinct commands to PJ for opening, writing and closing the jobtape, and will allow PJ to return a result indication to P. Specifically, the result indication which PJ may return to P on a write command is "end of jobtape", returned when PJ has processed the log-off record for the job.

The new form for P is therefore:

```
P     seq
        open logtape;
        read logtape;
      PB   iter until eof-logtape
            read sv (job-number);
            PSVA   select not-found
                    create dummy sv;
                    insert sv (job-number);
                    open PJ (sv, comm, record);
            PSVA   end
            write PJ (sv, comm, record);
           .PSVB   select end-of-jobtape
                    close PJ (sv, comm, record);
                    delete sv (job-number);
            PSVB   or not end-of-jobtape
                    update sv (job-number);
            PSVB   end
            read logtape;
       PB   end
        close logtape;
P     end
```

The "close" invocation of PJ is equivalent to a write invocation in which the record passed to PJ is the end marker for the jobtape.

The associated changes to PJ are these. First, PJ must set the result in the communication area: this result is always "OK" except when PJ returns after processing the log-off record, when we require:

. . .

SUBTRACT X FROM LOGOFFTIME GIVING JOBTIME.

```
        MOVE "EF" TO RESULT.
        MOVE 5 TO QS.        GOBACK.
Q5.
        WRITE JOBINF.
        GOBACK.
PJEND.
```

Second, PJ must recognize the "open" invocation and, when it occurs, initialize QS. Thus we require:

```
. . .
        ENTRY "PJ" USING STATE-VECTOR, COMM, RECORD.
        IF OPEN-OP
          MOVE 1 TO QS
          GOBACK.
        GO TO Q1, Q2, Q3, Q4, Q5 DEPENDING ON QS.
. . .
```

This, or equivalent coding, is inescapable. Having introduced the "open" invocation specifcally to allow PJ to initialize its own state variable, we must examine the opcode before using the value of QS.

10.5

So far, we have chiefly considered Version 1 of the problem. In Version 2, arbitrary sets of consecutive records may be missing from the logtape, and there is therefore no longer any assurance that the first record of each job will be a log-on record, or that the last will be a log-off.

The effect on the design of PJ is substantial. The structure of the jobtape is shown on p. 230.

This will evidently need the use of backtracking in the program structure of PJ. The end-of-file marker has been shown explicitly because of its importance: without it, there would be no way of recognizing the end of an incomplete job, and hence no way of arranging for PJ to write the jobinf record to the output file.

The jobinf record, and the printed report, are both more elaborate for Version 2, because they now include information for both complete and incomplete jobs. More significantly, a further complication arises in the design of the program P. In the form of P given in Section 10.4 above, P closes the jobtape (that is, it writes the end-of-file marker) when PJ indicates that end-of-jobtape has been reached. But this indication is given by PJ

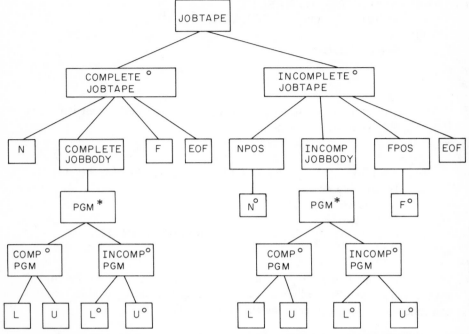

when the log-off record is processed; for an incomplete job, there may be no log-off record. We must therefore arrange in P to write an end-of-file marker for every incomplete job.

This may be done conveniently at the end of P by running through all of the state vectors which have been created but not yet deleted. We need to be able to invoke HSV to read back serially the currently existing state vectors. The new form of P is then:

```
P      seq
         open logtape;
         read logtape;
      PB   iter until eof-logtape
           read sv (job-number);
           PSVA   select not-found
                      create dummy sv;
                      insert sv (job-number);
                      open PJ (sv, comm, record);
           PSVA   end
                 write PJ (sv, comm, record);
           PSVB   select end-of-jobtape
```

```
                    close PJ (sv, comm, record);
                    delete sv (job-number);
        PSVB    or not end-of-jobtape
                    update sv (job-number);
        PSVB    end
                read logtape;
    PB    end
            open HSV for serial read;
            read next sv;
    PSVSET    iter until eof-svfile
                close PJ (sv, comm, dummy-record);
                delete sv (job-number);
                read next sv;
        PSVSET    end
            close logtape;
    P        end
```

10.6

Finally, we come to consider the program SUM, which we must design and then invert with respect to the output file. The basic form of SUM is:

```
SUM    seq
            open output;
            read record from output; (jobinf or eof)
            write report headline;
            initialize totals;
        SUMBODY    iter until eof-output
                    add jobinf to totals;
                    read record from output; (jobinf or eof)
        SUMBODY    end
            calculate averages;
            print report;
            close output;
    SUM    end
```

It should be clear to the reader that when this program is coded in an inverted form its state variable will have two values, one corresponding to the first invocation and the other corresponding to the read statement within SUMBODY.

Thus we will have:

```
    . . .
        ENTRY "SUM" USING JOBINF.
```

```
          GO TO Q1, Q2 DEPENDING ON QS.
     SUMSEQ.
     Q1.
          WRITE HEADLINE.
          MOVE 0 TO TOTALS.
     SUMBODYITER.
          IF EOF-OUTPUT GO TO SUMBODYEND.
          ADD JOBINF TO TOTALS.
          MOVE 2 TO QS.     GOBACK.
     Q2.
          GO TO SUMBODYITER.
     SUMBODYEND.
          CALCULATE AVERAGES.
          WRITE REPORT LINES.
          GOBACK.
     SUMEND.
```

The end-of-file record for the output file must be written by program P: none of the programs PJJ can recognize when the output file is complete. However, it seems inefficient to introduce an operation code (or end-file indicator) into the interface of SUM, when we can easily arrange to calculate the averages and write the report lines in P directly. And while we are doing so, we might as well write the headline and initialize the totals directly in the beginning of P. Every invocation of SUM will then be a simple "write jobinf" invocation, issued by PJ.

The new form of SUM is:

```
     . . .
          ENTRY "SUM" USING JOBINF.
          GO TO Q1, Q2 DEPENDING ON QS.
     SUMSEQ.
     Q1.
     SUMBODYITER.
          ADD JOBINF TO TOTALS.
          MOVE 2 TO QS.     GOBACK.
     Q2.
          GO TO SUMBODYITER.
     SUMBODYEND.
     SUMEND.
```

It is not difficult to see that the code executed at Q1 is identical to the code executed at Q2. We may therefore combine the two values of QS into one.

Obviously, a variable which has only one value need never be set or tested, and we arrive at the final, highly optimized form of the program SUM:

```
  . . .
        ENTRY "SUM" USING JOBINF.
        ADD JOBINF TO TOTALS.
        GOBACK.
```

It seems sensible to give PJ access to the totals, so that it may update them from jobinf directly, and need not call the program SUM at all. We therefore have a stage of optimization beyond the final stage: the program SUM disappears altogether.

EXERCISE 10.1 (c)

Design and implement two compatible versions of HSV, one using disk and the other main storage only. Each version should check its file of invocations for errors such as direct-access invocations following "open for serial reading".

EXERCISE 10.2 (b)

Design and code a complete solution to Problem 14 (System Log) using your solution to Exercise 10.1.

EXERCISE 10.3 (b)

Describe very carefully the problems of addressing the totals in Problem 14 as the program SUM goes through the successive versions suggested in Section 10.6 above. Explain why the problems become harder as the program SUM becomes more trivial.

EXERCISE 10.4 (c)

Suppose that the input file of Problem 11 (Good and Bad Branches) has been sorted into ascending order by card type only. Design and code a solution which produces the error listing and the good data file in a single pass of the input file.

QUESTION 10.1

Suppose that we have a complete solution to Problem 14 (System Log), and that we use it on a logtape which, by chance, happens to be sorted into chronological order within job-number order. (The logtape would be sorted in this way if there were only one terminal or if there were only one terminal in use at any one time.) What would happen to the state vector file? Does it matter whether or not there are missing blocks?

QUESTION 10.2

The input–output procedure for state vectors (HSV in Problem 14 solution) was neither closed nor opened (except for the "open for serial reading"). Should it have been? Why? Suppose that Problem 14 were different in the following way: the time-sharing system runs continuously, but logtapes are taken off and analysed once every 24 hours; a job may have its log-on in one 24-hour period and its log-off in another. How would you then handle the state vectors?

QUESTION 10.3

Section 10.6 discusses how the program SUM can be reduced to nothing by distributing its instructions between the programs P and PJ. Find other examples in this book of this process of reducing a program to nothing. What are the benefits and what are the penalties of carrying out the process? What would a system be like in which we resolved never to do so?

QUESTION 10.4

Why does a data processing system need master files?

QUESTION 10.5

Find out (from the book "Structured Programming" by O.-J. Dahl, E. W. Dijkstra and C. A. R. Hoare, Academic Press, 1972) what is meant by a *class* in the programming language SIMULA 67. How are the procedures declared in a *class* declaration related to one another? Can a *class* have a state variable?

11. SYSTEMS AND PROGRAMS

11.1

The concepts of serial file processing are fundamental to the design technique presented in this book. We base our program structures on data structures, and those data structures are structures of serial files. Sometimes we are dealing with files stored on peripheral devices, such as card readers, line printers or tape or disk drives; sometimes with files held in main storage, such as character strings or tables of serially arranged entries. But there are always serial files to be processed. The technique of program inversion allows us to design a program to process a complete file, taking full account of the relationships among the records of the file, and then to code that program in the form of a record handling routine, which processes only one record of the file at each invocation. Further, by separating out the state vector, we can use the record handling routine to process several instances of the file simultaneously.

At first sight it may seem that the applicability of the technique is strictly limited. Clearly, it is relevant to serial batch processing programs. But what about system design at the higher levels, where the elementary components are themselves application programs? What about software design at the lower levels? What about on-line systems? The purpose of this chapter is to indicate the wider relevance of the technique, and to suggest an underlying unity of system design at all levels.

The chief obstacles to recognition of this unity are these:

Problems are often posed in such a way that the designer is given a worm's eye view of the system: he is encouraged to think about individual records when he should be thinking about the file, about characters when he should be thinking about the string;

For various reasons, some good and some bad, the software environment is radically different at different levels: it is not too difficult to see what is common to COBOL and machine language, but much harder to see what is common to COBOL and the Job Control Language;

K

There is a real need for efficiency, especially at the highest and lowest levels of a system: design thinking often begins by optimizing the use of the available facilities, thus stressing the unique characteristics of those facilities, instead of beginning by reaching a full understanding of the problem, thus stressing its general structure, and only then moving on to consider its efficient implementation.

Much of the discussion in this chapter will be based on the following example problem. The main purpose of the problem is to serve as a source of illustration of various points; very little detail is provided in the problem statement, and no unified complete solution is attempted.

PROBLEM 17—LOANS SYSTEM

The Bank of Timbuktu is in the business of making loans to commercial customers.

Each new customer must go through a process of negotiation with the bank, in which the general terms are agreed for all loans to that customer. Each round of negotiations is recorded in a transaction of type TN, and submitted to the computer system for evaluation. After the final round of negotiations, agreement is reached (the Bank never loses a customer) and the agreed terms are submitted to the system in a TA transaction. The customer is then permitted to receive any number of loans, but only one loan may be current at any one time. The transactions submitted for each loan are a loan initiation (TI), followed by a number of repayments (TR), followed by a loan termination (TT). Naturally, each loan may be in existence for several years, and some of the Bank's customers have been borrowing money from the Bank for over 50 years.

The system should be capable of processing transactions on a daily basis, producing any output appropriate to each transaction. Monthly and yearly summaries will also be required.

11.2

We will begin by considering the design of the daily transaction processing program. We will suppose that each transaction is keypunched as it is received, and that a magnetic tape file of transactions is created, the transactions being written to the tape in strict chronological order. No attempt is made to sort the transactions into customer number sequence.

Our first step is to recognize that we are, as so often, presented with a worm's eye view of the problem. We are required to design a program which will be run once a day, but a day is too small a timeslice: we need to consider a span of time which will encompass the complete existence of every loan and every customer. Certainly, a day is a meaningful timeslice: the calculation of interest will depend on the exact day of the intiation of a loan and on the exact day on which each repayment is made. So we will suppose that each transaction will carry a date field. But we will design the transaction processing program as if its input file contained all the transactions occurring in the whole lifetime of the system.

We imagine, then, that the program runs perpetually. Its input file consists of all the input transactions which ever occur, arranged in chronological order. Its output file consists of the computer-produced documents (payment acknowledgements, requests for overdue payments, etc) arising from the input transactions. To fix the ideas, we may imagine that the program runs on a dedicated computer which is never switched off: the input file is a multi-reel file, with an infinite number of reels—one for each day's transactions; at the end of each reel the program waits until the operator mounts the next reel.

The system flow diagram for this perpetual program is:

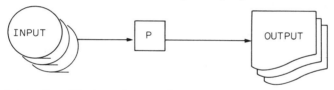

There is no other file than the two shown; in particular, there is no master file, either for customers or for loans.

The problem of designing this perpetual program is similar to Problem 14 (System Log). The only structure we can impose on the input file is:

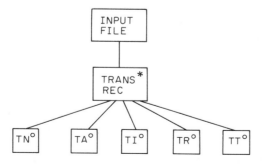

but clearly there are various operations which must be performed once per customer and others which must be performed once per loan. The analogy

with Problem 14 is straightforward: customer is analogous to job and loan
is analogous to program. So we redraw the system flow diagram as:

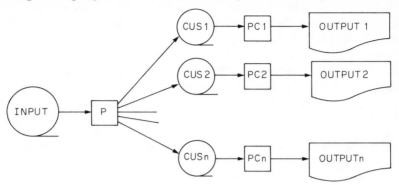

Program P splits the input file into n transaction files, CUS1, CUS2, ... CUSn,
one for each customer. Each of these n transaction files is processed by a
program PC, which produces the associated output. The structure of each
of the transaction files CUS1, CUS2, ... CUSn, is:

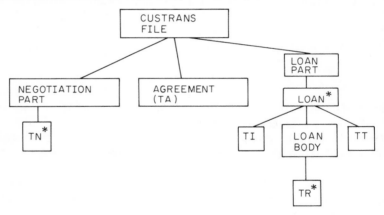

We may, of course, elaborate this structure to take error data into account:
indeed, in a practical system, we must. Usually, this will involve backtracking,
and the question of backtracking in system design is discussed briefly later
in this chapter. For the moment we will assume that the above structure is
adequate.

Following the pattern of our solution to Problem 14, we design the
programs PC1, PC2, ... PCn, invert them with respect to their customer
transaction files, and separate out their state vectors. We are left as a result
with a program PCT ("process one transaction for a customer"), a set of

state vectors SV1, SV2, . . . SVn, and a main program P. Because there is an indefinite number of customers, we decide that the state vector file should be held on disk rather than in main storage. We create two additional programs: HSV, to handle the state vector file, and HOPT, to handle the printed output file. The configuration of our solution is now:

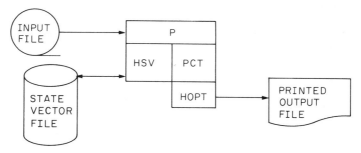

P invokes HSV to retrieve and replace each state vector, and invokes PCT to process each transaction against the associated state vector; PCT invokes HOPT to produce the printed output. We could equally well have chosen to invoke HOPT directly from P; in some ways that is a better solution, but it involves inverting PCT with respect both to the customer transaction file and to the output file.

11.3

This solution turns out to be surprisingly versatile. We produced it as a perpetually running program, but it can clearly be converted into the originally required daily transaction processing program with a minimum of effort.

For the perpetually running program, the state vector file is an internal work file. Space need not be allocated for it before the start of execution of P, and may be released when P terminates. The basic form of P is:

```
P   seq
        create state vector file;
        process input file;
        destroy state vector file;
P   end
```

in which the instruction "create state vector file" allocates space to the file and initializes the file so that it initially contains no records, while the instruction "destroy state vector file" releases the space for other purposes, thus losing any information still stored in the file.

To convert P into the daily processing program, we need only remove these instructions: the state vector file must be in existence when each daily run begins, and must be kept after termination so that it is available for the next daily run. Traditionally, we would rename the state vector file: we would call it the "Customer Master File". Provided that there are no significant instructions remaining at the beginning and end of P—we would have to remove them, as we removed the "create" and "destroy" instructions—we now have the daily processing program:

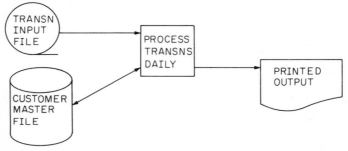

The transaction input file is a slice of the perpetual input file, covering one day's transactions. It is arranged in strict chronological order, and is not sorted by customer number. The customer master file records are the state vectors for the program component PCT: in particular, they contain a field QS, the state variable of PCT; traditionally this field would be named "Customer Status Indicator".

By making other changes to the main program P we can create other configurations for transaction processing. One important such change is to invert P with respect to the transaction input file: this would give a transaction processing routine PT which could be used in an on-line system:

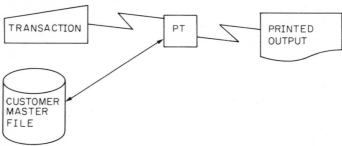

The printed output could be produced centrally or transmitted to the terminal from which the associated transaction is received.

Another important change is to convert the customer master file from direct-access to serial-access. By pre-sorting the input tranactions into chronological order within customer number order we may, in some circumstances, be able to improve the speed of program execution. The new serial version of P, PS, is:

```
PS      seq
        open transfile;
        read trans;
        open old cusfile; ⎫
        read old cusfile;  ⎬(open CMF)
        open new cusfile;  ⎭
      PSBODY   iter until eof-trans
          PCUSGRP   seq
                  cn:=transaction-cus-no;
                  copy old cusfile ⎫
                  to new until rec  ⎪
                  for cn found or   ⎬ (read CMF (cn))
                  not-found;       ⎭
              PCUSBODY   iter until eof-trans or cus-no ≠ cn
                         do PCT;
                         read trans;
              PCUSBODY   end
                  do nothing; (update CMF (cn))
          PCUSGRP   end
      PSBODY   end
        copy old cusfile ⎫
        to new until eof;  ⎪
        close old cusfile; ⎬(close CMF)
        close new cusfile; ⎭
        close trans;
PS      end
```

The groups of operations bracketed together are implementations in serial form of the operations necessary for the state vector file. There is no reason why a version of HSV should not be produced which would conceal from the program PS the fact that the state vector file (customer master file) is held on tape: the design of such a version was set as Exercise 4.3 above.

11.4

So far, we have concerned ourselves only with one program. But the system must include at least monthly and yearly summaries in addition to the transaction processing. To provide these we return to the idea of the perpetual program, processing the infinite transaction file.

Essentially, what we need to do is to elaborate the structure of the transaction input file to show the chronological arrangement of days within months and months within years. But we have no guarantee that there will be at least one transaction on every month-end day and on every year-end day. So it becomes necessary to introduce a new file: the calendar file, each record of which corresponds to a day. The records of the calendar file are, of course, in chronological order, and may be readily collated with the records of the transaction file.

The system has the form:

```
    SYSTEM   seq
                 create state vector file;
                 open trans
                 read trans;
                 open calendar file;
                 read calendar;
          SYSBODY   iter until eof-calendar
              PYEARBODY   iter until end-of-year
                  PMTHBODY   iter until end-of-month
                              process 1 day's transactions;
                              read calendar;
                  PMTHBODY   end
                              do mnth-end summary;
              PYEARBODY   end
                          do year-end summary;
          SYSBODY   end
                 close trans;
                 close calendar file;
                 destroy state vector file;
    SYSTEM   end
```

There are two ways of producing the month-end and year-end summaries. The first way is to treat them as we treated the output report in problem 14 (System Log). We modify the inverted program PCT (process one transaction for a customer) so that it writes records to a summary output file. The summaries may then be produced by reading and analysing this file. The second way is, in some respects, less attractive. We make no modification to PCT. Instead, we produce the summaries by scanning serially through the state vector file (the customer master file). The reason for considering this solution less attractive is that the state vector file is, in an important sense,

private to PCT: although, for historical reasons, it is traditional to regard a
master file as being available without restriction to every program, there are
benefits in regarding it as private to the program whose state vectors it
contains.

Implementation of the program shown above is not difficult. We fragment
the infinite transaction file into an infinite set of finite daily transaction files.
We invert the program SYSTEM with respect to the calendar file, giving a
program SYSC: SYSC may be invoked to carry out the processing appropriate to one record of the calendar file, that is, the processing approriate
to one day. Finally, we arrange to run a very general program OPSYS:

```
OPSYS   seq
            open calendar file;
            read calendar file;
        OPBODY   iter until eof-calendar
                     retrieve state vector of SYSC;
                     do SYSC;
                     store updated state vector of SYSC;
                     read calendar;
        OPBODY   end
            close calendar file;
OPSYS   end
```

The generality of OPSYS is obvious. Into the iterated part of OPBODY
we may insert the statements necessary to invoke systems other than our
commercial loan system:

```
    . . .
OPBODY   iter until eof-calendar
             retrieve state vector of SYSC;
             do SYSC;
             store updated state vector of SYSC;
             retrieve state vector of XSYSC;
             do XSYSC;
             store updated state vector of XSYSC;
             retrieve state vector of YSYSC;
                  . . .
                  . . .
             store updated state vector of ZSYSC;
             read calendar;
OPBODY   end
    . . .
```

In effect, the basic algorithm of the iterated part of OPBODY is:

> look at today's date;
> do whatever has to be done today;

and everything is beautifully simple.

11.5

But, of course, everything is not quite so simple. There are two complicating factors. First, practical systems are not so trivial as our commercial loan system: the program SYSTEM would, in practice, be much larger and much more complex. This, in itself, would not matter very much—we have the necessary tools to master complexity—if it were not for the second factor. The second factor is that the programming system, at the level of our present discussion, is inadequate to our needs.

There is an obvious analogy between the invocation of a COBOL subprogram with a list of parameters and the invocation of a main program with a list of files. Just as we write:

> CALL "SUBPGM" USING AREA1, AREA2, AREA3.

so we write:

```
//    EXEC PGM=MAINPROG
//FILEA DD DSNAME=FILE1, ...
//FILEB DD DSNAME=FILE2, ...
//FILEC DD DSNAME=FILE3, ...
```

Unfortunately, we cannot carry the analogy as far as we would like to.

When we implement a program whose elementary operations are invoked by "//   EXEC" statements, we are quickly forced to abandon the Job Control Language and to resort to natural language instructions to the computer operator:

> "Job 1234 (Daily Transaction Processing) must be run every day, unless there is no input for the day. Job 5678 (Month-end Summary) must be run on the last working day of each calendar month, using the Customer Master File as updated by Job 1234 if Job 1234 is run on that day. . . ."

Of course, we can adopt various palliatives. We can make sure that we have written the schematic logic of the program and satisfied ourselves that it is correct before translating it into operators' instructions. We can write programs to punch out the JCL statements needed for each day's work. We can even make a serious effort to read the JCL Manual. But perhaps the task shouldn't be quite so difficult.

11.6

The main theme of this chapter is that system design is an extension of the program design task, and that the same techniques can usefully be applied to both. In principle, we may think of a system as a large program:

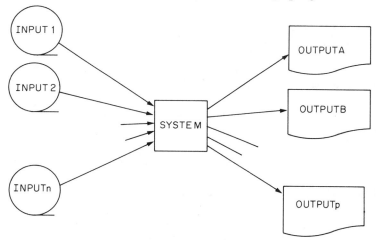

The input files are all pictured as tape files, because they are necessarily serial: the chronological ordering of the input is always significant. Physically, the inputs may arrive on cards, tapes, terminals, disks, computer-readable documents, or any other medium. The outputs are all pictured as print-out, because they are destined to be read by some human being (or, perhaps, another computer system).

The design task consists of devising a structure for the system which corresponds correctly to the data structures of the input and output files. The executable operations, whether they are COBOL statements, transaction-processing routines, or complete jobs, must be allocated to appropriate components of the system structure.

The problems of structure clashes and of backtracking are important at all levels of the system. In Chapters 5 through 10 these problems are discussed in the context of the lower levels of the system, conventionally thought of as the programming context. The solutions proposed there have counterparts in the context of the higher levels too.

The chief techniques for solving structure clashes at the higher levels of the system are:

The introduction of master files to hold state vectors;

Sorting input or output files;

The use of file organizations, especially those provided by data-base management systems, which permit different logical structures to be imposed on the same physical file.

In backtracking problems the difficulties centre on the handling of side effects. The chief techniques here are:

Use of generation data groups (the grandfather, father, son method) to allow backspacing over an array of files;

Dumping a database; this is a "note" operation, anticipating the need for a later "restore" in the event of erroneous operation;

Use of the "checkpoint" and "restore" facilities of the operating system;

Retention of transaction input records, either in a special file or in master file records; this may be thought of as a multiple read ahead device, and is often implemented in a highly optimized form in which only the minimum information is retained from each record.

EXERCISE 11.1 (c)

The system flow diagram of a daily updating system is:

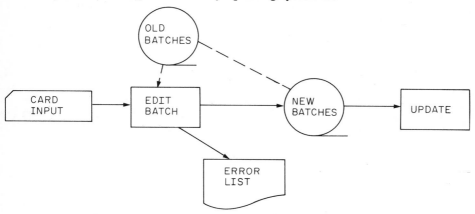

The card input arrives in several batches during the day. Each batch is edited and added to the "new batches" file together with any batches previously edited on the same day. After the final batch has been edited, the resulting new batches file is used in an update run. The "edit batch" program may fail due to an intermittent fault in the operating system, in which case it must be run again.

Design the system in schematic logic as if it were a single program of the form:

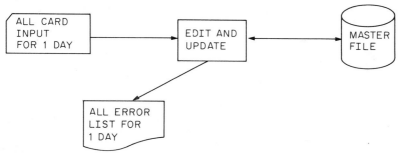

Implement your design in the form of Job Control statements and instructions to the operator, to give the system originally specified above.

EXERCISE 11.2 (c)

Design and specify a language for operators' instructions.

QUESTION 11.1

Why was it possible in Section 11.3 above to configure several different versions of the program (perpetual batch, on-line, daily batch) without changing the component PCT?

QUESTION 11.2

If the "Customer Status Indicator" is really the state variable for the program PCT, what precautions should we take in using it? What would happen if there were another system sharing the same customer master file?

QUESTION 11.3

Examine the Job Control Language available in your installation. What facilities does it have for implementing sequences, iterations and selections? How are files passed as parameters to programs? How is it determined whether a file is to be kept or deleted? Why is the control of file space so much more elaborate than the control of main storage space in a COBOL environment?

QUESTION 11.4

What programming facilities would you like to find in an on-line environment?

QUESTION 11.5

If the suggested solution to Problem 17 (Loans System) were implemented, how could we arrange to produce summary reports on request rather than at predetermined intervals? How could we arrange to add a new program to the system—such as a weekly summary—once the system is in operation?

12. OPTIMIZATION

12.1

The word "optimization" is ill-chosen. Its Latin derivation implies that to optimize a program is to make it as good as it can be; but what we mean by an optimized program is one which is as small or as fast as it can be. In making it small or fast, or, if we can, both, we are liable to make it bad in various ways: it may become harder to understand, harder to maintain and more prone to error.

In short, optimization costs money. We may define our basic attitude to optimization in two rules:

Rule 1: Don't do it.

Rule 2: Don't do it yet.

The first rule tells us that we need a positive quantified justification before we optimize, and that often the justification simply does not exist. There is no sense in making a program run faster if the result is merely to increase the proportion of unused CPU cycles. There is no sense in making a program smaller if the result is merely to increase the number of unused locations in a standard-size partition of store. There is no sense in reducing the execution time by 5% if the result is to increase by 5% the likelihood of a production rerun due to program error.

The second rule tells us that we must always begin with an unoptimized design, even if we intend to optimize it eventually. Only an unoptimized design can have the clarity and simplicity that are necessary for full understanding: and we must understand our program fully if we are to optimize it without introducing logical errors. Anyone who has worked on program maintenance knows how dangerous it is to change a program which is less than transparently simple: apparently innocuous changes can have surprising, and disastrous, effects.

For these reasons the problem solutions presented in this book have been almost entirely unoptimized, sometimes perversely so. In this chapter we explore some of the transformations which can be used to make the programs faster or smaller.

12.2

We will concern ourselves essentially with transformations of the program structure. We will not consider two important techniques: optimization by tuning and optimization by algorithm.

Optimization by tuning consists of adjusting parameters which affect the execution characteristics without affecting the structure. Some obvious examples are:

adjusting blocking factors of files to obtain the best compromise between the storage space needed for buffers and the number of physical data transfers to be executed;

allocation of multiple buffers to improve the overlapping of channel and CPU activity;

adjusting queue sizes, especially in on-line systems, to obtain the best compromise between space requirements and device utilization;

choice of data types to minimize storage requirements on files or to minimize the use of data conversion routines;

segmentation of programs to permit overlaying or to improve use of virtual storage.

None of these forms of tuning affects program structure (except possibly the last), and we will not consider them further.

Optimization by algorithm is of greater relevance to mathematical than to data processing programs. The following problem provides an illustration.

PROBLEM 18—BUBBLE SORT

A table in main storage has the form:

```
01   TABLE.
   02   MAX PIC S9(4) COMPUTATIONAL.
```

```
  02  TABLE-BODY.
    03  ENTRY OCCURS 500.
      04  EKEY PIC X(4).
      04  EVAL PIC X(8).
```

There are 500 locations available for holding entries, but at any moment only the locations ENTRY (1), ENTRY (2), . . . ENTRY (MAX) are occupied. The value of MAX is always non-negative, but may be zero.

It is required to design a problem component which will sort this table; that is, arrange it so that the values of EKEY (S) are in ascending order for increasing S. The sorting method to be used is the bubble sort. A number of passes are made over the table. In each pass, which may be from left to right (that is, increasing the subscript) or from right to left, successive pairs of adjacent entries are examined, wrongly ordered pairs being swapped. Thus, for example, if the values of EKEY are

$$6 \quad 1 \quad 4 \quad 5 \quad 3 \quad 2 \quad 7 \quad 0 \quad 8$$

then after a left-to-right pass they will be

$$1 \quad 4 \quad 5 \quad 3 \quad 2 \quad 6 \quad 0 \quad 7 \quad 8$$

Note that after the first left-to-right pass the highest entry must arrive in the rightmost position, and that after the first right-to-left pass the lowest entry must arrive in the leftmost position. It follows that the table can be completely sorted in MAX-1 passes at most.

The simplest possible algorithm to solve this problem is one in which we make MAX-1 left-to-right passes over the complete table. The program would be:

```
P1     seq
       NP:=0;
   PB   iter until NP ⩾ MAX-1
       S:=1;     T:=2;
       PASS   iter until S ⩾ MAX
           PPAIR   select EKEY (S) > EKEY (T)
                   swap;
           PPAIR   end
               S:=S+1;     T:=T+1;
       PASS   end
       NP:=NP+1;
```

PB **end**
P   **end**

The most effective optimization available to us now is to improve the algorithm itself. For example, we may make the following changes:

stop when a null pass is made instead of waiting until MAX-1 passes have been executed;

reduce the area of the table over which each successive pass is made: if in the Nth pass the leftmost swapped pair is at SN and SN+1, then the N+1'th pass may begin at SN−1, SN, and similarly for the rightmost swapped pair;

depending on the expected forms of misordering, it may be useful to execute alternate left-to-right and right-to-left passes;

stop when the table is sorted instead of waiting until an unnecessary null pass has been made.

We will regard these improvements as examples of optimization by algorithm: they require new program structures rather than transformations of an old structure. The distinction is not precise, and it would not be useful to make it so. We may perhaps say that we are concerned in this chapter with the kind of optimization that could in principle be carried out by a good compiler working on well-structured programs.

12.3

Most of our optimization techniques will be directed to reducing the program size. For a given algorithm, the structuring technique presented in this book tends to produce the fastest possible program, and there are rarely major improvements to be made in execution speed. However, some minor improvements are available.

The program given in Section 8.6 as a solution to Problem 15 (Generating Test Data) is:

PROGZ   **seq**
        ...

    PZBODY   **iter**
        PGROUPZ   **seq**

```
                        flagZ: = 1;
                        write  X;
                        read FX;
          PGXBODY    iter until flagX = 1
                        flagZ: = 0;
                        write  X;
                        read FX;
          PGXBODY    end
                        flagZ: = 0;
                        write  Y;
                        read FY;
          PGYBODY    iter until flagY = 1
                        flagZ: = 0;
                        write  Y;
                        read FY;
          PGYBODY    end
        PGROUPZ   end
      PZBODY   end
          ...
  PROGZ   end
```

The value 1 is assigned to flagZ at the beginning of PGROUPZ; subsequently, the value 0 is assigned several times. If we can be certain that no other assignments are made to flagZ (for example, during the write operations), then we can greatly reduce the number of assignments executed by rewriting the program as:

```
  PROGZ   seq
          ...
    PZBODY   iter
      PGROUPZ   seq
                   flagZ: = 1;
                   write X;
                   read FX;
                   flagZ: = 0;
          PGXBODY    iter until flagX = 1
                       ...
                       ...
          PGYBODY    end
        PGROUPZ   end
      PZBODY   end
          ...
  PROGZ   end
```

We have already used a similar technique to handle the usual end-of-file flag. Instead of coding the read operation as:

```
PROCREAD.
    MOVE SPACE TO FILE-EOF.
    READ FILE AT END MOVE "E" TO FILE-EOF.
```

we reduce the number of executions of the "move space" instruction by writing the whole program as:

```
PROGSTART.
    MOVE SPACE TO FILE-EOF
    OPEN INPUT FILE.
    READ FILE AT END MOVE "E" TO FILE-EOF.
    ...
    ...

    ...
    READ FILE AT END MOVE "E" TO FILE-EOF.
    ...
    READ FILE AT END MOVE "E" TO FILE-EOF.
    ...
```

And we may go further by initializing the value of FILE-EOF at compile time.

What we are doing in these examples is to move operations from their natural place in the program structure. A value of flagZ is associated with every record of the fileZ; the natural place to set the value of flagZ is therefore at the point at which the record is written. A value of FILE-EOF is obtained as the result of every read operation; the natural place to set that value is therefore at the point of the read operation. The possibility of optimization depends on being able to deduce that the assignment is otiose in its natural place, that the value to be assigned is already set. In the two examples above the deduction is not difficult, and the optimization is unlikely to cause trouble. An example in which the optimization does cause trouble is provided by Problem 1 (Multiplication Table).

In the first version of this problem we have to print the table

```
1
2    4
3    6    9
...  ...  ...  ...
10   20   ...  ...   100
```

An operation "clear print line" must be allocated, and the correct place for it is undoubtedly in the component "process line". However, we may choose instead to place the operation at the beginning of "process table", where it will be executed once only: this optimization is based on the fact that each line of the table overwrites all the non-space characters of the immediately preceding line. The fact is correctly observed, and the optimized program works. However, when we come to modify the program for the second version, to print the table

1	2	3	...	10
	4	6	...	20
		...	...	...
			81	90
				100

the facts have changed, and the optimization no longer works. We are forced to restore the "clear print line" operation to its natural place.

Another method of reducing the number of instructions to be executed is to make a single instruction serve two or more purposes. In Problem 13 (Telegrams Analysis) the component "process word" in P1 is:

```
PROCWORD    seq
                ws: =1;
                cct: =0;
PWORDBODY    iter until bchar(bs) = space or eob
                wch(ws): =bchar(bs);
                ws: =ws+1;
                bs: =bs+1;
                cct: =cct+1;
PWORDBODY    end
                write word;
PROCWORD    end
```

Three distinct variables—bs, ws and cct—are used, each of which must be incremented in the iterated part of PWORDBODY. If our programming language allows subscript expressions (COBOL does not), we can make a substantial improvement to the number of executed instructions:

```
PROCWORD    seq
                wbs: =bs;
PWORDBODY    iter until bchar(bs) = space or eob
                wch(bs+1—wbs): =bchar(bs):
```

```
                    bs: = bs + 1;
   PWORDBODY   end
                    cct: = bs − wbs;
                    write word;
   PROCWORD   end
```

Whether the resulting program will execute any faster depends on how the compiler treats the subscript expression. But in any case we have produced a program which is potentially harder to maintain. The optimization depends on the equality of three distinct quantities:

the number of characters to be counted as belonging to the word (cct),

the difference between the initial and current values of the word-string subscript (ws − 1), and

the difference between the initial and current values of the block-string subscript (bs − wbs).

These equalities hold in the problem as specified. But they may no longer hold in a later version: for example, we may allow backspace-erase characters in the block-string.

Execution speed may sometimes be improved by careful ordering of condition tests. For example, consider the structure

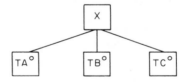

where TA is defined by a value 1, 3, 8 or 9 in a certain variable, TB by a value 2 or 4, and TC by a value 5. If the parts TA, TB and TC occur with equal frequencies, the the most efficient ordering of the parts in the selection is:

```
   PROCX   select value 5
              process TC;
   PROCX   or value 2 or 4
              process TB;
   PROCX   or value 1 3 8 or 9
              process TA;
   PROCX   end
```

because it minimizes the number of value tests to be executed. If the value 8 occurs 94% of the time, and the other values occur 1% each, the most efficient ordering is

```
PROCX     select value 8
          process TA;
PROCX     or value 5
          process TC;
PROCX     or value 2 or 4
          process TB;
PROCX     or value 1 3 or 9
          process TA;
PROCX     end
```

in which we have chosen to improve execution speed at the expense of main storage space, accepting the additional penalty of splitting the processing of TA into two parts.

12.4

Reducing the length of the program text, and hence the size of the compiled program, is usually more important than increasing the speed of execution. The basic method of reducing the text size is to conflate distinct program components so that they can be implemented by the same physical text. We will consider three approaches. The first is to simplify the data structures so that they contain fewer distinct components to be processed; the second is to manipulate the program text by amalgamating states which are historically different but for which the subsequent processing is identical; the third is to generalize program components so that they can serve more than one purpose. The three approaches lead to the same basic method, as will become apparent; but they have different flavours, and are used at different stages of the design process.

The first approach, simplifying data structures, is the most dangerous: it is used at the earliest stage of the design process, and therefore demands great foresight if it is not to undermine the whole structure of the program. We have already seen a successful example in the solution of Problem 13 (Telegrams Analysis). The structure of the paper tape file is shown on p. 260.

In part, this structure is already optimized. It expresses the fact that a block begins with zero or more leading spaces, and then consists of alternate words and trailing spaces followed by the terminating EOB character. It

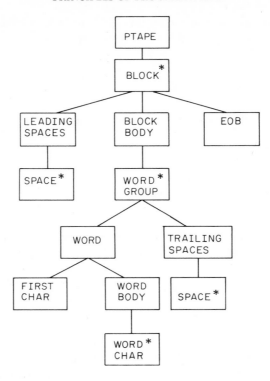

expresses the fact that a word must consist of at least one character. But it does not express the fact that the trailing spaces after each word except the last word in the block must consist of at least one space.

We need not express this last fact directly in the data structure. We know that the iteration "word body" will consume all of the characters of the word; the next character must therefore be a space or EOB; it can be EOB only if the current wordgroup is the last in the block, because there is, by definition, no EOB character except at the end of block. So the structure shown will suffice. But by similar reasoning we can show that the structure may be further simplified as shown at the top of p. 261.

This structure, which is the structure used in our solution of the problem, does not express the alternation of space groups and word groups, nor does it express the fact that a word group must contain at least one character and a space group must contain at least one space. We may even make a further simplification of character group as shown at the bottom of p. 261.

Here each space is treated as a complete character group. We will not

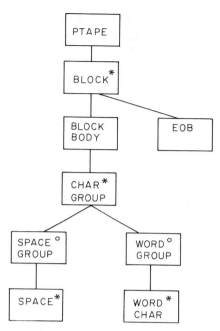

therefore require an iteration component "process space group" in the program structure.

These optimizations of the data structure are harmless, because we are confident that:

the position and grouping of sets of consecutive space is, and will continue to be, irrelevant to the problem;

the processing of a word does not, and will not, depend on whether it is preceded or followed by any particular form of delimiter.

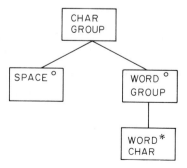

A very different example, in which optimization would be very dangerous, can be found in Problem 8 (Source Statement Library). We might argue superficially that the card types in the card input file can be treated simply as if they were commands to carry out certain actions: an insert card is a command to copy the library member to a specified point; a basis card is a command to find and open a specified library member; a source card is a command to reproduce that card in the output text file; and so on. We might then adopt the structure:

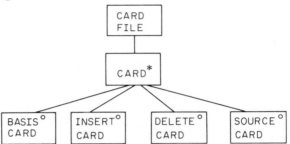

This structure is quite inadequate to solve the problem. The processing of each card type is highly dependent on its context in the card file. For example, the processing of a source card depends on whether the first card of the file was a basis card, and, if so, on whether the specified library member was found, and, if so, on whether at least one insert or delete card had intervened between the basis card and the source card to be processed. All of these distinctions can be drawn in the program by setting and testing switches: but to adopt the structure shown and then introduce the distinctions later is to reverse the proper order of design. The data and program structures should exhibit all of the necessary distinctions explicitly; optimization by removing distinctions or by reducing their expression to the values of switches is a step which should be taken much later if at all.

12.5   Common Action Tails

The second approach to reducing program size is to manipulate the program text directly. We may be able to identify points in the text for which subsequent processing is identical although previous processing may have differed.

The simplest illustration is provided by a selection component:

P   **select** condition-1
      do A;
      do B; $-(x1)$
      do C; $-(y1)$

P   **or** condition-2
    do D;
    do E;
    do C; —(y2)
P   **or** condition-3
    do F;
    do B; —(x3)
    do C; —(y3)
P   **end**

The points marked y1, y2 and y3 are all followed by execution of component C and the end of P. The points marked x1 and x3 are both followed by execution of components B and C and the end of P. We may code an optimized version as:

```
PSLCT.
      IF NOT CONDITION-1 GO TO POR1.
      PERFORM A.
X.    PERFORM B.
Y.    PERFORM C.
      GO TO PEND.
POR1.
      IF NOT CONDITION-2 GO TO POR2.
      PERFORM D.
      PERFORM E.
      GO TO Y.          NOTE COMMON ACTION TAIL.
POR2.
      PERFORM F.
      GO TO X.          NOT COMMON ACTION TAIL.
PEND.
```

The statements "GO TO X" and "GO TO Y" infringe every conceivable rule of structured coding. And they are intended to. They are written purely for purposes of optimization, and they are therefore coded in such a manner that they cannot be mistaken for structure-defining statements. It would be a serious error to restructure the selection to conform to our usual conventions:

PP   **seq**
    PQ   **select** condition-2
        do D;
        do E;
    PQ   **or** condition-1 or condition-3

```
        PR    select condition-1
              do A;
        PR    or condition-3
              do F;
        PR    end
            do B;
      PQ    end
          do C;
PP      end
```

This restructing implies, quite falsely, that the common operations "do B" and "do C" indicate the fundamental structure of the problem: they do not; they are merely an optimization device and must be clearly marked as such.

Plentiful examples of this type of optimization are provided by iteration components. It happens often that the first or last iterated part is structurally distinct, and has therefore been placed outside the iteration in the program structure. With a little manipulation we may be able to identify two common points, one inside and the other outside the iteration. Consider, for example, our original solution to Problem 15 (Generating Test Data), given in Section 8.6 above:

```
PROGZ   seq

            ...
   PZBODY   iter
      PGROUPZ   seq
                    flagZ: = 1;
                    write X;          - (x1)
                    read FX;
            PGXBODY   iter until flagX=1
                          flagZ: =0;
                          write X;     - (x2)
                          read FX;
            PGXBODY   end
                          flagZ: =0;   - (y1)
                      write Y;
                      read FY;
            PGYBODY   iter until flagY = 1
                          flagZ: =0;   - (y2)
                          write Y;
                          read FY;
            PGYBODY   end
```

```
          PGROUPZ  end
       PZBODY  end
          ...
    PROGZ   end
```

The points x1 and x2 correspond, as do the points y1 and y2. We may treat the coding as we did in the selection P discussed above:

```
       ...
    PGROUPZSEQ.
          MOVE 1 TO FLAGZ.
    X.    write X.
          read FX.
    PGXBODYITER.
          IF FLAGX = 1 GO TO PGXBODYEND.
          MOVE 0 TO FLAGZ.
          GO TO X.          NOTE COMMON ACTION POINT.
    PGXBODYEND.
       ...
```

However, there is a reasonable case for restructuring on this occasion:

```
    PGROUPZ   seq
                 flagZ: = 1;
          PGXBODYX   iter
                     write X;
                     read FX;
                     quit PGXBODYX if flagX = 1;
                     flagZ: = 0;
          PGXBODYX   end
                 ...
```

The case is reasonable, but not entirely convincing. We have abolished the original distinction between the first and other records of FX, and we may come to regret its abolition.

Another example is seen in Problem 10 (Delimited Strings); this time the distinction is between the last and other parts. The solution suggested in Section 6.7 includes the text:

```
       ...
       ps: = 1;
    PS1BDY   iter until schar(ss) = "@"
```

```
                quit MAINST if schar(ss) = "%";
                pchar(ps): =schar(ss);
                ps: =ps+1;       ss: =ss+1;
PS1BDY    end
        pchar(ps): =schar(ss);
        ps: =ps+1;       ss: =ss+1;
        line-2: ="S1=" printstring;
        ...
```

with similar text for the component PS2BDY.

There is obvious duplication of text here: the statements

```
    pchar(ps): =schar(ss);
    ps: =ps+1;       ss: =ss+1;
```

appear both inside and outside the iteration PS1BDY. But there is no common action point: inside PS1BDY the duplicated statements are followed by the condition test of the iteration, while outside they are followed by the assignment to line-2. To eliminate the duplication we must arrange to test the distinguishing conditions after and not before executing the duplicated statements.

We therefore need to change the condition test from "is the next character @?" to "was the previous character @?", and to make the test after, and not before, processing each character. Drawing on the perverted ingenuity which is the stock-in-trade of the optimizing programmer, we write:

```
            ...
        ps: =1;
PS1BDY    iter
                quit MAINST if schar(ss) = "%";
                pchar(ps): =schar(ss);
                ss: =ss+1;
                quit PS1BDY if pchar(ps) = "@";
                ps: =ps+1;
PS1BDY    end
        line2: ="S1=" printstring;
        ...
```

Note that we chose to inspect the character in the printstring rather than in the source string: the source string subscript (ss) must be incremented after every character, while we can afford not to increment the printstring subscript (ps) after the "@".

There is a further change to be made. We have a conditional branch for the "**quit** PS1BDY" statement, and, after incrementing ps, an unconditional branch to the head of the iteration. We may be tempted to write:

```
        ...
        ps:=0;
PS1BDY   iter
        quit MAINST if schar(ss) = "%";
        ps:=ps+1;
        pchar(ps):=schar(ss);
        ss:=ss+1;
        quit PS1BDY if pchar(ps) = "@";
PS1BDY   end
        line2:="S1=" printstring;
        ...
```

so that we can eventually code:

```
        MOVE 0 TO PS.
PS1BDYITER.
        ...
        IF PCHAR (PS) NOT = "@" GO TO PS1BDYITER.
PS1BDYEND.
        ...
```

This is thoroughly undesirable: 0 is not a legitimate value for a COBOL subscript, and we have no business using it.

12.6   Generalization

Another approach to the same example is to recognize that the statements

```
pchar(ps):=schar(ss);
ps:=ps+1;     ss:=ss+1;
```

form a "common subroutine". We code the paragraph

```
PMOVECHAR.
        MOVE SCHAR (SS) TO PCHAR (PS).
        ADD 1 TO PS.        ADD 1 TO SS.
```

and invoke it from the four places in the text at which the common operations occur.

This is the very simplest illustration of the third approach to reducing the length of the program text. We recognize that certain operations occur more than once in conjunction, and we devise a routine which is sufficiently general to handle every occurrence. In the present simple illustration the four occurrences are already identical, and there is no need to generalize.

This form of optimization is often misunderstood, and mistaken for a fundamental design technique. There is a crucial, though not perfectly precise, distinction between common subroutines which are the result of bottom-up design activity and common subroutines which are the result of optimization. The former arise from a recognition that the hardware/software machine is not ideally suited to solving a given problem: by providing ourselves with new elementary operations, implemented as common subroutines, we rebuild the machine nearer to our ideal. We may expect these routines to remain valid for the lifetime of the system which motivated them—and often to outlive the system. The latter, by contrast, arise from a detailed consideration of the text of a particular program. We may expect them to be invalidated by changes to the program specification, and we will not often find that they can be used in any other program.

Problem 3 (Cantor's Enumeration of Rationals) provides a more elaborate illustration of this third approach to optimization. The program given in Section 3.1 above is:

```
PNSET    seq
         Z:=1;
    PSBODY   iter until Z > 50
       PZIGZAG   seq
          PROCZIG   seq
                    S:=2*Z−1;
                    T:=1;
             PZIGBODY   iter until S < 1
             PZIGNUM   seq
                       display S/T;
                       S:=S−1;
                       T:=T+1;
             PZIGNUM   end
             PZIGBODY   end
          PROCZIG   end
          PROCZAG   seq
                    S:=1;
                    T:=2*Z;
             PZAGBODY   iter until T < 1
             PZAGNUM   seq
```

```
                              display S/T;
                              S:=S+1;
                              T:=T-1;
                  PZAGNUM  end
               PZAGBODY  end
            PROCZAG  end
                    Z:=Z+1;
         PZIGZAG  end
      PSBODY  end
            stop;
   PNSET  end
```

There are evident similarities between the text of PROCZIG and the text of PROCZAG: we will exploit these similarities and devise a common subroutine for both. We begin by making the following observations:

> although the variables S and T are global to PROCZIG and to PROC-ZAG (they are local to PZIGZAG), they are used as if they were local; we could replace them by two other pairs of variables, SI, TI and SA, TA, for use in PROCZIG and PROCZAG respectively;

> further, we could use TI to do duty for SA, and SI to do duty for TA; the components PROCZIG and PROCZAG would then be:

```
PROCZIG  seq
         SI:=2*Z-1;
         TI:=1;
      PZIGBODY  iter until SI < 1
         PZIGNUM  seq
                  display SI/TI;
                  SI:=SI-1;
                  TI:=TI+1;
         PZIGNUM  end
      PZIGBODY  end
PROCZIG  end
PROCZAG  seq
         SI:=2*Z;
         TI:=1;
      PZAGBODY  iter until SI < 1
         PZAGNUM  seq
                  display TI/SI;
```

```
                              SI:=SI−1;
                              TI:=TI+1;
            PZAGNUM  end
      PZAGBODY  end
 PROCZAG  end
```

PROCZIG and PROCZAG are then identical components except for the assignment statements

$$SI:=2*Z-1; \qquad SI:=2*Z:$$

and the display statements

$$\text{display } SI/TI; \qquad \text{display } TI/SI;$$

Having identified the essential differences between PROCZIG and PROCZAG, we now require to devise a suitably generalized component of which they will be special cases. The specialization must depend on a parameter which we can set. After some experiment, we devise the following scheme.

We declare SI and TI in the form:

```
01   SITI.
   02   SI PIC 9(6).
   02   TI PIC 9(6).
01   NN REDEFINES SITI.
   02   N PIC 9(6) OCCURS 2.
```

which allows us to refer to SI as N (1) and to TI as N (2). We also declare a variable U, which can take the values 1 and 2; U will take the value 1 for PROCZIG, and the value 2 for PROCZAG. The generalized component is:

```
PROCZUG  seq
            SI:=2*Z−(2−U);
            TI:=1;
      PZUGBODY   iter until SI < 1
         PZUGNUM   seq
                     display N(U)/N(3−U);
                     SI:=SI−1;
                     TI:=TI+1;
            PZUGNUM  end
      PZUGBODY  end
 PROCZUG  end
```

We could use this component directly in the existing program, writing

MOVE 1 TO U.   PERFORM PROCZUG.

in place of PROCZIG, and similarly for PROCZAG. However, by generalizing we have removed the necessity of treating PZIGZAG as a sequence: we could treat it as an iteration instead:

PZIGZAG.   PERFORM PROCZUG VARYING U FROM 1 BY 1
                                          UNTIL U > 2.

Further, we could merge together the two iterations PSBODY and PZIGZAG: instead of having an iteration of two occurrences within an iteration of 50, we could have a single iteration of 100 occurrences:

```
PNSET    seq
            Z:=1;
            U:=1;
     PSBODY    iter until Z > 100
         PROCZUG    seq
                       SI:=Z;
                       TI:=1;
                  PZUGBODY   iter until SI < 1
                     PZUGNUM    seq
                                   display N(U)/N(3−U);
                                   SI:=SI−1;
                                   TI:=TI+1;
                     PZUGNUM    end
                  PZUGBODY    end
         PROCZUG    end
                       Z:=Z+1;
                       U:=3−U;
     PSBODY    end
            stop;
PNSET    end
```

Note that the meaning of Z has changed: Z now counts the zugs whereas previously it was counting the zigzags; happily, the new value of Z gives the exact value to be assigned to SI at the beginning of each zug. Note too that the statement "U:=3−U;" causes the value of U to alternate between 1 and 2.

Further optimization of this program is suggested in an exercise at the end of this chapter.

12.7

Selections with backtracking often give opportunities for optimization by generalizing: the **posit** part of the selection is often tantalizingly similar to the **admit** part. A simple version of Problem 18 (Bubble Sort) illustrates the point.

Taking the first improvement to the algorithm, as suggested in Section 12.2 above, we consider the table, at each pass, to be either a sorted or a misordered table:

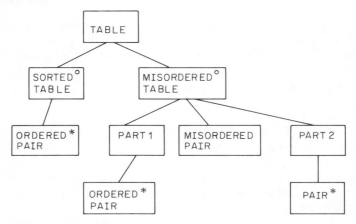

The reader should be able to reconstruct the design steps leading to the schematic logic:

```
P2    seq
      PB   iter
           S:=1;     T:=2;
         PASS   posit null pass (sorted table)
            PSORT   iter until S ≥ MAX
                    quit PASS if EKEY (S) > EKEY (T);
                    S:=S+1;      T:=T+1;
            PSORT   end
                quit PB;
         PASS   admit misordered table
            PMISP   seq
                    swap;
                    S:=S+1;      T:=T+1;
            PMISP   end
            PPART2   iter until S ≥ MAX
```

```
            PPAIR    select EKEY (S) > EKEY (T)
                     swap;
            PPAIR    end
                     S:=S+1;      T:=T+1;
         PPART2   end
      PASS   end
   PB   end
      stop;
P2      end
```

Processing of part1 of the misordered table has been eliminated as a beneficent side effect. The resulting program, as shown above, contains three distinct components which process entry pairs: the iterated part of PSORT, the iterated part of PPART2, and the sequence PMISP. Each contains the statements

$$S:=S+1; \qquad T:=T+1;$$

to increment the subscripts to point at the next potential entry pair.

It is easy to see that the component PMISP can be removed: the misordered pair, by definition, must satisfy the condition tests of the iteration PPART2 and the selection PPAIR, and will therefore be swapped as required. We are now left with the following text for PASS:

```
PASS   posit null pass (sorted table)
   PSORT   iter until S ⩾ MAX
              quit PASS if EKEY (S) > EKEY (T);
              S:=S+1;      T:=T+1;
   PSORT   end
      quit PB;
PASS   admit misordered table
   PPART2   iter until S ⩾ MAX
      PPAIR    select EKEY (S) > EKEY (T)
                  swap;
      PPAIR    end
              S:=S+1;      T:=T+1;
   PPART2   end
PASS   end
```

The two parts of the selection are identical, except that:

the first part is followed by the "quit PB" statement, and

for a misordered pair, the second part executes a swap, while the first executes a branch to the second.

We may readily generalize the two parts by introducing a switch. The switch has two values, corresponding to the two parts of the selection; initially it takes the value corresponding to the first part. The resulting text for the complete program is:

```
P3      seq
    PB   iter
        S:=1;     T:=2;
        PASS   seq
                switch:= "posit"
            PASSB   iter until S ⩾ MAX
                PPAIR   select EKEY (S) > EKEY (T)
                            switch:= "admit"
                            swap;
                PPAIR   end
                        S:=S+1;     T:=T+1;
            PASSB   end
                quit PB if switch= "posit"
        PASS   end
    PB   end
        stop;
P3      end
```

The statement "switch:='admit';" is executed more often than it should be: however, it is more expensive to determine that the statement need not be executed than to execute it unconditionally.

12.8

An extreme form of generalization is the construction of interpretive schemes. Consider, for example, the file structure:

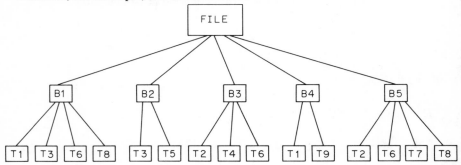

Clearly we could write a long and boring program to process this file. But it will be more agreeable to devise a generalization which will save some main storage space. We may choose to regard the file as having the structure:

The special features of each batch will be described in a "record table" for that batch. For example, the record table for the B1 batch will be:

| T 1 |
| T 3 |
| T 6 |
| T 8 |
| END |

Similarly, there will be a "batch table" describing the arrangement of the file in batches. Each entry of the batch table will be a pointer to a record table. The resulting program to process the file is:

```
P      seq
         open file;
         read file;
         point to start of batch-table;
       PB   iter until end-of-batch-table
              point to record-table start;
              process batch start;
              PBTCH   iter until end-of-record-table
                        process record against record-table-entry;
                        read file;
                        point to next record-table-entry;
              PBTCH   end
              process batch end;
              point to next batch-table-entry;
       PB   end
         close file;
         stop;
P      end
```

We may change the program by changing only the entries in the batch table and record tables. But there are tight constraints on the changes we may make in this way: the file must be a sequence of batches, and each batch must be a sequence of records. By changing only the tables we could not arrange to process a file whose batches were iterations of records, or which contained selections: for that we would need to change both the tables and the form of the tables and the program P.

Essentially, what has happened is this. The program P plays the role of a special-purpose computer: this computer is programmed in a special language, namely the language in which we define the batch table and record tables. When we allow the file structure to contain selections or iterations, we find that the special-purpose computer, and its programming language, are no longer adequate. We have built a computer whose programs consist only of sequences, whose parts in turn must also be sequences.

Interpretive schemes, in which a fixed program (P in the example above) interprets data (the batch and record tables) describing the required processing, can save large amounts of main storage space. But their effective design is governed by our second rule for optimization: we must always start from the unoptimized form, from a consideration of the programs which we will want to write in the interpreted data.

EXERCISE 12.1 (b)

The program shown in Section 12.3 above for Problem 3 (Cantor's Enumeration of Rationals) can be further optimized. Also, we may invert it with respect to the file of displayed rationals, giving a subroutine which, on each invocation, returns a pair of integers S and T such that the next rational to be displayed is S/T. Here, in the form of a COBOL paragraph, is such a subroutine:

```
...
77   R PIC 9 VALUE 2.
77   Q PIC 9 VALUE 1.
...
01   SITI.
   02   SI PIC 9(6) VALUE 2.
   02   TI PIC 9(6) VALUE 0.
01   NN REDEFINES SITI.
   02   N PIC 9(6) OCCURS 2.
...
...
PCANTORNEXT.
     SUBTRACT 1 FROM SI.
     ADD 1 TO TI.
     IF SI < 1,
         MOVE Q TO R
         SUBTRACT R FROM 3 GIVING Q
         MOVE TI TO SI
         MOVE 1 TO TI.
     MOVE N (Q) TO S.
     MOVE N (R) TO T.
...
```

Show how such a version can be derived from the version given in Section 12.3 by a number of provably correct steps.

EXERCISE 12.2 (b)

Rewrite the solution to Problem 10 (Delimited Strings) so that the same text is used to process both of the substrings S1 and S2.

EXERCISE 12.3 (b)

Devise a suitable format for the batch table and record tables discussed in Section 12.8 above, and write the interpreter program P.

QUESTION 12.1

Choose some typical programs in your installation. Discover as accurately as possible, for these programs, the answers to the following questions:

What is the cost of a single compilation?

What is the annual cost of running the program? How would this cost change if the program were 10% larger? If it used 10% more CPU cycles?

How many changes have been made since the program was put into production? How many of them were to correct programming errors? How many compilations were needed for each change?

Has the program ever failed in production running? If so, how much did the failure cost in machine time, manpower and other resources?

What do the user departments think of the program? How satisfied are they with its reliability and ease of maintenance?

QUESTION 12.2

If you intend eventually to optimize a program, why not produce it originally in the optimized form?

QUESTION 12.3

How much optimization does your present compiler carry out? Is it enough? If not, why does it not do more? Which of the optimization devices discussed in this chapter could be used by a compiler?

13. RETROSPECT

13.1

The central theme of this book has been the relationship between data and program structures. The data provides a model of the problem environment, and by basing our program structures on data structures we ensure that our programs will be intelligible and easy to maintain.

The data structures used are limited in two ways. Firstly, we have avoided recursive structures, in which a component may contain itself, directly or indirectly, as a part. For example, a COBOL program may contain COPY statements, whose meaning is that the specified library member is to be inserted into the program text. If we allow library members themselves to contain COPY statements, then the resulting structure of a program is:

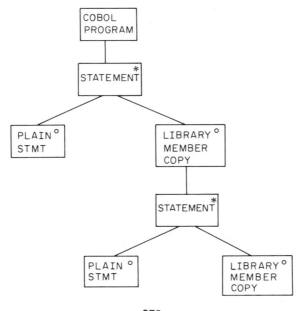

The structure of a library member is recursive, because it contains a library member as a component.

Inherently recursive structures occur only rarely in data processing. Indeed, apart from the parts explosion problem ("a product is made from a number of parts, which are made from parts, which . . .") it is difficult to think of important examples. For that reason, and also because recursion is very inconvenient to implement in COBOL, we have accepted the limitation. However, the limitation can be easily removed if we adopt a language such as PL/I which allows recursive programs to be written conveniently; the techniques presented in this book are largely unaffected.

The second, and more important, limitation on data structures is that they are hierarchical and must be explored sequentially. The serial file is fundamental. At first sight this emphasis on serial files may seem to some readers to be absurdly out of date. Surely tapes have long since been superseded by disks, batch processing by on-line systems, discrete files by database management software? Yes, they have; but these changes are relatively superficial. A useful program must have a serial input file. An on-line conversational program has a serial input file of messages from the user, and outputs to him a serial output file of replies. An interrupt-handling routine has a serial input file of interrupts. A software routine to provide a sophisticated access method has a serial input file of access requests. A program which updates a customer's master record has a serial input file of transactions initiated by or for that customer. All of these files are serial because the reality which they model is chronologically ordered: if we ignore or distort the serial nature of the file we cannot deal correctly with the reality,

We may think of a system as an aggregate of many individual programs— one program for each individual entity in the real world with which the system is concerned. Each individual program has a serial input file of transactions pertaining to the corresponding entity, and a serial output file of the responses to those transactions. Thus we would have a program for each customer, a program for each employee, a program for each supplier, a program for each insurance policy, and so on. We also need an overall control program to direct the transactions to the appropriate individual programs, and to transfer the outputs either to the final system output or to the input of other individual programs. When we come to implement the system in practice we make two major changes. We group together the individual programs for the entities of one class—such as the class of employees—by inverting the programs and storing their state vectors as a master file—the employee master file. Also, for reasons of efficiency, we may batch the transactions in various ways and disseminate the work of the control program over various parts of the operating system, of the file management system and of the special-purpose control programs which we call "batch processing programs". As a result it is usually hard to identify the underlying simple serial programs, especially if we have taken the final step of using the same master record to serve as the state vector of more than one program.

13.2 Coding

Some readers may have been offended by the uncouth appearance of many of the COBOL solutions. The inverted programs, in particular, bristle with labels and GO TO statements, and are unashamedly equipped with an internal switch.

It is vital to distiguish surface appearance from underlying substance. When we write:

PXITER.　IF NOT CONDITION-1 GO TO PXEND.

　　　　　...

　　　　　GO TO PXITER.
PXEND.

we are writing an iteration no less well-formed than

PX:　DO　WHILE (CONDITION 1);

　　　...

　　　...

　　END PX;

We are merely forced, because of shortcomings in the language (which it shares with PL/I and ALGOL), to code our well-formed iteration in an unusual manner. We are writing by hand the text which we would prefer our compiler to generate automatically. The true objection to GO TO statements is, of course, that they permit unrestrained branching from one part of a program to another. The two GO TO statements in the example above do no such thing: they are an utterly standardized implementation of the schematic logic.

But might it not be better, nonetheless, to reshape the code of an inverted program to conform to the accepted rules of GO TO-less programming style? Definitely not. The inverted program is designed, and should be read, as if it were not inverted. The coding

　　　MOVE 5 TO QS.　　GOBACK.
　Q5.

must be read as a "read" or as a "write" statement, which is what it is. By reshaping the code we would lose the direct correspondence with the schematic logic; we would no longer have a program in which the structure of the program text exhibited clearly the structure of the data it processes.

The use of the state variable QS presents another, similar, issue. Surely we should avoid the use of internal switches, and create programs which are re-entrant, pure procedures? Again, definitely not. We cannot avoid solving problems which demand the use of inversion. The resulting programs must have some mechanism which allows them to resume execution at the point at which execution was last suspended. So long as we use COBOL, PL/I, ALGOL or FORTRAN, we must provide that mechanism explicitly in the form of a state variable. By moving the state variable out of the text of the inverted program into the parameter list we achieve nothing of real value unless we need to handle multi-threading. Indeed, we may be doing ourselves an injury: we make the state variable visible and accessible to other programs, thus undermining its essentially private purpose.

A more substantial question concerns the use of the **quit** statement in backtracking. This is certainly a genuine GO TO; it branches from one context into another without passing through the upwards and downwards path which we normally demand, and that is why backtracking gives rise to side effects problems. Should we then forbid the use of the **quit** statement? Only if we are prepared to tolerate the very cumbersome solutions from which backtracking technique saves us. For example, in Problem 9 (A Daisy Chain) we must be prepared to tolerate the solution in a six-level structure; when the problem grows to 20 files instead of three we must be prepared to tolerate a 40-level structure. What we should not on any account do is to replace the **quit** statement by a switch and imagine that we have improved matters. We have merely made the program a little more obscure by choosing to record in the setting of the switch what would otherwise have been re-corded in the value of the program sequence counter.

13.3

Our objective above all has been to create programs which are self-evidently correct. There is still plenty of scope for error: we may suffer a slip of the pen in writing a program statement; the statement may be wrongly keypunched; the operator may drop a card on the floor of the computer room when he loads our program text in the card reader. All of these things may go wrong, and we will need to test our program to ensure that all is well. But we cannot afford any significant probability that our program contains a logic error. All the logic errors must have been eliminated during the design process.

We cannot hope to find logic errors by testing. Logic errors are concerned with combinations of circumstances, and there are too many combinations to test. Instead of testing we must think and plan and design so that testing becomes unnecessary.

Consider, for example, Problem 13 (Telegrams Analysis). If we were asked to devise a good set of test data to check out a purported solution to this problem, we might wish to include these cases among many others:

telegram exactly filling one block;

telegram starting in the middle of a block and ending in the middle of the next block;

telegram starting at the beginning of a block and ending in the middle of the next block;

telegram starting at the beginning of a block and ending in the middle of the same block;

telegram starting in the middle of a block and ending in the middle of the next block but one, the intervening block being full of spaces;

telegram starting in the middle of a block and having its terminating ZZZZ word as the first word of the next block.

These test cases seem reasonable They are concerned with a point of potential difficulty in the problem: the interaction between blocks and telegrams. But the solution to this potential difficulty lies in the program design. We designed a program, in Chapter 8 above, in which all interaction between blocks and telegrams is excluded. We split the program into two parts, P1 and P2; P1 deals only with blocks, and knows nothing of telegrams; P2 deals only with telegrams, and knows nothing of blocks. The test cases suggested above are quite irrelevant to such a program; the errors which they might reveal have been eliminated in the design. We know that the program is correct, because we designed it correctly.

APPENDIX

COBOL Language

The preceding chapters contain many example solutions coded in COBOL. The notes in this appendix are intended to help readers who are unfamiliar with COBOL to understand the solutions.

That is their sole intent and purpose. They do not present an exhaustive or definitive description of the language; they do not even contain enough information to guide the reader in writing the simplest possible program. Features and facilities which have not been used in the examples are ignored. Those which are described are described informally and usually in a simplified form. Obscure features are distorted for clarity.

The COBOL dialect described is, more or less, the IBM version of ANS COBOL.

A1. Card Format

The text of a COBOL program is arranged as a series of card images. Columns 1 through 6 of each card contain a sequence number; columns 73 through 80 contain a name by which the file of card images may be known. Neither of these fields is a part of the program text proper, and we will ignore them. Column 7 is used to indicate that a word (such as a long character string constant) has been split between cards, much as words are hyphenated in ordinary printed text so that they may be split between lines. This facility is known as "continuation", and is not used in the examples. We will therefore ignore column 7 also.

The remainder of the card image is available for program text. The first four columns, columns 8 through 11, are thought of as constituting a special area called Area A; the rest, columns 12 through 72, is called Area B. Certain elements of the text, such as division headers and paragraph names, must be written so that they start in Area A; most of the text is written in Area B.

A2. General Structure

A program has four divisions: IDENTIFICATION or ID division; EN-VIRONMENT division; DATA division; PROCEDURE division. Each division begins with a header card, such as

IDENTIFICATION DIVISION.

in which the word "identification" starts in Area A. There is no way of indicating the end of one division except by the beginning of the next, or by the end of the program.

The identification division contains the program name, the name of the programmer, and other similar information. It has been omitted from the examples.

The environment division is intended to describe the physical environment in which the program is to be executed. It therefore contains such information as the allocation of files to specific devices. The environment division has been omitted from most of the examples.

The data division contains all the data declarations.

The procedure division contains all of the executable coding.

A program may be either a main program or a sub-program. A main program is invoked by the operating system, which fetches a fresh unused copy of the program text for each execution. It is therefore impossible to remember anything from one execution of a main program to the next execution of the same program except by storing the information on a file. A sub-program is like a FORTRAN subroutine or a PL/I external procedure. It is invoked by a main program or by another sub-program. The invocation statement is of the form

CALL "PGMA" USING PARAM1, PARAM2, PARAM3.

where PGMA is the name of the entry point in the invoked sub-program and PARAM1, PARAM2 and PARAM3 are the names of actual parameters for the invocation. At the entry point of the invoked sub-program there must be a matching statement

ENTRY "PGMA" USING X, Y, Z.

where X, Y and Z are the names of dummy or formal parameters, declared in the data division of PGMA. Call is always by reference; that is, references to X, Y and Z in the above example are references to the actual data areas

PARAM1, PARAM2 and PARAM3 as declared in the invoking program. At machine code level, the parameter list consists of the addresses of the actual parameters in main storage.

All data declared in the data division is global within the compilation. Each program, whether it is a main program or a sub-program, must be separately compiled.

A3. Data Division

The data division begins with the division header card

DATA DIVISION.

It is arranged in three sections: FILE section; WORKING-STORAGE section; LINKAGE section. Each section begins with a section header card, such as

WORKING-STORAGE SECTION.

in which the word "working-storage" starts in Area A.

The file section declares the files which the program handles, and the formats of their records. The working-storage section declares local variables. The linkage section contains the declarations of dummy or formal parameters, and is therefore required only for sub-programs.

The fundamental concept in COBOL data declarations is the record. A record is a hierarchical structure of data items which occupy fixed relative locations in main storage. Each component of the structure is described in a data item description, consisting of a level indicator, a name and certain other (optional) information. For example, in the record description:

```
01   CUSREC.
     02   CUST-NO...
     02   AMOUNT...
     02   DATE.
          03   DAY...
          03   MTH...
          03   YEAR...
```

the name of the record is CUSREC; it consists of CUST-NO, AMOUNT and DATE, in that order; DATE consists of DAY, MTH and YEAR, in that order. The significance of the level indicators may be easily seen by comparing the above description with the structure diagram:

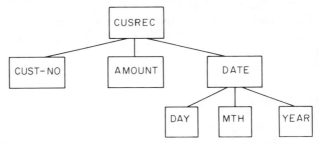

The items at the lowest levels of a structure are elementary items, which may be of various types. The type of an elementary item is specified by PICTURE and USAGE clauses in the item description: broadly, the picture clause specifies the values which the item may take, and the usage clause specifies the internal representation. Here are some examples of elementary data item descriptions:

> 02 CUST-NO PIC X(8).   8 alphanumeric characters; only one internal representation is available, so no usage clause is required.

> 02   AMOUNT PIC S9(6)V99 COMP-3.   8 decimal digits, signed, with an implied decimal point between the sixth and seventh; the usage clause COMP-3 specifies internal representation in packed decimal form.

> 02   DAY PIC 99.   2 decimal digits, representing an unsigned integer in the range 0 through 99; in the absence of a usage clause, internal representation is in character form, but arithmetic is still possible (though inefficient).

> 04   INT PIC Z(4)9.   5 decimal digits, representing an unsigned integer in the range 0 through 99999; the Z's in the picture specify that leading zeros are to be replaced by spaces; only character representation is meaningful, so no usage clause is required.

Generally, usage clauses are relevant only for numeric items. The most important usage clauses in IBM COBOL, and the only ones used in the examples in this book, are COMP-3 (packed decimal) and COMP (binary).

In addition to the information discussed above, an item description may contain an OCCURS clause and/or a REDEFINES clause. The occurs clause specifies that the item is iterated, as in

```
01   A.
   02   ACHAR PIC X OCCURS 100.
```

in which the record A is an iteration of 100 occurrences of ACHAR. The redefines clause specifies that storage is to be allocated to the item in the same main storage locations as a previously described item of the same level. Thus

```
01   A.
   02   Z PIC 99999.
   02   Y REDEFINES Z.
      03   YCHAR PIC X OCCURS 5.
```

specifies that the five-character group item Y is to be allocated the same main storage locations as the five-digit integer Z.

A4. File Section

The file section of the data division contains a file description entry for each file to be handled by the program. A file description entry has a special level indicator "FD", and is followed by a record description for each record format in the file. Thus, for example,

```
FD   INFILE . . .
01   RECA.
   02   . . .
         . . .
01   RECB.
   02   . . .
         . . .
```

specifies that the file name "INFILE" contains records in the two formats RECA and RECB. The additional information in the FD entry itself (following the file name) is concerned with labels, blocking factors and other physical characteristics of the file. It is also possible, redundantly, to list the names of the record formats, so that the above FD entry could have been written

```
FD   INFILE DATA RECORDS ARE RECA, RECB.
```

```
01   RECA.
  02   . . .
```

When an input file is read, the record is thought of as being placed in main storage in the area described by the appropriate record description in the file section. Where a file contains records of more than one format, the same storage locations are allocated to all of the formats. When a file is written, the record is thought of as being written from the appropriate record area described in the file section.

A5. Working-storage Section

The working-storage section contains declarations of local variables in the form of record descriptions. These local variables are like ALGOL "own" variables or STATIC variables in PL/I: storage is allocated for them at the beginning of the main program, and is not released until the main program has completed execution. Working-storage in a sub-program may therefore be used to hold information from one invocation of the sub-program to the next.

In addition to record descriptions, the working-storage section may contain descriptions of elementary items which are not grouped into records or any composite structures. These items are declared in the same way as ordinary elementary items, but their level indicator is 77.

Elementary items in the working-storage section, whether they are level-77 items or parts of records, may receive initial values at compile time. These values are specified by writing a value clause in the item description, as in

```
77   WW PIC 99 VALUE 1.
77   ZZ PIC X(6) VALUE "MONDAY".
01   RECC.
  02   RECCF1 PIC S9(7)V9(3) VALUE 2349651.004.
  02   . . .
```

If an item has an occurs or a redefines clause in its description, then no value clause may be written in the description of that item or of any of its lower-level components.

A6. Linkage Section

The linkage section contains declarations of dummy or formal parameters. Each parameter is described either as a level-77 item or as a level-01 record. Naturally, initial values may not be specified for linkage section items.

A7. Referring to Data Items

Data items are referred to by the name written in the item description entry. If the same name has been used in more than one description, as in

```
01   RECA.
  02   FLD1 PIC XX.
  . . .
01   RECB.
  02   FLD1 PIC 99.
  . . .
```

unique reference must be achieved by qualifying the ambiguous name, as in

MOVE X TO FLD1 IN RECA.

If a data item has an occurs clause in its description, or is a lower-level component of an item which has an occurs clause in its description, it must be referred to by a subscripted name. Thus, given the data description

```
01   Z.
  02   Y OCCURS 10.
    03   W1 PIC 99.
    03   W2 PIC XX.
```

we may refer to the second occurrence of W1 as

W1   (2)

to the eighth occurrence of W2 as

W2   (8)

and so on. Subscripts may be themselves data items, so that we may write

```
77   SUB1 PIC 99.
01   Z.
  02   Y OCCURS 10 PIC X.
  . . .

  . . .
     MOVE SPACE TO Y (SUB1).
```

However, subscript expressions are not permitted.

A8. Condition Names

To simplify the writing of condition tests in the procedure division, conditions may be named and described in the data division. For example, we may have an item

    05   CODE PIC XX.

which can take any of the values "T2", "4R", "GG" and "9L", corresponding to four transaction types "debit", "credit", "refund" and "cancel" respectively. We may define each transaction type as a condition name associated with a value of CODE:

    05   CODE PIC XX.
        88   DEBIT VALUE "T2".
        88   CREDIT VALUE "4R".
        88   REFUND VALUE "GG".
        88   CANCEL VALUE "9L".

The special level indicator 88 is used to define condition names in this way. Having defined the condition names, we may use them in the obvious way:

    IF DEBIT MOVE P TO Q
    ELSE IF CANCEL ADD R TO S
        ELSE IF REFUND MOVE T TO U
        ELSE ADD V TO W.

This statement is in all respects equivalent to

    IF CODE = "T2" MOVE P TO Q
    ELSE IF CODE = "9L" ADD R TO S
        ELSE IF CODE = "GG" MOVE T TO U
        ELSE ADD V TO W.

The usefulness of condition names is greatly reduced by the fact that they cannot be used to set the conditions, only to test them.

A9. Procedure Division

The procedure division contains all of the executable coding. It exhibits, more than any other part of COBOL, the frustrated hopes of the language designers that a program could be written and understood in much the same way as natural language English text. The basic components of the procedure division are statements; statements may be grouped into sentences, sentences into paragraphs and paragraphs into sections. Only sentences are equipped with an end marker: a sentence terminates with a full stop, as in English. Statements, paragraphs and sections are terminated only by the beginning of the next component at the same or a higher level of grouping, or by the physical end of the program text.

The simplest statements are the imperative, unconditional statements such as:

```
MOVE X TO Y
DIVIDE P INTO Q GIVING R
OPEN INFILE
WRITE TOTAL-RECORD
DISPLAY PRINT-LINE
```

In general, such statements are self-explanatory; the more obscure imperative statements have been avoided in the examples. The DISPLAY statement is particularly useful in illustrative programs, because it permits output to be written to the line printer without a formal file definition and without execution of OPEN and CLOSE operations.

More complex are the conditional statements. We have used only two: the IF statement and the READ statement. The READ statement has the form

```
READ INFILE AT END imperative-statements
```

while the IF statement has the form

```
IF condition-1 statements-1 ELSE statements-2.
```

Serious anomalies arise from the fact that there is no end marker for a statement, that statements-1 and statements-2 in an IF statement may themselves be conditional statements, and that the ELSE clause may be omitted. A null statement is provided ("NEXT SENTENCE") so that the ELSE clause can always be written where it is required for correct pairing of IF and ELSE clauses, as in:

```
IF X = Y
   IF P = Q
      MOVE A TO B
   ELSE NEXT SENTENCE
ELSE ADD R TO S.
```

However, the NEXT SENTENCE statement is not merely a null statement: it does actually transfer control to the next sentence. It is therefore not permissible to write

```
IF X = Y
    IF P = Q
        MOVE A TO B
    ELSE NEXT SENTENCE
    IF T = U
        MOVE C TO D.
```

A10. Logic Flow

Apart from the use of conditional statements, there are two ways of modifying the normal sequential flow of control. The PERFORM statement allows paragraphs or sections to be invoked as local subroutines (without parameterization); the GO TO statement allows arbitrary transfers of control. Section and paragraph groupings serve to define local subroutines for the PERFORM statement; section and paragraph names serve also as branch points for the GO TO statement. This ambivalence in the meaning of sections and paragraphs causes many difficulties when PERFORM and GO TO statements are used in an undisciplined manner.

A paragraph is defined by writing a paragraph name, starting in Area A, immediately before the first statement of the paragraph. Thus, in the text

```
PARA-1.
    ADD A TO B.
    MOVE C TO D.
PARA-2.
    ADD E TO F.
    . . .
```

the paragraph PARA-1 consists of the statements ADD A TO B and MOVE C TO D.

A section is a sequence of paragraphs, prefaced by a section header, as in

```
P1 SECTION.
P1-1.
    ADD A TO B.
    MOVE C TO D.
P1-2.
```

    DISPLAY E.
    SUBTRACT P FROM Q.
P2 SECTION.
    . . .

The section P1 consists of the paragraphs P1-1 and P1-2.

The PERFORM statement may be used to execute, as subroutines, either sections or paragraphs. Thus the sentences

    PERFORM P1.   and   PERFORM P1-1,
                              PERFORM P1-2.

have identical effect, where the section P1 is defined as above. Because all data within a compilation is global, no recursion is possible.

There are more elaborate forms of the PERFORM statement. Instead of specifying a single paragraph or section, it may specify a sequence of paragraphs or sections, as in:

    PERFORM P1-1 THRU P1-2

but this facility is undesirable and is not used in the examples.

More useful are the iterative forms of the statement. We may write, with obvious meaning

    PERFORM P1-1 5 TIMES
or PERFORM P1-1 X TIMES.

Instead of a simple repetition specification of this kind, a terminal condition may be specified, with or without a control variable. Without a control variable the statement is:

    PERFORM sec-or-para UNTIL condition-1

which has the meaning of the schematic logic:

    P   **iter until** condition-1
        do sec-or-para;
    P   **end**

With a control variable the statement is

    PERFORM sec-or-para VARYING cvar FROM init BY incr
                        UNTIL condition-2

which has the meaning of the schematic logic:

```
P     seq
        cvar: =init;
    PB    iter until condition-2
            do sec-or-para;
            cvar: =cvar+incr;
    PB    end
P       end
```

The GO TO statement is used to execute a transfer of control to the beginning of a named section or paragraph. It has two useful forms. The simple form is

GO TO sec-or-para

which transfers control to the first statement of sec-or-para. Section and paragraph names, like data names, are known globally within a compilation. There is therefore no syntactic restriction on the destination of a GO TO statement.

The second form of the GO TO statement is

GO TO p-1, p-2, p-3, . . . p-n DEPENDING ON var

which transfers control to p-1 if var = 1, to p-2 if var = 2, and so on. If var has a value outside the range 1 through n, no transfer of control is made, and execution proceeds with the statement following the GO TO statement. P-1, p-2 etc. may be section or paragraph names.

A11. Procedure Division Structure

Execution of a main program begins at the point immediately following the procedure division header, and continues sequentially, subject to PERFORM and GO TO statements, until a STOP RUN statement is executed. Execution of a sub-program begins at the entry point (which should immediately follow the procedure division header), and continues sequentially, subject to PERFORM and GO TO statements, until a GOBACK statement is executed. The sequential flow may pass through sections and paragraphs which are the objects of PERFORM statements, as in:

PROCEDURE DIVISION.
P1.

```
        MOVE X TO Y.
        ADD P TO Q.
P2.
        MOVE R TO S.
        PERFORM P1.
        SUBTRACT T FROM U.
    . . .
```

Clearly, this arrangement is error-prone. It is usually considered good practice to place sections and paragraphs which are the objects of PERFORM statements at the end of the program text, and to avoid executing them by sequential flow of control.

A difficulty arises in the internal design of sections which are the objects of PERFORM statements. There is no form of return statement corresponding to the PERFORM; execution of the PERFORMed section terminates when execution of its last paragraph terminates. A special null paragraph is therefore provided:

```
        para-name.
            EXIT.
```

This may be written as the physically last paragraph of the section. Execution of the section may then be terminated by the statement

```
        GO TO para-name.
```

READING LIST

The following books are concerned with the same subject as this book, or with related subjects. The list does not pretend to be complete in any respect: it is a personal choice of a few books which I have found interesting and illuminating.

1. Structured Programming. O.-J. Dahl, E. W. Dijkstra and C. A. R. Hoare. Academic Press 1972.
2. Systematic Programming: An Introduction. N. Wirth. Prentice Hall 1973.
3. Software Engineering: Report on a NATO Science Committee Conference. Edited by J. N. Buxton and B. Randell. Scientific Affairs Division, NATO, Brussels 39. 1970.
4. Modular Programming—Proceedings of a National Symposium. Edited by L. L. Constantine. Information and Systems Institute Inc, Cambridge, Mass. 1968.
5. The Elements of Programming Style. B. W. Kernighan and P. J. Plauger. Bell Telephone Laboratories, Murray Hill, New Jersey. 1974.
6. The Psychology of Computer Programming. G. M. Weinberg. Van Nostrand Reinhold. 1971.